WILSON COUNTY
TENNESSEE
MISCELLANEOUS RECORDS
1800-1875

Compiled by:
Thomas E. Partlow

SOUTHERN HISTORICAL PRESS
%The Rev. S. Emmett Lucas, Jr.
P. O. Box 738
Easley, South Carolina 29640

ISBN 0-89308-283-X

This Book

Is Dedicated To The One

Who Most Realized The Work Involved

My Mother

NANNIE JOHNSON PARTLOW

(1910--1981)

PREFACE

This book is part of a continuing effort to
compile all Wilson County records available. This is
particularly true of the period prior to 1865. Probably, Wilson County is closer to achieving this goal
than any other county in Tennessee.

The majority of information in this book was
taken from the records at the Courthouse. Most of
the books are found in the County Court Clerk's Office.
Some are from old records in the basement of the
Courthouse. In many cases, only portions of these
books remain. Rarely are these books indexed.

The other records were obtained from private
sources. These include the cemetery records, church
records, war records, etc. Much of this information
is not available elsewhere.

Thomas E. Partlow

TABLE OF CONTENTS

GUARDIAN SETTLEMENTS 1836-1841

WILSON HEARN Guardian. Guardian of Spencer C.,
Alfred W., and Michael M. Harris who are the minor heirs
of Michael Harris deceased. Recorded 10 March 1840.
(P. 1)

JAMES HOLMES Guardian. Guardian for Lucinda Holmes,
a minor heir of John Barbee. Recorded 12 May 1836. (P. 1)

BURRELL NETTLES Guardian. Guardian for the minor
heirs of Benjamin Nettles, to wit, Elizabeth and William
Nettles. Lucretia Nettles paid for boarding and clothing
the heirs. Recorded 12 May 1832. (P. 1)

BENNETT BABB Guardian. Guardian for Sally G. Newby.
Recorded 12 May 1836. (P. 2)

JOHN GUTHRIE Guardian. Guardian for (Jredah),
Delila, Zachariah, and Abigal Newby. Recorded 12 May
1836. (Pp. 2-4)

RICHARD W. CARTRIGHT Guardian. Guardian for the
minor heirs of William F. Bennett, to wit, Micajah, William, Nancy, and Oliver. Recorded 12 May 1836. (Pp. 4-
5)

PARKER (ADAMS) Guardian. Guardian for Eliza Putman.
Recorded 12 May 1836. (P. 5)

JAMES MARKS Guardian. Guardian for the minor heirs
of Amelia Snider, to wit, Joseph and Nancy Snider. Recorded 28 March 1836. (P. 6)

NANCY HARRIS Guardian. Guardian for Elizabeth E.
and Nancy L. Harris. Recorded 13 May 1836. (Pp. 6-7)

ELIZABETH HARRISON Guardian. Guardian for Landon,
Temperance, and Elizabeth Harrison. Recorded 12 May
1836. (P. 7)

THOMAS LEECH Guardian. 28 March 1836. Guardian for
the minor heirs of John Luck deceased. Recorded 13 May
1836. (P. 8)

LEWIS CHAMBERS Guardian. Guardian for John and
Lewis Chambers, the minor heirs of Alexander Chambers.
Recorded 13 May 1836. (P. 8)

BRITAIN DRAKE Guardian. Guardian for James Hunter.
Recorded 13 May 1836. (P. 9)

ARCHEMACK (ALEXANDER) BASS Guardian. 28 March 1836.
Guardian for the minor heirs of Jacob Vantreese, to wit,
William and Ezekiel Vantreese. (P. 9)

JAMES C. BONE Guardian. Guardian for James W. Bone.
Recorded 13 May 1836. (P. 10)

JOHN ROACH Guardian. 27 March 1836. Guardian for
Thomas C. Telford, a minor heir of Robert Telford. (P.
10)

JAMES R. THOMPSON Guardian. Guardian for Nancy
Thompson or Nancy Airhart, Henry R. Thompson, and Margaret
Thompson, minor heirs of John Thompson. Recorded 13 May ·

1

1836. (P. 11)

W. T. WATERS Guardian. Guardian for the minor heirs
of Wiatt Lindsey, to wit, Elisha, Wiatt, and Josiah Lindsey. Recorded 13 May 1836. (P. 12)

LEWIS WRIGHT Guardian. Guardian for John Hughley.
Recorded 13 May 1836. (P. 12)

JAMES SHANNON Guardian. 28 March 1836. Guardian
for the heirs of Jeptha Clemmons. (P. 13)

MORRIS BREWER Guardian. 28 March 1836. Guardian
for the minor heirs of Jehu Climer. (P. 13)

WILLIAM THOMPSON Guardian. Guardian for Alexander
Cloyd, minor heir of Stephen Cloyd. Recorded 14 May 1836.
(P. 14)

ALFRED DUKE Guardian. 28 March 1836. Guardian for
the heirs of Sion Duke. (P. 14)

JOSEPH BRYSON Guardian. 28 March 1836. Guardian
for John Bryson, Jr. (P. 15)

BENJAMIN ALEXANDER Guardian. Thomas R. Roach and
Nancy W. Roach received their equal portion of the estate
of John and Lettice Cloyd. Recorded 14 May 1836. (P.
15)

JONAS SWINGLEY Guardian. 26 March 1836. Guardian
for Thomas Curd. (P. 16)

THOMAS CLIFTON Guardian. Guardian for Benjamin
Clifton who is a minor heir of Benjamin Clifton deceased.
Recorded 14 May 1836. (P. 17)

ALEXANDER ESKEW Guardian. Guardian for the minor
heirs of Bird Guille. Recorded 14 May 1836. (P. 17)

JOHN BASS Guardian. 28 March 1836. Guardian for
Ezekiel Gaddy, a minor heir of Elijah Gaddy. (P. 18)

GEORGE F. McWHIRTER Guardian. 20 March 1836.
Guardian for William, Frederick, and Manerva Wall, minor
heirs of Bird Wall. (P. 18)

CHARLES WADE Guardian. 23 February 1836. Guardian
for Kitty Harrison, Betsy Ann Lane, and Petro Harrison.
Recorded 16 May 1836. (Pp. 19-22)

THOMAS MILES Guardian. 28 March 1836. Guardian
for his ward, Mary Underwood. Recorded 16 May 1836.
(Pp. 22-23)

THOMAS MILES Guardian. Guardian for Mary, Martha
Elizabeth, and Newton Underwood. Recorded 16 May 1836.
(P. 23)

TOWNES SPRADLEY Guardian. Guardian for the minor
heirs of Hez Archer. Recorded 16 May 1836. (P. 23)

E. A. WHITE Guardian. Guardian for Sarah Johnson.
Recorded 16 May 1836. (P. 24)

GUARDIAN SETTLEMENTS 1836-1841

JOHN BAIRD Guardian. Guardian for William Baird. Recorded 16 May 1836. (P. 24)

E. A. WHITE Guardian. Guardian for William N. Bilbo. Recorded 16 May 1836. (P. 25)

WILLIAM H. PEACE Guardian. 25 March 1836. Guardian for Kesiah Walker dr. Recorded 17 March 1836. (P. 26)

MARY M. COWAN Guardian. 28 March 1836. Guardian for Samuel M., George W., and Joseph W. Cowen. (P. 27)

SILAS TARVER Guardian. 28 March 1836. Guardian for William E., Eleanor, and Henry Walker dr. (P. 28)

THOMAS E. MORRIS Guardian. Guardian for the heirs of Samuel W. Sands, to wit, Eliza C., Margaret A., and Richard B. Sands. Recorded 17 May 1836. (P. 29)

GEORGE H. BULLARD Guardian. Guardian for Helen and James Edwards who are the minor heirs of William Edwards. Recorded 17 May 1836. (P. 30)

ALFRED ENOCH Guardian. 29 March 1836. Guardian for John G. Enochs. (Pp. 30-31)

EDWARD TRAVELLIAN Guardian. Guardian of Thomas C. Breedlove, minor heir of Thomas Breedlove. Recorded 21 May 1836. (P. 31)

WILLIAM MOSS Guardian. Guardian of James Calvin Moss, a minor heir of Thomas Moss. Recorded 21 May 1836. (P. 32)

POLLY WALKER Guardian. Guardian for Thomas P. Walker, minor heir of William Walker. Recorded 21 May 1836. (P. 33)

JAMES McFARLAND Guardian. Guardian for Jourdain L, Burwell, and Archibald Moseley, the minor heirs of Burwell Moseley. Recorded 21 May 1836. (Pp. 33-34)

G. R. ASHWORTH Guardian. Guardian for Lewis D. Barry, a minor heir of Mark Barry. Recorded 23 May 1836. (Pp. 34-35)

WILLIAM MOSS Guardian. Guardian of Matthew Carr, a minor heir of Walter Carr. Recorded 3 May 1836. (P. 35)

STEPHEN McDONALD Guardian. Guardian of Samuel L. Eason. Recorded 2 June 1836. (P. 36)

DAWSON HANCOCK Guardian. Guardian for Ann and Drucilla Hancock. Recorded 22 June 1836. (P. 36)

P. HUBBARD Guardian. 1 June 1836. Mentions Mary P. Cage and Claiborne Cage. "Received of the hands of Wilson Cage from her mother." Of Sumner County. (Pp. 37-38)

JAMES TIPTON Guardian. Guardian of Isaac N. Stewart, heir of James Stewart. Recorded 10 August 1836. (P. 39)

JAMES TIPTON Guardian. Guardian of Sirena Tipton, heir of Rachael Tipton. Recorded 10 August 1836. (P. 39)

FANNY BRANCH Guardian. Guardian for James H. Branch, a minor heir of Robert Branch. Recorded 12 October 1836. (P. 40)

WILLIAM LAWRENCE Guardian. Guardian for Frances Nunley. Recorded 12 October 1836. (P. 40)

T. SPRADLEY Guardian. Guardian for the heirs of Hezekiah Archer. Recorded 12 October 1836. (P. 41)

ISBEL ALEXANDER Guardian. Guardian for the heirs of Robert Alexander, to wit, Polly, Joseph, and Jesse Alexander. Recorded 13 October 1836. (P. 41)

R. P. COMER Guardian. 4 July 1836. Guardian for Nancy, Katharine, and Anna Marrs who are the minor heirs of William Marrs. (P. 42)

SAMUEL HILL Guardian. Guardian of Hiram H. Alsup, one of the heirs of John and Elizabeth Alsup. Recorded 29 November 1836. (P. 43)

HUGH ROBERTSON Guardian. Guardian for Mary Falker. Recorded 29 November 1836. (P. 45)

WILSON HEARN Guardian. 2 December 1836. Guardian for Colman, Alfred, and Monroe Harris, the heirs of Michael Harris. (P. 46)

BENJAMIN ALEXANDER Guardian. Guardian for the minor heirs of Lettice Cloyd. Recorded 5 January 1837. (P. 46)

G. A. WILLIFORD Guardian. Guardian of Anthony Hagan, heir of Anthony Hagan. Recorded 5 January 1837. (P. 46)

JAMES P. THOMPSON Guardian. Guardian for the minor heirs of John Thompson. Recorded 5 January 1837. (P. 47)

JOSEPH CLOYD Guardian. Guardian of the minor heirs of Nancy Cloyd. Recorded 5 January 1837. (P. 47)

SILAS TARVER Guardian. Guardian for William E., Eleanor D., and Nancy Walker, minor heirs of Henry Walker. Recorded 2 January 1837. (P. 48)

WARNER LAMBETH Guardian. Guardian of William Harris who is a minor heir of John B. Harris. Recorded 6 January 1837. (P. 48)

MARY M. COWEN Guardian. Guardian of the minor heirs of William Cowen. Recorded 6 January 1837. (P. 49)

WILLIAM BAIRD Guardian. Guardian of (Miles), Wilson, Elizabeth, and Sally Baird, heirs of James Bostick. Recorded 6 January 1837. (P. 50)

EDMONT CRAWFORD Guardian. 2 January 1837. Guardian for the minor heirs of Ransom Word. (P. 50)

NANCY HARRIS Guardian. 2 January 1837. Guardian for the minor heirs of Michael Harris. (P. 50)

4

GUARDIAN SETTLEMENTS 1836-1841

THOMAS ESTES Guardian. 2 January 1837. Guardian of his children for and in a legacy bequeathed to them by Martha Atkinson. (P. 51)

SALLY OZMENT Guardian. 2 January 1837. Guardian for Katharine Ozment, a minor heir of Jonathan Ozment. (P. 51)

EDMONT CRAWFORD Guardian. 2 January 1837. Guardian for Margaret T. Smith, minor heir of William Smith. (P. 52)

LINA WARREN Guardian. Guardian for the heirs of Charles Warren. Recorded 7 January 1837. (P. 52)

JOHN BONE Guardian. Guardian for Thomas, George, and Margaret Scott, minor heirs of Samuel and Ann Scott. Recorded 9 January 1837. (P. 53)

CHARLES BRADLEY Guardian. 1 January 1837. Guardian for James, Abigal, and John Calhoun, minor heirs of John Calhoun. (P. 54)

HOPE H. HANCOCK Guardian 2 January 1837. Guardian for Martin, Robert, Elizabeth, Rosel, and Boid Edwards, minor heirs of Eli Edwards. (P. 55)

COLEMAN TALLY Guardian. 2 January 1837. Guardian for Westley T. Harris, minor heir of Michael Harris. (P. 55)

LEVI DONNELL Guardian. Guardian for Emsley D. Foster. Recorded 9 January 1837. (P. 55)

DAWSON HANCOCK Guardian. Guardian for the minor heirs of Lesley Hancock. Recorded 10 January 1837. (P. 56)

G. A. WILLIFORD Guardian. 2 January 1837. Guardian for Jane E. Carlin, a minor heir of Spencer Carlin. (P. 56)

THOMAS GUTHRIE Guardian. Guardian of Jeremiah F. Newby, a minor heir of John Newby. Recorded 10 January 1837. (P. 57)

RIAL J. ATKINSON Guardian. Guardian for the children of Rebecca Hunt. "To the whole amount due to said children for Joseph Atkinson." Recorded 11 January 1837. (P. 58)

EDMONT CRAWFORD Guardian. 2 January 1837. Guardian for the minor heirs of Lewis McCartney. (P. 58)

SIMON HANCOCK Guardian. Guardian for John Newby. Recorded 11 January 1837. (P. 59)

E. R. HARRISON Guardian. Guardian for Vicy F. Harrison. Recorded 11 January 1837. (P. 59)

EDMONT CRAWFORD Guardian. 2 January 1837. Guardian for Polly McCartney, minor heir of John McCartney. (P. 60)

GEORGE E. FRAZIER Guardian. Guardian for Mary P. Cage and Benjamin M. Cage. Recorded 11 January 1837. (Pp. 60-

61.

ELIJAH WILLIAMS Guardian. Guardian for the heirs of
Green Tucker, to wit, Jarrett, Elizabeth, Hiram, Foster,
Green H., Martha, Jeremiah, James, John, and Priscillar.
Recorded 26 January 1837. (P. 62)

ANTHONY OWEN Guardian. 6 February 1837. Guardian
for Christeny Bryan, minor heir of Nelson Bryan. The
heir has received property from Joshua Lester Estate bequeathed to Christeny. (P. 63)

JOSEPH B. WYNN Guardian. Guardian of Jesse McHenry,
and James McHenry, heirs of Jesse McHenry. Recorded 10
February 1837. (P. 63)

W. T. WATERS Guardian. Guardian for the minor heirs
of Wiatt Lindsey, to wit, Wiatt Lindsey and Joseph Lindsey.
Recorded 1 February 1837. (P. 64)

JOHN B. BRYAN Guardian. Guardian for (Aljournal)
Bryan, minor heir of Nelson Bryan. Recorded 10 February
1837. (P. 64)

THORNTON LAIN Guardian. Guardian for the minor heirs
of Ephraim Harrelson, to wit, Gency Ann Guill and William
Harrelson. Recorded 13 February 1837. (P. 65)

JULIUS WILLIAMS Guardian. Guardian for Joseph Cason,
minor heir of Joseph Cason. Recorded 13 February 1837.
(P. 65)

MORRIS BREWER Guardian. 6 February 1837. Guardian
for John P., Elizabeth, Noah, James, Ausbun, Christiana
Climer, the minor heirs of John Climer. (P. 65)

BENNETT BABB Guardian. Guardian for Sarah Newby, a
minor heir of John Newby. Recorded 13 February 1837. (P.
66)

NANCY A. CRUTCHFIELD Guardian. Guardian for the
minor heirs of S. B. Crutchfield, to wit, John, George,
and Lucy. Recorded 13 February 1837. (P. 67)

JOHN M. ALEXANDER Guardian. 6 February 1837. Guardian of Esther Alexander and Ezekiel Alexander, minor heirs
of Abner Alexander and heirs at law of Ezekiel Sharp. (P.
67)

A. BASS Guardian. Guardian for the minor heirs of
Jacob Vantreese, to wit, William and Ezekiel Vantreese.
Recorded 14 February 1837. (P. 67)

E. TALLY Guardian. Guardian of Emily, Jane, and Edwin C. Tally. Recorded 14 February 1837. (P. 68)

JOSEPH CLOYD Guardian. 7 December 1836. Slaves divided so that Samuel A. Hays and his wife, Jane, daughter
of said Nancy Cloyd may receive their part. (P. 69)

JAMES SWINGLEY Guardian. Guardian for Thomas Curd.
Recorded 14 February 1837. (P. 69)

E. A. WHITE Guardian. Guardian for Reymond and Green

GUARDIAN SETTLEMENTS 1836-1841

Proctor. Recorded 15 February 1837. (P. 70)

M. T. CARTRIGHT Guardian. Guardian for James N. Cartright and Thomas Atwood, minor heirs of Hezekiah Cartright. Recorded 15 February 1837. (P. 71)

A. SIMMONS Guardian. 6 February 1837. Guardian for the children of Dudley Ware. Recorded 15 February 1837. (P. 71)

SOLS DEBOW Guardian. Guardian for Margaret, James, John, and Ann Elizabeth Debow, children of A. Debow. Recorded 15 February 1837. (P. 72)

SAMUEL TRIGG Guardian. 6 February 1837. Guardian of William Word. (Pp. 72-73)

JOHN P. HUGHS Guardian. Guardian for the minor heirs of Gedalech Hughs, to wit, Littleberry and Gedalech Hughs. Recorded 16 February 1837. (Pp. 73-74)

JOHN GADDY Guardian. Guardian for Ezekiel Gaddy, a minor heir of Elijah Gaddy. Recorded 17 February 1837. (P. 75)

JOSEPH M. HEARN Guardian. 6 February 1837. Guardian for Louisa W. Edwards, minor heir of William Edwards. (P. 76)

NELSON J. BRYAN Guardian. 6 February 1837. Guardian for William M. Bryan, minor heir of Nelson Bryan. (P. 76)

HUGH H. BRADLEY Guardian. Guardian of Robert Van Buren Holland, minor heir of Alexander Holland. Recorded 17 February 1837. (P. 77)

WILLIAM H. GRIMMETT Guardian. 6 February 1837. Guardian for Sary Bryan, minor heir of Nelson Bryan. Heir has received property from Joshua Lester. (P. 78)

JAMES SHANNON Guardian. 6 February 1837. Guardian for Jeptha and Caroline Clemmons, minor heirs of Jeptha Clemmons. (P. 78)

LEWIS PATTERSON Guardian. Guardian for his children, the legatees of the Estate of Jacob Jennings. Recorded 25 February 1837. (P. 78)

THOMAS TELFORD Report. 3 February 1837. A true return of the estate of the heirs of H. Telford. "There is three heirs, two are over twenty." (P. 79)

STEPHEN McDONALD Guardian. Guardian for Samuel L. Eason. Recorded 21 February 1837. (Pp. 80-81)

WILLIAM PHILLIPS Guardian. Guardian for the minor heirs of Samuel Dodds. Recorded 21 February 1837. (P. 81)

THOMAS MILES Guardian. Guardian for Martha and Newton Underwood, heirs of Berry Underwood. Recorded 21 February 1837. (P. 81)

THOMAS R. WYNN Guardian. Guardian for Sarah Johnson.

GUARDIAN SETTLEMENTS 1836-1841

Recorded 21 February 1837. (P. 82)

ALEXANDER ESKEW Guardian. 6 March 1837. Guardian for the heirs of Bird Guill. (P. 83)

CHARLES COMPTON Guardian. Guardian for the heirs of Skine Hancock, to wit, Lennie, Eleanor, Porter, and Jacob Hancock. Recorded 20 March 1837. (P. 83)

JOHN ORGAN Guardian. 6 March 1837. Guardian of Mary Ann Johnson, minor heir of Watkins Johnson. (P. 84)

SOLOMON CAPLINGER Guardian. 6 March 1837. Guardian of Elizabeth Lindsey, a lunatic. (P. 85)

WILLIAM C. ODOM Guardian. Guardian for Alexander Weatherspoon's heirs. Recorded 21 March 1837. (P. 86)

ROBERT CAMPBELL Guardian. Guardian for Allen and Elizabeth Webb, minor heirs of William Webb. Recorded 21 March 1837. (P. 86)

SAMUEL VICK Guardian. Guardian for James Little. Recorded 21 March 1837. (P. 86)

WILLIAM TARVER Guardian. Guardian for Nathan Ames, minor heir of Thomas Ames. Recorded 21 March 1837. (P. 87)

MARY REESE Guardian. Guardian of Mary Barbee, Jr., Eliza Barbee, Elizabeth J. Barbee who are the minor heirs of John Barbee. By Thomas B. Reese. Recorded 22 March 1837. (P. 89)

EDWARD TRAVILLIAN Guardian. Guardian of James, Anderson, Grasty, and Matthew Breedlove, the minor heirs of Thomas C. Breedlove. Recorded 22 March 1837. (Pp. 89-90)

BRITAIN DRAKE Guardian. Guardian of Caroline and James Hunter, minor heirs of William Hunter. Recorded 22 March 1837. (Pp. 90-91)

JOSIAH SMITH Guardian. Guardian for Benjamin Clifton, minor heir of Jesse Clifton. Recorded 23 March 1837. (P. 91)

WILLIAM P. DONNELL. 6 March 1837. Guardian for the minor heirs of Dr. Kelly, to wit, Eliza, Jane, Martha, and William D. Kelly. (P. 91)

PHILLIP SHORES Guardian. 6 March 1837. Guardian for his own children, to wit, Richard, Patsy, W. M., Jonathan, and Jane Shores as heirs of their sister Rachel Craton. (P. 92)

JOSHUA PRUETT Guardian. Guardian for the minor heirs of Warrington O'Neal, to wit, Jane and Martha Ann O'Neal. Recorded 24 March 1837. (P. 93)

ROBERT SWEATT Guardian. 6 May 1837. Guardian for Nancy Sweatt, minor heir of George Sweatt. (P. 94)

EDWARD SWEATT Guardian. Guardian for the minor heirs

of Thomas Tuggle. Recorded 24 March 1837. (P. 95)

WILLIAM McGRIGOR Guardian. Guardian of Eliza Brown. Recorded 28 March 1837. (P. 96)

ENNIS DOUGLASS Guardian. Guardian of the heirs of E. B. Corley. Recorded 10 April 1837. (P. 97)

B. G. NETTLES Guardian. Guardian for the heirs of Benjamin Nettles, to wit, Elizabeth and William C. Nettles. Recorded 10 April 1837. (P. 98)

RANSOM GWYNN Guardian. 6 March 1837. Guardian for Rebecca Gwynn, (P. 98)

JOHN R. WILSON Guardian. 6 March 1837. Guardian for Andrew W. and Margaret E. Thompson, minor heirs of John Thompson. (P. 98)

EDWARD B. WHEELER Guardian. 6 March 1837. Guardian for the heirs of John Wheeler. (P. 99)

ALLEN ROSS Guardian. Guardian for the heirs of Henry Rieff, to wit, Katherine and Darthula Rieff. Also, for the heirs of Samuel Bryant, to wit, Julia and Miseble Bryant. Recorded 10 April 1837. (P. 101)

REBECCA PUCKETT Guardian. Guardian for Rebecca Puckett, minor heir of Shippy A. Puckett. Recorded 10 April 1837. (P. 101)

A. R. DILLARD Guardian. 1 March 1837. Guardian of Thomas B. Taylor, minor heir of Thomas Taylor. (P. 104)

LEVI DONNELL Guardian. 3 April 1837. Guardian for Hiram L. Sherrell, minor heir of A. ?. Sherrell. Guardian reported that the return of Shelah Waters as Executor of Hugh Sherrell who was the previous guardian was included. (P. 104)

WILLIAM P. DAVIDSON Guardian. Guardian of Baby Bell. Recorded 11 April 1837. (P. 105)

DUNCAN JOHNSON Guardian. Guardian of William Neal, Margaret J. Neal, and Isaac Neal, the children and heirs of Isaac Neal. Recorded 11 April 1837. (P. 106)

ISAIAH COE Guardian. 1 March 1837. Guardian of William Compton, minor heir of William Compton. (P. 107)

SYRUS STUART Guardian. Guardian of the minor heirs of Samuel Cunningham. Recorded 8 June 1837. (P. 108)

SYRUS STUART Guardian. Guardian of the minor heirs of John Gleaves, to wit, Malvina, William, and John Gleaves. Recorded 8 June 1837. (P. 108)

GEORGE ALEXANDER Guardian. 3 July 1837. Guardian of the minor heirs of Robert Alexander, to wit, Joseph and Jesse Alexander. (P. 109)

JOHN SPINKS Guardian. 3 July 1837. Guardian for the minor heirs of Aaron Sherin. No effects accruing to said minors until the death of Joanah Sherin. (P. 109)

9

SARAH STUART Guardian. 7 August 1837. Guardian for Isaac N. Stuart. By James Tipton. (P. 110)

HANNAH FRAZER Guardian. Guardian of Henry S. Frazer and Martha J. Frazer. Recorded 13 September 1837. (Pp.

JAMES TIPTON Guardian. Guardian of Sireny Tipton. Recorded 4 June 1838. (P. 111)

WILLIAM LAWRENCE Guardian. 7 August 1837. Guardian of Sarah Lawrence. (P. 113)

ALLIGOOD WOOLARD Guardian. Guardiah for the heirs of Hezekiah Archer, to wit, Hezekiah, William, Eli, Mary, and Laney Archer. Recorded 29 November 1837. (P. 114)

JEFFERSON BELL Guardian. Guardian for his children, to wit, John L., Edward D., Harriet L., and Sarah Ann Bell. Money from the first sale of James Johnson deceased. Recorded 26 December 1837. (P. 115)

NELSON BRYAN Guardian. Guardian of Melchesdec Francis, minor heir of Micajah Francis. Recorded 16 January 1838. (Pp. 116-117)

JOSEPH CLOYD Guardian. 26 December 1837. Guaraian for the heirs of David Cloyd. (P. 118)

AZARIAH CORDER Guardian. 1 January 1838. Guardian of the minor heirs of George Allen. (P. 118)

JAMES D. WHITE Guardian. Guardian of Daniel, Isaac, and Amanda Bradley, minor heirs of David Bradley. Recorded January 1838. (P. 119)

ALEXANDER SIMMONS Guardian. Guardian of Dudley Ware's children, to wit, John R., James, Thomas, Granberry, Lovell, Devy, Sally, Dudley, Jerusha, Cintha, and Polly Ware, to whom a legacy has been bequeathed by their grandfather, Thomas Ware of Montgomery County, North Carolina. There were eleven children. John R., James, and Thomas are of age. Devy and Granberry are dead. First two guardians were Adnah Donnell and James Porterfield. Recorded 15 October 1839. (Pp. 120-121)

ISRAEL MOORE Guardian. Guardian of Sophia and Martha Hunt. Recorded 17 January 1838. (P. 120)

THOMAS ESTES Guardian. Guardian of his children, to wit, Martha, J. T., Elizabeth J., Joshua A., and William P. Estes. Recorded 17 January 1838. (P. 120)

NELSON D. HANCOCK Guardian. Guardian for (Druritha) Hancock. Recorded 17 January 1838. (P. 120)

JACOB CASTLEMAN Guardian. Guardian for the minor heirs of Bird Wall, to wit, William and Sarah Wall. One note on Christian Wall (interest due to the widow). Recorded 17 January 1838. (P. 121)

MARY M. COWAN Guardian. Guardian of the minor heirs of William M. Cowan. Recorded 17 January 1838. (Pp. 121)

GUARDIAN SETTLEMENTS 1836-1841

E. R. HARRISON Guardian. Guardian for Dicy F. Harrison. Recorded 18 January 1838. (P. 122)

COLEMAN TALLY Guardian. Guardian for Wesley Harris. Recorded 18 January 1838. (P. 122)

GEORGE SMITH Guardian. Guardian for Robert B. Smith. Recorded 18 January 1838. (P. 122)

MATTHEW T. CARTRIGHT Guardian. Guardian for James W. Cartright who is the minor heir of Hezekiah Cartright. Recorded 18 January 1839. (P. 123)

MATTHEW T. CARTRIGHT Guardian. Guardian for Thomas Atwood, minor heir of Edwin Atwood. Recorded 18 January 1838. (P. 123)

LINA WARREN Guardian. Guardian of Elizabeth, Elvira, and Eliza Jane Warren, heirs at law of Charles Warren. Recorded 18 January 1838. (P. 124)

THOMAS DRENNAN Guardian. Guardian for Hardenia L. Drennan, minor heir of Thomas Drennan deceased. Recorded 18 January 1838. (P. 124)

SOLOMAN HARTSFIELD Guardian. 1 January 1838. Guardian for Mary M. Adkinson. (P. 125)

CHARLES BRADLEY Guardian. Guardian for James and John Calhoun, minor heirs of John Calhoun. Recorded 19 January 1838. (P. 126)

THOMAS BABB Guardian. Guardian for Hicksey C. T. Babb. Recorded 19 January 1839. (P. 127)

SAMUEL WALKER Guardian. Guardian for Thomas Walker. Recorded 19 January 1838. (P. 127)

A. H. WYNN Guardian. Guardian for John A. and William G. Wynn. Recorded 19 January 1838. (Pp. 128-129)

ROBERT P. SWEATT Guardian. Guardian for Nancy Sweatt. Recorded 24 January 1838. (P. 131)

M. C. HANKINS Guardian. Guardian for Elizabeth Grissim, one of the children and heirs of Rowland W. Grissim. Recorded 24 January 1838. (P. 132)

RIAL J. ATKINSON Guardian. Guardian for the children of James Hunt. Recorded 24 January 1838. (P. 132)

JAMES W. GRISSIM Guardian. Guardian of John D., Wilson T., and Julia Ann Grissim, minor children of Rolland W. Grissim. Recorded 24 January 1838. (P. 133)

N. SANDERS Guardian. Guardian for Robert, Agnes, Rolpha, Nancy, and George Sanders, heirs of Richard Sanders. Josias P. Sanders, Executor (father of said wards except George). Recorded 24 January 1838. (Pp. 134-135)

LEWIS WRIGHT Guardian. Guardian for Richard J., James J., and Rachel J. Tate. Recorded 26 January 1838. (P. 135)

11

GUARDIAN SETTLEMENTS 1836-1841

EPHRAIM TALLY Guardian. Guardian for Edwin C. Tally. Recorded 26 January 1838. (P. 136)

GEORGE A. WILLIFORD Guardian. Guardian for Sam E. Tally Recorded 26 January 1838. (P. 137)

EDMONT CRAWFORD Guardian. 1 January 1838. Guardian of the heirs of Ransom Ward. (P. 138)

JAMES T. PENNY Guardian. Guardian of Napoleon B. Patton. Recorded 26 January 1838. (P. 138)

ISAIAH COE Guardian. Guardian of Jemima Sweatt, one of the children of William Sweatt. Recorded 26 January 1838. (P. 139)

EDMONT CRAWFORD Guardian. 1 January 1838. Guardian of Margaret Smith. (P. 139)

EDMONT CRAWFORD Guardian. 1 January 1838. Guardian of the minor heirs of Gilbert Young. (P. 140)

REUBEN P. COMER Guardian. 1 January 1838. Guardian of Catharine Marrs. (P. 142)

NANCY CRUTCHFIELD Guardian. Guardian for John, George, and Lucy Crutchfield. Recorded 15 February 1838. (P. 146)

WILLIAM WORD Guardian. Guardian for Samuel Trigg, a minor heir of Daniel Trigg. Recorded 15 February 1838. (P. 147)

WILLIAM VANTREASE Guardian. Guardian for Susan Lawrence, minor heir of John Lawrence. Recorded 15 February 1838. (P. 147)

THOMAS TELFORD Guardian. 5 February 1838. Guardian of Washington Telford. (P. 149)

THORNTON LAIN Guardian. Guardian of William and Jency Ann Haraldson, minor heirs of Ephraim Haraldson. There is one other heir. Recorded 16 February 1838. (P. 150)

DANIEL GLENN Guardian. 19 September 1837. Guardian of Harriet Eagan, one of thirteen heirs of Hugh Eagan. (P. 151)

J. N. ALEXANDER Guardian. Guardian of Esther and Ezekiel Alexander. Recorded 28 October 1838. (P. 156)

ROBERT CAMPBELL Guardian. Guardian of Hugh, Jane, and Eliza Eagan, minor heirs of Hugh Eagan. Recorded 6 November 1838. (P. 156)

ALLEN ROSS Guardian. Guardian for Masible Griffith, formerly Masible Bryant who has intermarried with ____ Griffith. Neither wife nor husband are of age, but cannot commence housekeeping without assistance. (Pp. 157-158)

SUTTON E. Belcher Guardian. Guardian for Abigail Hicks Ellis and Rebecca Jane Ellis, minor heirs of Rebecca

12

GUARDIAN SETTLEMENTS 1836-1841

Ellis. Recorded 6 November 1838. (P. 158)

WILLIAM DAVIS Guardian. Guardian for his children, to wit, Anderson T., Lucy G., and Nancy C. Davis who are heirs of George Webb. Recorded 12 November 1838. (P. 162)

JAMES McFARLAND Guardian. Guardian for Betsy Ann, Mary Jane, Benjamin, and James Castleman, minor heirs of John McFarland. Was also guardian of Arthur Castleman, but he is now of age. Recorded 12 November 1838. (Pp. 166-170)

NATHAN WHEELER Guardian. Guardian of the heirs of Harris Reeder. Recorded 14 November 1838. (P. 173)

WILLIAM C. ODOM Guardian. Guardian of Martha Jane Johnson, a minor heir of Coleman Johnson. Recorded 20 November 1838. (P. 176)

L. B. MOORE Guardian. Guardian of Andrew Nelson Johnson and John B. Johnson, minor heirs of Coleman Johnson. Recorded 20 November 1838. (P. 177)

JAMES S. ODOM Guardian. Guardian of Elizabeth M. Johnson, minor heir of Coleman Johnson. Recorded 20 November 1838. (P. 178)

JAMES M. ARMSTRONG Guardian. Guardian for Garrett Bumpass, a lunatic. Robert Bumpass was the guardian until his death. Recorded 20 November 1838. (P. 179)

JOHN W. GARRETT Guardian. Guardian of Robert C., Franklin E., and David R. Garrett, minor heirs of David Garrett. Recorded 21 November 1838. (P. 182)

MARY BARBEE Guardian. Thomas B. Reese who has married Mary Barbee who was heretofore guardian of her children. (Pp. 187-188)

WILLIAM BYRN Guardian. 29 January 1839. Guardian of Rebecca Ann and Nancy E. Luck, minor heirs of James Luck. The mother was appointed previous guardian, but made no report. (P. 192)

EDMONT CRAWFORD Guardian. Guardian of Peggy T. Smith. The guardian received for her ward money from the estate of said ward's grandfather and grandmother, William and Margaret Smith. Recorded 6 March 1839. (P. 193)

AZARIAH CORDER Guardian. Guardian of Susan and Jesse Allen, minor heirs of George Allen. Recorded 6 March 1839. (P. 197)

WILLIAM C. ODUM Guardian. Guardian for Wilson, Emeline, and Calvin Weatherspoon. Recorded 6 March 1839. (P. 205)

GEORGE E. FRAZER Guardian. Guardian of Benjamin M. and Mary P. Cage, minor heirs of John Cage. Recorded 13 September 1839. (Pp. 210-211)

JAMES PENNY Guardian. 10 January 1839. Guardian for Napoleon B. Patton. The guardian paid for his ward to

C. B. Caldwell, one of the heirs of William Patton deceased who was the father of Napoleon B. (Pp. 217-218)

LEWIS PATTERSON Guardian. 1 January 1839. Guardian of his children, to wit, Nancy, Elizabeth P., Mary Jane, William Carroll, and (Uriah) Patterson, minor heirs of Jacob Jennings. (P. 220)

JAMES L. ODOM Guardian. Guardian of Elizabeth and Malinda Johnson, minor heirs of Coleman Johnson. Recorded 21 September 1839. (P. 221)

ANTHONY OWEN Guardian. Guardian of Peter P. Johnson, minor heir of Coleman Johnson. Recorded 21 September 1839. (P. 222)

WILLIAM C. ODOM Guardian. Guardian of Marthy Jane Johnson, minor heir of Coleman Johnson. Recorded 21 September 1839. (P. 223)

L. B. MOORE Guardian. Guardian of Andrew N. and J. B. Johnson, minor heirs of Coleman Johnson. Recorded 21 September 1839. (P. 224)

JOHN REA Administrator. 23 January 1839. A settlement with John Rea, administrator of William Rea deceased. (P. 225)

ISRAEL MOORE Guardian. Guardian of Sphea (Sophie) and Martha Hunt, minor heirs of Leatty Hunt. Recorded 23 September 1839. (P. 227)

ALFRED ENOCHS Guardian. Guardian of Joseph W. and Elijah Dickens, minors of Etheldred P. Horn, their former guardian now deceased. Recorded 23 September 1839. (P. 229)

EDMOND CRAWFORD Guardian. Guardian of James W. and Andrew McCartney, minor heirs of Lewis McCartney. Recorded 23 September 1839. (Pp. 231-232)

GEORGE SMITH Guardian. Guardian of Isaac N. Johnson, minor heir of Coleman Johnson. Recorded 24 September 1839. (P. 234)

SUTON BUCKNER Guardian. Guardian of (Usley), Jacob, and Richard Buckner, minor heirs of Richard Buckner. Recorded 25 September 1839. (P. 235)

ELIJAH WILLIAMS Guardian. Guardian for Jarratt, Elizabeth, Hiram, Foster, Martha, Jeremiah, James D., John W., Priscilla, and Green H. Tucker, minor heirs of Green Tucker. Recorded 25 September 1839. (P. 229)

PRISCILLA TUCKER Guardian. Guardian of her children, to wit, Jarratt, Elizabeth, Hiram, Foster, Martha, Jeremiah, James D., John W., Priscilla, and Green H. Tucker. Guardian also received from the amount of George Tucker the grandfather of said heirs. . . Recorded September 1839. (Pp. 231-232)

SOLOMON DEBOW Guardian. Guardian of James, John, and Elizabeth Debow. Recorded 26 September 1839. (Pp. 232-233)

14

GUARDIAN SETTLEMENTS 1836-1841

RANSOM GWYNN and JOHN REA Executors. Executors for Benjamin Dobson deceased. Recorded 26 September 1839. (Pp. 234-235)

WILLIAM DAVIS Guardian. Guardian for the minor heirs of Noah Walker, to wit, Parthena, (Lureny), High C., William, Mourning, Martha, Ann, and Noah Walker. Recorded 26 September 1839. (P. 236)

DANIEL GLEN Guardian. 7 February 1839. Guardian for Harriet Eagan, a minor heir of Hugh Eagan. (P. 237)

DANIEL GLEN Guardian. 7 February 1839. Guardian of Carroll, Manah, Isaac, and Nicholas Preston Wray, the minor heirs of Ely Wray. (P. 238)

ISAAC E. GIBSON Guardian. 27 February 1839. Guardian for George, Francis, Jane, and Louisianea Gibson, minor heirs of Arch Gibson. (P. 244)

ALEXANDER ESKEW Guardian. 24 February 1839. Guardian of William, Mary, Ann, Josiah, Nancy, and Isbel Guill, the minor heirs of Bird Guill. (P. 245)

ROBERT BRYSON Administrator. 4 February 1839. A settlement with Robert Bryson, the administrator of D. Bryson deceased. (P. 246)

JAMES ALLEN Administrator. A settlement with James Allen, administrator of George Allen deceased. Recorded 4 October 1839. (P. 249)

WILSON C. WATERS Guardian. Guardian of the heirs of Wiat Lindsey, to wit, John, Peggy, Polly, Elisha, Joseph, and Wiat Lindsey. Recorded 4 October 1839. (Pp. 250-251)

JOHN BATES Guardian. Guardian to Hiram G. Hester, a minor orphant of Benjamin Hester and heir at law of Zachariah Hester, his grandfather, from whose estate he received his legacy in the State of North Carolina. The said John Bates is also guardian for his children, to wit, William, John, Susan, Eliza, and Candia Bates. Recorded 2 October 1839. (Pp. 252-253)

SHELA WATERS Guardian. Guardian for Saraphine, Elizabeth, Josephine, Rebeca, (Dolphine), (Geonie), and Hugh L. White Sherrell, the minor heirs of Hugh Sherrell. The widow is to have a child's part. Recorded 2 October 1839. (Pp. 256-257)

SION BASS Administrator. Administrator of William G. Bass. The widow's share is one third, there being but one child. Recorded 2 October 1839. (Pp. 258-259)

HUGH (CALIN) Administrator. Administrator of Isham (Calin) deceased. Recorded 2 October 1839. (Pp. 260-261)

WILLIAM D. MORRISON Guardian. 22 February 1839. Guardian of Mary, Ann, and Hugh H. Marrs, the minor heirs of Martin Marrs. (P. 261)

ROBERT P. SWEATT Guardian. Guardian of Mary Sweatt.

GUARDIAN SETTLEMENTS 1836-1841

Recorded 3 October 1839. (Pp. 264-265)

WILLIAM H. PEACE Guardian. Guardian for Kiziah Walker, minor heir of William Walker. Recorded 4 October 1839. (Pp. 268-269)

WILLIAM WORD Guardian. Guardian for the minor heir of Daniel Trigg. Recorded 5 October 1839. (Pp. 274-275)

ARCHEMACK BASS Guardian. Guardian for the minor heirs of Jacob Vantrease. Recorded 4 October 1839. (Pp. 276-278)

STEPHEN McDANIEL Guardian. Guardian for the minor heirs of Green Warren, to wit, Martha, Adelea D., and Benjamin G. Warren. Recorded 8 October 1839. (Pp. 279-280)

ELIZABETH REDDIT Guardian. Elizabeth Reddit, formerly Harrison, guardian for Elizabeth Harrison, a minor heir of Sterling Harrison. Recorded 8 October 1839. (P. 281)

JOHN M. ALEXANDER Guardian. Guardian of Ann Eliza McAdow, a minor heir of Newborn McAdow. Recorded 9 October 1839. (P. 284)

LEO DONNELL Guardian. Guardian of Hiram T. Sherrell, a minor heir of Alexander Sherrell. April Term 1839. (P. 286)

EPHRAIM Tally Guardian. Guardian of Edwin C. Tally, a minor heir of Henry Tally. April Term 1839. (P. 287)

THOMAS LEECH GUARDIAN. Guardian of Preston James and John Coffe Leech, minor heirs of John Leech. Recorded 9 October 1839. (P. 288)

ELIZABETH HARRISON Guardian. Guardian for Lansdon Harrison, a minor heir of Sterling Harrison. Another heir, Temperance Harrison, married a man of age. Recorded 9 October 1839. (P. 289)

ISAAC PEAK Guardian. Guardian of the minor heirs of Stokes Zackary, to wit, Joshua and Josephine Zackary. Recorded 11 October 1839. (P. 294)

NELSON HANCOCK Guardian. Guardian of Drucilia Hancock, a minor heir of Nancy Hancock. Recorded 11 October 1839. (P. 295)

*CYRUS SWEATT Guardian. Guardian for the minor heirs of Samuel Cunningham. Said Cunningham's children are heirs at law of Thomas Wray. Recorded 12 October 1839. (P. 296)

NATHAN WHEELER Guardian. Guardian of the minor heirs of Harris Reeder, to wit, William, Mary, and Rachael Reeder. Recorded 12 October 1839. (P. 297)

JOHN B. BRYAN Guardian. Guardian for (Aljurnal) Bryan, a minor heir of Milford Bryant. Recorded 12 October 1839. (P. 304)

*Poor legibility may have made this entry inaccurate.

16

BENJAMIN ALEXANDER GUARDIAN. Guardian of Mary Ann and Robert N. Cloyd, minor heirs of Lettice Cloyd. Recorded 15 October 1839. (P. 306)

JAMES C. BONE Guardian. Guardian for his son, James W. Bone. The guardian received a legacy from the grandfather of said minor, James Smith. Recorded 9 December 1839. (P. 317)

WILLIAM SHANKS Guardian. 25 November 1839. Guardian of Mary, (Mark), and William Joplin. William Joplin is still a minor. (P. 320)

WILLIAM W. CARTER Guardian. Guardian of the minor heirs of Daniel Trigg, to wit, Stephen and Abram Trigg. Recorded 11 December 1839. (Pp. 329-330)

WILLIAM L. S. DEARING Guardian. Former guardian of Kitty, Betsy, and Peter Harrison who are the minor heirs of Thweatt Harrison. Recorded 11 December 1839. (Pp. 331-332)

E. A. WHITE Guardian. Guardian of Dudley, Green, and Raymond Proctor. Recorded 8 January 1840. (Pp. 334-335)

ECLEMUEL SULLIVAN Guardian. Guardian of the minor heirs of Levi Holland, to wit, Sarah, Noah, and William Holland. Recorded 29 January 1840. (P. 336)

STEPHEN WRAY Guardian. Guardian for James W. Setter. Recorded 4 March 1840. (P. 347)

E. A. WHITE Guardian. Guardian for Green L. Ball. Recorded 4 March 1840. (P. 349)

JAMES THOMAS Guardian. Guardian for the minor heirs of W. B. Thomas, to wit, Catharine who has married Andrew McKee, Mary Elanor, Hugh, and Amy Eliza who has married M. Ewing. One other child, Lucinda, has married. Recorded 5 March 1840. (P. 355)

JOSEPH RUTLAND Guardian. Guardian for Sally and Margaret Cloyd. Recorded 5 March 1840. (P. 356)

WILLIAM B. BYNE Guardian. Guardian for the minor heirs of James L. Leach, to wit, Rebecca Ann and Nancy B. Leach. Recorded 5 March 1840. (P. 359)

JOHN B. SCOBY Guardian. Guardian of James L. Goodall, a minor heir of Hardin Goodall. Recorded 5 March 1840. (P. 363)

WILLIAM C. MOORE Guardian. Guardian of the minor heirs of Isham Carlin, to wit, Elizabeth, Martha, Evaline, Louisa, John, and Hugh Carlin. Recorded 6 March 1840. (P. 367)

William Davis Guardian. Guardian of his children, Anderson L., Lucy G., and Nancy C. Davis who are the minor heirs at law of John Webb. Recorded 6 March 1840. (P. 370)

GUARDIAN SETTLEMENTS 1836-1841

JAMES B. TAYLOR Guardian. 27 January 1840. Guardian of Francis Ann and Joshua B. Taylor, children of Jeremiah Taylor, son of (Joshua) Taylor who was the grandfather of these minors. The guardian reported that the said children now live in Mississippi. (P. 371)

MARK JACKSON Guardian. Guardian for his son, John M. Jackson to whom a legacy was bequeathed by his uncle John M. Jackson. Recorded 9 March 1840. (P. 374)

WOOD H. SHERRON Guardian. Guardian of Amanda G. E. Hunt, a daughter of Jesse and Martha Hunt. Said Amanda received a family of negroes willed to Mrs. Hunt by her mother, Martha Baker, for and during her lifetime which are to descend to the heirs of her body or for want of such to the brothers of said Martha Hunt, to wit, Edward and Thomas Drenton. Recorded 9 March 1840. (P. 375)

LEWIS Wright Guardian. Guardian of James J. and Rachel J. Tate, children of Zidekiah Tate and legatees of Winneford Johnson. Recorded 9 March 1840. (Pp. 378-379)

CHARLES WADE Guardian. 20 February 1840. Guardian of the minor daughters of Thweatt Harrison, to wit, Kitty, Elizabeth, and Petro Quincy Harrison. Their late guardian was William L. S. Dearing. (Pp. 382-383)

BENNETT BABB Guardian. 12 February 1840. Guardian of Margaret A. White, a minor heir of Edward White. (P. 385)

ROBERT L. MILLS Guardian. Guardian of Charles, Malvina, and Peggy Bonner (two others married and settled). They are the minor heirs of Thomas L. Bonner. Recorded 10 March 1840. (P. 385)

SAMUEL JOHNSON Guardian. Guardian of Mary Ann and Theophelus J. Johnson, children of John M. Johnson and heirs at law of Theophelus Gray deceased. Recorded 11 March 1840. (P. 390)

EDMOND CRAWFORD Guardian. 8 February 1840. Guardian of Martha Jane, Parallee, Catharine, Nancy, Emaline, Louisa, and Gilbert Young, minor heirs of Gilbert Young. (P. 398)

JAMES J. FREEMAN Guardian. Guardian of the minor heirs of Matthew Dew, to wit, William C., Nancy Jane, Thomas B., and John M. Dew. Recorded 13 March 1840. (Pp. 401-404)

THOMAS TURNER Guardian. Guardian of Adalin, Matilda, and William P. Turner, the minor heirs of William Turner. Recorded 13 March 1840. (P. 405)

L. W. WHITE Trustee. 27 October 1840. Trustee of E. A. White who was the guardian of William Bilbo. (P. 408)

CLAIBORNE W. NEAL Guardian. Guardian of William C. Branch, a minor heir of Robert C. C. Branch. The widow's

18

GUARDIAN SETTLEMENTS 1836-1841

part is one-third. Recorded March 1840. (P. 413)

NAT SANDERS Guardian. 17 January 1840. Guardian
for George Sanders who was a son of William Sanders and
Robert, Agnes, Rolpha, and Mary Sanders who are the
children of Josia P. Sanders who had a legacy bequeathed by
their grandfather, Richard Sanders. (P. 420)

ISREAL MOORE Guardian. Guardian of Sopha and Martha
Hunt, the minor heirs of Altha Hunt. Recorded 21 January
1841. (P. 423)

WILLIAM MOSS Guardian. Guardian of James C. Moss,
a minor heir of Thomas Moss. Recorded 21 January 1841.
(P. 427)

WILLIAM WILLIS Guardian. Guardian for the minor heirs
of John Smith, to wit, Warren M., Mary A. H., Phebe F.,
and Daniel E. Smith. Sophia Smith is the mother of these
children. Recorded January 1841. (Pp. 430-431)

E. A. WHITE Guardian. Guardian for Sarah Clifton.
Cash paid her husband, William C. Clifton. Recorded 3
January 1841. (P. 431)

GEORGE WILLIAMSON Guardian. 10 May 1840. Guardian
of Elizabeth J. Crutchfield, a minor of Dr. H. C. Crutchfield. (P. 431)

DAVID McMURRY Guardian. Guardian of David M. Blythe,
a minor heir of Richard Blythe deceased. The infant has
been raised from a baby by his guardian. He is now about
thirteen years old. Settlement made in Sumner County,
Tennessee on 7 November 1837. Cash notes on Turner
Barnes which are doubtful having been given a long time
ago. The drawer is now living in Texas. A sum advanced
to James E. Blythe as one of the heirs. Recorded 3
January 1841. (Pp. 437-438)

A. G. MUIRHEAD Guardian. Guardian of Martha Jane
Frazer. Recorded 4 January 1841. (P. 440)

BURRELL PATTERSON Guardian. Guardian of his children, to wit, Martha and Marinda Patterson who are heirs
at law of their brother William Patterson. Recorded 5
January 1841. (P. 443)

MOSES ELLIS Guardian. Guardian of the heirs of
Thomas B. Chappell, to wit, Lucinda, Thomas B., and Nancy
J. Chappell. Recorded 5 March 1841. (P. 447)

RUTHERFORD R. BARTON Guardian. Guardian of John H.
McLarin, a minor heir of John W. H. McLarin. His ward is
about four years old. The guardian has paid since he
married his mother 1838. Recorded 5 March 1841. (P. 449)

JOHN SMITH Guardian. Guardian of Robert, Andrew, and
Margaret Smith, minor heirs of John Smith. Hugh Robertson
was the administrator of Mary Smith who was the mother of
these children. Recorded 5 March 1841. (P. 450)

HICKS ELLIS Guardian. Guardian of Pamelia Ellis,

19

Elizabeth Ellis, and Samuel P. Ellis who are minor heirs of Rebecca Ellis. Recorded 10 March 1841. (P. 455)

MICHAEL E. JONES Guardian. Guardian of Pamelia Ellis, a minor heir of Rebecca Ellis. Recorded 10 March 1841. (P. 455)

WILLIAM JENNINGS Guardian. Guardian of Clem Jennings, a minor heir of (m Jennings. This ward is about twenty years of age and is a farmer. Recorded 10 March 1841. (P. 456)

SAM HILL Guardian. Guardian of John, Charles, and Elizabeth Simpson, minor heirs of Nathan Simpson. The guardian reported that he has from their grandfather's estate their part of the proceeds of a tract of land in the State of Kentucky. Recorded 10 May 1841. (P. 457)

GUARDIAN SETTLEMENTS 1841-1845

WILLIAM F. JONES Guardian. Guardian for his children, to wit, Martha, Calvin, Emily, Alfred, Richard, Rachel, Fathy, and William F. Jones, minor heirs of his wife, Lucy Jones, who was a daughter of Richard and Rachel Wommack deceased. Recorded 7 December 1841. (P. 3)

ANDERSON LOYD Guardian. Guardian of the minor orphans of (Charity) Chappell, to wit, Samuel, Alfred, Robert, and William Chappell. Said Charity was a daughter of Phillip Johnson. Recorded 7 December 1841. (P. 3)

MARY J. FOSTER Guardian. Guardian of (Missouri) Ellin and William Foster, the minor heirs of Richard Foster. The widow (who is the guardian) and two children are all the heirs. Recorded 6 January 1842. (P. 10)

WILLIAM WORD Guardian. Guardian of Samuel (Sugg). Recorded 6 January 1842. (P. 13)

JOHN B. SCOBY Guardian. Guardian of James L. Goodall, a minor heir of Hardin Goodall. James Scoby, the grandfather of this child has raised him. Recorded 6 January 1842. (P. 13)

RHODA BELL Guardian. Guardian of Rebecca Eliza and Parthena Maria Bell, the minor heirs of Amzi Bell. Recorded 6 January 1842. (Pp. 15-16)

SOLOMON DEBOW Guardian. Guardian for the minor heirs of Archibald Debow, to wit, James, John, and Ann Elizabeth Debow. Recorded 7 January 1842. (Pp. 19-20)

P. ANDERSON Guardian. Guardian who was appointed guardian of Garrison Sweatt. Said Garrison now deceased was the heir of William Sweatt. Recorded 7 January 1842. (P. 21)

ISAAC E. GIBSON Guardian. Guardian of George, Francis Jane, and Louisa Gibson who are minor children of Archibald Gibson. Minors had a legacy bequeathed to them by Polly Ann Moseley now deceased. Recorded 7 January 1842. (P. 22)

RANSOM GWYNN Guardian. 27 March 1830. Guardian of Newton Underwood, a minor heir of Perry Underwood. Including the widow, there were ten distributees. (P. 31)

ELI S. CARUTH Guardian. Guardian of William and George Caruth, the minor heirs of William S. Caruth. The heirs are the widow and two children. Recorded 11 January 1842. (P. 39)

PRESTON HENDERSON Guardian. Guardian of the minor heirs of John Bone, to wit, Elihu C., James F., Aceneth M., Robert D., Samuel N., John H., and Levice J. Bone. Recorded 5 February 1842. (P. 40)

RUFUS H. FOSTER Guardian. Guardian (who is related to the Clerk) for the minor heirs of John D. Foster, to wit, Benjamin, John D., Martha R., Elizabeth, Anderson E.`,

21

and Mary E. Foster. Recorded 13 January 1842. (P.

ISRAEL MOORE Guardian. Guardian of the minor heirs of Aletha Hunt. Recorded 14 January 1842. (P. 48)

DUNCAN JOHNSON Guardian. Guardian of the minor heirs of Isaac Neal, to wit, Wilson, Margaret J., and Isaac Neal. Recorded 14 January 1842. (P. 48)

CYRUS STEWART Guardian. Guardian of William and John Gleaves, the minor heirs of John Gleaves. Recorded 14 January 1842. (P. 50)

WILLIAM BILBO Guardian. Guardian for his children, to wit, Mary Ann, Elizabeth, and Berryman H. Bilbo who are heirs at law of John McFarland who was also appointed for his son James M. Bilbo who has since died. Recorded 15 January 1842. (P. 55)

ROBERT D. REED Guardian. Guardian of the minor children of Henry Reed, to wit, Mary J. and Walter Reed and heirs at law of Walter Carruth deceased. Their mother who was a daughter of the deceased is dead. Recorded 12 January 1842. (P. 56)

S. E. BELCHER Guardian. Guardian of the minor heirs of Richard Belcher, to wit, Usly, Jacob, and Richard Belcher. Recorded 7 January 1842. (P. 63)

SUTTON E. BELCHER Guardian. Guardian of the minor children of Phillip Johnson, to wit, Jarrett, James, Joseph, and Sarah Ann Johnson. Recorded 17 January 1842. (P. 63)

WILSON L. WATERS. Administrator of William Phillips who was guardian for the minor heirs of Samuel Dodd. Said deceased left a widow and seven minor children. Recorded 17 January 1842. (P. 65)

JOSEPH FREEMAN Guardian. 1 December 1841. Guardian of the minor heirs of Matthew Dew. The guardian married the widow. (Pp. 66-67)

WILLIAM M. GRAY Guardian. Guardian for his brothers, to wit, John J., David J., Hiram C., and Samuel Gray. Recorded 21 April 1842. (P. 68)

WILLIAM J. JENNINGS Guardian. Guardian for Clem Jennings, a minor heir of Clem Jennings. Recorded 21 April 1842. (P. 69)

THOMAS WYNNE Guardian. Guardian of Edney Bell, a minor heir of Jefferson Bell. Recorded 23 April 1842. (P. 77)

JOHN A. MAJOR Guardian. Guardian of the minor heirs of Henry A. Major, to wit, Martha A. and Samuel W. Major. Recorded 23 April 1842. (P. 78)

JOHN A. CLOPTON Guardian. 22 January 1842. Guardian of William S. and Eliza Ann Clopton who are the minor heirs of Walter Clopton. There is a negro woman belonging

GUARDIAN SETTLEMENTS 1841-1845

to five of the heirs. (Pp. 78-79)

EDWARD SWEATT Guardian. Guardian of the minor heirs of Thomas Tuggle, to wit, Sally, Polly, John, Fanny, and Martha Tuggle. Recorded 26 April 1842. (Pp. 87-92)

ALBERT H. WYNNE Guardian. 31 January 1842. Guardian of John A. and William Wynne, minor heirs of John L. Wynne. (P. 93)

WILLIAM B. BYRN Guardian. Guardian of Rebecca Ann and Nancy B. Luck, minor heirs of J. S. Luck. Recorded 28 April 1842. (P. 98)

NANCY JOHNSON Guardian. Guardian of Samuel A. and Clementary D. Johnson, minor heirs of Phillip Johnson. Recorded 28 April 1842. (P. 102)

E. A. WHITE Guardian. Guardian for Sarah Clifton. A note on William Clifton who was the husband of said Sarah Clifton. Recorded 28 April 1842. (P. 103)

WILLIAM CURD Guardian. Guardian for Robert A., Doshea, and Marian Davis, heirs at law of J. M. Davis. There are five distributees. Recorded 28 April 1842. (P. 106)

W. H. PEACE Guardian. 9 January 1842. Guardian for Kiziah Walker, a lunatic. (P. 107)

ALFRED McCLAIN Guardian. Guardian of Josiah, Frances, Elizabeth, Washington, (Moore), and Samuel Houston Stevenson, the minor heirs of Isaac T. Stevenson. Recorded 28 April 1842. (Pp. 109-110)

JOHN W. HEWGLEY Guardian. Guardian of James S., Thomas C., Elen M., Washington Lafayette, and Sarah A. Whitsitt, minor heirs of William D. Whitsitt. The said William D. died in the State of Kentucky and administration was granted there. Recorded 6 May 1842. (P. 112)

WILLIAM YANDLE Guardian. 6 June 1839. Guardian of James N. Yandle, his minor son who is an heir of William Barr deceased. Recorded 7 May 1842. (P. 114)

ARCHIBALD REA Guardian. Guardian of Jourdan and Louisa Rea, heirs of Archibald Rea, Sr. There were eleven distributees. The guardian was appointed guardian for Martha who has since married Thomas K. Roach. Received of Archibald Rea, Executor of the Estate of Rhea, Sr. deceased and administrator of Susan Rhea deceased. Recorded 9 May 1842. (P. 118)

WILLIAM CAMPBELL Guardian. Guardian of Olivia Rhea, a minor heir of Archibald Rhea. Recorded 9 May 1842. (P. 119)

WILEY E. (JONES) Administrator. 12 March 1842. Administrator of Polly (Jones). The said Polly at the time of her death had in her possession a negro woman given by her father to be divided among her children at her death. (P. 138)

23

BENJAMIN G. BARCLAY Guardian. Guardian of Joseph Lindsey, a minor heir of Wyett Lindsey. Recorded 16 November 1842. (P. 140)

JOSEPH RUTLAND Guardian. Guardian of the minor heirs of Joseph Pew, to wit, William G., Mary J., J. F., E. B., M. A., J. F., and G. W. Pew. There are nine distributees. The guardian has paid the mother of these children. Recorded 16 November 1842. (P. 143)

JAMES CUNNINGHAM Guardian. Guardian of William N. and Andrew T. Underwood. Recorded 16 November 1842. (P. 144)

THOMAS THORN Guardian. Guardian of Cornelia A. and Elisha P. Underwood. Recorded 19 November 1842. (P. 144)

THOMAS KIRKPATRICK Guardian. Guardian of the minor heirs of Ann Zackary, to wit, Elizabeth L., Nancy, and Cinthea Zackary. Recorded 7 June 1842. (Pp. 147-148)

REBECCA SUBLETT Guardian. Guardian of Rebecca Puckett, a minor heir of (Shepp) A. Puckett. Recorded 27 November 1842. (P. 149)

M. CARTRIGHT Guardian. Guardian of Mary Atwood. Recorded 17 December 1842. (P. 155)

HENRY B. WILLIAMS Guardian. Guardian of John Rea, a minor heir of Archibald Rea. Recorded 17 December 1842. (P. 156)

FINIS E. SHANNON Guardian. Guardian of Rachel C. Hearn, a minor heir of Milbrey Hearn. Recorded 13 December 1842. (P. 160)

THOMAS S. Hill Guardian. Guardian of Thomas A. Hill. Recorded 13 December 1843. (P. 165)

THOMAS VAUGHN Guardian. Guardian of Joel N. Vanhook who was a grandson of Jacob Vanhook, now deceased of the State of Virginia and him and his sister are the representatives of their father entitled to a distributive share of the said deceased he having died intestate. The guardian also conveyed their interest in a tract of land in North Carolina for a negro woman who was conveyed to him for them by a bill of sale made by Kendal Vanhook. Recorded 14 December 1842. (P. 165)

JAMES D. WHITE Guardian. Guardian for Robert, Kiziah, and John Hamlet, minors. Recorded 14 December 1842. (P. 167)

ELIZABETH W. HORN Guardian. Guardian of the minor heirs of Etheldred P. Horn, to wit, Elizabeth Ann, Mary B., Charlotte B., Rebecca P., James B., and Etheldred P. Horn. Recorded 14 December 1842. (Pp. 170-171)

ROWLAND G. ANDREWS Guardian. Guardian of the minor heirs of Thomas Webb, to wit, Elizabeth and Thomas J. Webb. They are entitled under the pension laws of the United States to a pension for five years which the mother of these child-

24

ren drew during her widowhood. She married the fourth of
June 1841. Since that time, the children are entitled
to the pension. Recorded 15 December 1842. (P. 171)

JAMES B. TAYLOR Guardian. Guardian of Martha,
Louisa, and John P. Taylor, minor heirs of Joshua V. Taylor. Recorded 15 December 1842. (P. 173)

PETER HUBBARD Guardian. Guardian of Mary P. Barry,
formerly Mary P. Cage. Recorded 15 December 1842. (P.
175)

BENJAMIN ALEXANDER Guardian. Guardian of Robert M.
Cloyd. Recorded 10 January 1843. (P. 176)

MAJOR E. A. WHITE Guardian. Guardian of Martha
Bradley. Recorded 10 January 1843. (P. 177)

ISAIAH ALLISON Guardian. Guardian of Harriet Ann
Allison, a minor heir of John L. Allison. Said Harriet
Ann received from the estate of William Bond. Recorded
10 February 1843. (P. 178)

NORMAN WALSH Guardian. Guardian of James W. Hearn,
a minor heir of Milbrey Hearn. Recorded 15 January 1844.
(P. 189)

THOMAS J. MUMFORD Guardian. Guardian of the minor
heirs of Charles A. Lewis, to wit, Hannah and Robert
Lewis. Recorded 16 January 1844. (Pp. 198-199)

WILLIAM DAVIS Guardian. Guardian of Anderson L.,
Lucy G., and Nancy C. his children heirs at law of John
Webb. Recorded 15 January 1844. (P. 202).

MOSES ELLIS Guardian. 11 February 1843. Guardian
of Lucinda E. and Elizabeth Jane Chappell, minor heirs of
Thomas B. Chappell. Since the last report one of the heirs,
improperly called Nancy Jane, has died. The mother raises
the children on the farm. (P. 205)

JOHN BROGAN Guardian. Guardian of Parrallee Brogan,
his daughter, who is the minor heir of Elizabeth Brogan.
The guardian has received for his said daughter, Parrallee
Brogan, from the estate of her grandfather, Abner Moore,
the 24th of February last year. (P. 207)

JAMES WILLIAMS Guardian. Guardian of Frazer Baker
Williams who will be 19 years old the 17th September next,
Raleigh (Brox) Baker Williams who was 17 years old the 2nd
January 1843, Newborn Stanley Guston Williams, 13 years old
the 27th this month. His children and heirs of Polly Wil-
liams deceased. The guardian has received from the estate
of Mary Baker in the State of Virginia. Recorded 17
January 1844. (P. 208)

JOSEPH B. WYNN Guardian. Guardian of the minor heirs
of Jesse McHenry, to wit, Eliza, Fanny, and Carroll McHenry.
Said Wynn was guardian of four other heirs, to wit, James,
Elizabeth, Jesse, and Rebecca McHenry who now are of age.
Recorded 17 January 1844. (Pp. 212-213)

25

ROBERT CAMPBELL Guardian. Guardian of Allen Webb.
Was the guardian of Elizabeth Webb, but who has married.
Also, guardian for two of Cyrus Stewart's children. One
of which has married and the other of age. They were en-
titled to a distributive share of the estate of Samuel
Motheral. Recorded 17 January 1844. (P. 216)

LEWIS WRIGHT Guardian. Guardian of Martha G. Lumpkin, a minor heir of Obadiah Lumpkin. Recorded 18
January 1844. (P. 219)

SOLOMON DEBOW Guardian. Guardian of the minor heirs
of A. A. Debow, to wit, John, Ann Elizabeth, and James
Debow. Recorded 18 January 1844. (P. 228)

WILLIAM L. REDDITT Guardian. Guardian of Elizabeth
Harrison, a minor heir of Sterling Harrison deceased.
Elizabeth Redditt, the wife of said William L. Redditt,
was formerly the widow of said Sterling Harrison. Recorded 18 January 1844. (P. 229)

THOMAS THORN Guardian. Guardian of the minor heirs
of Elisha Underwood, to wit, Cornelia Ann, William, Newton, Andrew T., and Elisha P. Underwood. Recorded 18
January 1844. (P. 230)

DUNCAN JOHNSON Guardian. Guardian of the minor
heirs of Charles Bradley, to wit, William, John, and
Mary Bradley. Recorded 18 January 1844. (P. 231)

ANDREW GWYNN Guardian. Guardian of the minor heirs
of James Rice, to wit, Fredonia, Esther, Elizabeth,
Sally, and James Thomas Rice. Recorded 19 January 1844.
(Pp. 235-237)

WILLIAM LAWRENCE Guardian. Guardian of Francis Newby. Recorded 19 January 1844. (P. 238)

JOHN C. LASH Guardian. Guardian of the minor heirs
of Elijah Jones, to wit, Pembrook, Harriet, Sarah, and
Samuel Jones. The minors are heirs at law of William
Bandy, late of the County of Smith in the State of Tenn.
Recorded 19 January 1844. (P. 239)

DOAK YOUNG Guardian. Guardian of Charles C. and Levi
Smith, two of the children of Jacob and Mary Smith deceased.
Recorded 19 January 1843. (P. 244)

ASHLEY NEAL Guardian. Guardian of (Sion) B., James
W., and Mary E. Smith, three of the children and heirs at
law of Jacob and Mary Smith. Recorded 19 January 1844.
(Pp. 244-245)

H. D. LESTER Guardian. Guardian of Robert and Benjamin Dellis and James Cropper, minor heirs at law of
Robert Dellis. Robert and Benjamin Dellis are entitled to
half and James Cropper to the other half they being grandchildren of said deceased. Recorded 20 January 1844. (P.
248)

CLAIBORN H. RHODES Guardian. Guardian of Joseph B.

Clopton, a minor heir of Jesse B. Clopton. Recorded 20 January 1844. (P. 250)

JAMES STEWART Guardian. Guardian to the minor heirs of Seth Thornton, to wit, Joseph, Ransom, and Houston Thornton. There are nine distributees. Andrew Gwynn is guardian for James Eskew's children, to wit, William, Hughey, Eliza, and James. Recorded 20 January 1844. (P. 251)

MERRETT CARAWAY Guardian. Guardian of his daughter, Elizabeth Caraway. The said Elizabeth is a granddaughter of William Anderson, late of Rutherford County, Tennessee. Recorded 20 January 1844. (P. 253)

JOHNATHAN HOOKER Guardian. Guardian of Christiana and John Clemmons, the minor heirs of Allen Clemmons. Recorded 20 January 1844. (P. 254)

WILLIAM L. WATERS Guardian. Guardian of John Lawrence, a lunatic who is now dead. Said William L. Waters moved "old lady Lawrence to his house." Recorded 20 January 1844. (Pp. 259-260)

JOHNATHAN SHORES Guardian. 23 September 1843. Guardian of Elizabeth McMullin, a minor heir of Andrew McMullin deceased. (P. 262)

JOHN W. ALEXANDER Guardian. Guardian of Martha E. and Margaret Jane Donnell, the minor heirs of Thomas Donnell. Recorded 7 February 1844. (Pp. 267-268)

JAMES D. WHITE Guardian. Guardian of Robert, Kiziah, and John Hamlet Waters, the minor heirs of John Waters. Recorded 7 February 1844. (P. 268)

DAVID PHILLIPS Guardian. Guardian of the minor heirs of William Phillips, to wit, Shelah, A__a, Sally Jane, Elizabeth, Malissa, Caroline, Margaret, Wilson, and Madison Phillips. Recorded 7 February 1844. (P. 270)

DAVID DODD Guardian. Guardian of the minor heirs of Albert Burton, to wit, Susan Frances Burton. The deceased lived in Smith County, Tennessee. Recorded 7 February 1844. (P. 275)

S. E. BELCHER Guardian. Guardian of Asley, Jacob, and Richard Belcher, minor heirs of Richard Belcher. Recorded 8 February 1844. (P. 277)

ROBERT D. REED Guardian. Guardian of Mary J. and Walter C. Reed, minor heirs of Nancy Reed deceased. Recorded 8 February 1844. (P. 279)

NATHAN NEWBETT Guardian. Johnson County, Arkansas. 18 July 1843. Guardian of the minor heirs of Radford Walker, to wit, Martha Ann, Saleno, Samuel, and Polly Walker. Recorded 8 February 1844. (Pp. 287-291)

SOLOMON MOORE Guardian. 16 January 1843. Amanda Jane Moore and Benjamin Franklin Moore, minor heirs who have an estate in Tennessee coming to them request that their father, Solomon Moore, be appointed their legal guardian. (Pp. 291-297)

ROBERT ALVIS Guardian. 1 April 1844. Guardian of Eliza, Nancy W., Ellen S., and William C. Sellars, the minor heirs of Alford Sellars. (P. 299)

HOPE H. HANCOCK Guardian. Guardian of the minor heirs of Jo B. Chance, to wit, Alexander, Charles C., William, and Martha Chance. Said minor heirs are legatees of Charles Braden. Recorded 7 May 1844. (P. 309)

JOEL SULLIVAN Guardian. Guardian of John M., Nancy A., Nathaniel B., and David L. Williams, the minor heirs of Judy Williams. Recorded 7 May 1844. (P. 311)

HIRAM DOBSON Guardian. Guardian of Sarah Ann and Esther Jane Dobson, the minor heirs of William Dobson. Recorded 7 May 1844. (P. 312)

ROBERT S. MILLS Guardian. Guardian of Charles and Margaret Bonner, the minor heirs of Thomas S. Bonner. Recorded 9 July 1844. (P. 331)

LEWIS CHAMBERS Guardian. 15 May 1844. Guardian for Tabitha Ann, Mary E., and Lavina McDonald who are minor heirs of Randell and Jane McDonald. Stephen McDonald is the administrator of the estate. (P. 333)

EDWARD CHAMBERS Guardian. 15 May 1844. Guardian of Joel and Lewis N. McDonald, the minor heirs of Randell and Jane McDonald. (P. 334)

ALEXANDER CHAMBERS Guardian. 15 May 1844. Guardian of John McDonald, a minor heir of Randell and Jane McDonald. (P. 334)

WILLIAM L. REDDITT Guardian. Guardian of Elizabeth Redditt, formerly Elizabeth Harrison, and a minor heir of Elizabeth Harrison deceased. Altho the ward has married, it is to a young man under age. Recorded 9 July 1844. (P. 338)

JAMES E. CROPPER Guardian. 13 July 1844. Guardian of the minor heirs of Adam Trout, to wit, William, Elizabeth, John, Thomas, Joseph, and Susan Trout. (P. 341)

L. W. OWEN Guardian. Guardian of the minor heirs of Richard Owen, to wit, Moses, Samuel, David, and Jane Owen. Recorded 13 August 1844. (P. 344)

ARMISTEAD BROGAN Guardian. Guardian for his children, to wit, Thomas, J. P., Pathea E., Julia Ann. Said children are minor heirs of Jane Brogan. The guardian received from the Estate of Abner Moore who was the grandfather of the minors on the 24th February 1843. Recorded 13 August 1844. (Pp. 346-347)

MARTHA H. BURTON Guardian. Guardian of Martha Mc-Gregor, a minor heir of John McGregor. Recorded 18 December 1844. (P. 355)

28

GUARDIAN SETTLEMENTS 1841-1845

JOHN MARKS Guardian. Guardian of Lucy Wilson, a
minor heir of Henry Thornton. Recorded 17 December 1844.
(P. 359)

JOHN POWELL Guardian. Guardian of Elizabeth Porter
and Lucy T. Hobson. Recorded 14 December 1844. (P. 362)

JOHN PALMER Guardian. Guardian of John A. Bennett.
Recorded 30 January 1845. (P. 363)

JAMES M. ARMSTRONG Guardian. 2 January 1845. Guardian of Garrett Bumpass, an idiot. (Pp. 364-365)

HENRY D. LESTER Guardian. 1 February 1845. Guardian of James C. Cropper and Benjamin Cropper, sons of
Elizabeth Cropper deceased and minor heirs of Robert and
Phebe Dellis deceased and of Robert Dellis, a minor son
of Joshua Dellis, also an heir at law of Robert Dellis
deceased. The names of the heirs were improperly put down
in the last settlement. (P. 371)

JOHN A. CLOPTON Guardian. Guardian of the minor
heirs of Walter Clopton, Jr., to wit, William L., Eliza
Ann, Benjamin, and John A. Clopton, Jr. William A. Clopton was guardian but died. The widow and these four
children were the distributees. Recorded 17 February
1845. (P. 372)

ROBERT CAMPBELL Guardian. Guardian of Hugh Eagan
and Jane Birmingham, formerly Jane Eagan. They are minor
heirs of Hugh Eagan. Recorded 17 February 1845. (P. 374)

WILLIAM B. BYRN Guardian. Guardian of the minor
heirs of James L. Luck, to wit, Rebecca Ann and Nancy B.
Luck. Recorded 7 February 1845. (P. 374)

JAMES SHANNON Guardian. Guardian of Henry Shannon,
now deceased. Recorded 15 October 1845. (P. 382)

JOHN B. SCOBY Guardian. 5 February 1845. Guardian
for James P. Goodall, a minor heir of Hardin Goodall.
(P. 383)

ZACHARIAH TOLLIVER Guardian. Guardian of Elizabeth
S. and William L. Andrews, the minor children of Purnel
H. Andrews. The Guardian replaced Purnel H. Andrews,
their former guardian. These wards have removed with
their father to Missouri. Recorded 16 October 1845. (P.
385)

R. L. WILBURN Guardian. Guardian of Frances G. Wilburn, a minor heir. Recorded 16 October 1845. (P. 387)

ANDREW J. McDONALD Guardian. Guardian of the minor
heirs of Elisha Walker, to wit, Elizabeth Jane, Celia F.,
and Mary Walker. The estate of said deceased was had in
Smith County, Tennessee where he died. The heirs received their mother's equal interest in said estate on
29 April 1844. (Pp. 396-399)

JAMES H. PEYTON Guardian. Guardian of Sarah, William,
Elizabeth, and Nancy Caple, the minor children of Rufus .

GUARDIAN SETTLEMENTS 1841-1845

Caple and legatees of William Eddings deceased. These children live with their father. Recorded 16 October 1845. (P. 398)

DAVID PHILIPS Guardian. Guardian of the minor heirs of Richard Cartwright, to wit, John, Polly, Edward W., Lucinda, and Manerva Cartwright. Recorded 17 October 1845. (Pp. 399-400.

JOHN KENNEDY Guardian. Guardian of William B. Kennedy. Recorded 17 October 1845. (P. 403)

JOSEPH RUTLAND Guardian. Guardian of Sally and Margaret Cloyd. Sally is now of age. She married _____ Hamlin. Recorded 17 October 1845. (P. 405)

JAMES WILLIAMS Guardian. Guardian for his children, to wit, Frazer Baker, Raleigh, B. B., and Newbern Williams. Also, S. G. Williams. Recorded 17 October 1845. (P. 407)

MILNER WALKER Guardian. Guardian of the minor heirs of William S. Walker, to wit, James Henry, Clinton, and William Harrison Walker. The widow purchased a negro from the estate. Recorded 17 October 1845. (Pp. 408-409)

THOMAS E. BONNER Guardian. Guardian of Margaret Bonner, a minor heir of Thomas S. Bonner. Robert S. Mills was the former guardian. Recorded 19 October 1845. (P. 411)

BENJAMIN LATIMER Guardian. Guardian for his child Mary Letitia Latimer. Recorded 18 October 1845. (P. 412)

WILIE ALFORD Guardian. Guardian of Thomas P. Walker, a minor heir of William Walker. Recorded 18 October 1845. (Pp. 413-414)

SAMUEL E. ESTES Guardian. Guardian of James L. Estes, an idiot and an heir of Robert Estes. Recorded 18 October 1845. (P. 414)

JAMES McFARLAND Guardian. Guardian for Marion Davis. William Curd was guardian for this minor who received his legacy and died. Recorded 20 October 1845. (Pp. 417-418)

WILLIAM H. GRIMMETT Guardian. Guardian for Susan Ellen, Mary Gregory, and William Walter Clopton, minor heirs of William A. Clopton. The mother of these wards is entitled to her part. Recorded 20 October 1845. (P. 418)

J. R. HAZARD Guardian. Guardian of S. Rives, a minor heir of William Rives deceased. Recorded 20 October 1845. (Pp. 425-426)

LEWIS CHAMBERS Guardian. Guardian of John McDonald deceased. Recorded 20 October 1845. (P. 428)

RIAL J. ATKINSON Guardian. Guardian of the minor heirs of James Hunt, to wit, Adolphus, Joseph, and Benjamin Hunt. A legacy was left them by Martha Atkinson. Recorded 20 October 1845. (P. 431)

GUARDIAN SETTLEMENTS 1841-1845

JAMES AYRES Guardian. Guardian of Garrett Bumpass, an idiot who is now deceased. Recorded 21 October 1845. (Pp. 432-433)

LEWIS WRIGHT Guardian. Guardian of James J. Tate and Rachel J. Harden, formerly Rachel J. Tate. Recorded 24 October 1845. (Pp. 437-438)

ROBERT M. BURTON Guardian. 1 October 1845. Guardian of Martha McGregor. There was a tract of land sold in Williamson County. (P. 11)

M. C. HANKINS Guardian. 23 October 1845. Guardian of Elizabeth R. Hankins, formerly Elizabeth R. Grissom, but now the wife of Drewry Hankins. (P. 13)

SILAS TARVER Guardian. Guardian of Benjamin F. and Silas N. Tarver, the minor heirs of Henry Hobson. There were four children of the deceased. Recorded 6 November 1845. (Pp. 14-15)

SOLOMON HARTSFIELD Guardian. Guardian of Matilda Johnson, a minor heir of Robert Johnson. Recorded 6 November 1845. (P. 15)

BENJAMIN G. BARCLAY Guardian. Guardian of Elizabeth and John Graves, the minor heirs of Susan Graves. Recorded 6 November 1845. (P. 16)

FINIS E. SHANNON Guardian. 1 January 1845. Guardian for Rachel C. Hearn who has departed this life. The young lady died with consumption. She had lived with her guardian for five years. (P. 17)

WILSON Y. WALKER Guardian. Guardian of John J. Walker, a minor heir of _____ Walker. Recorded 15 December 1845. (P. 22)

ALFRED McCLAIN Guardian. 5 January 1846. Guardian of Thomas H. and Mary E. Lindsey, the minor heirs of Isaac Lindsey. (P. 23)

BENJAMIN R. OWEN Guardian. 4 February 1846. Guardian of my wife, Martha M. McGregor, now Harris. TEMPLE O. HARRIS. (Pp. 28-29)

MATHEW C. HANKINS Guardian. Guardian of Mathew, C. R., (Lurana) Ann, Drucilla B., Samuel B., and Margaret C. Hearn, minor heirs of Stephen L. Hearn and heirs of Mary G. Hearn. Said heirs in right of their mother were entitled to a lot of land in the division of the lands of the estate of Richard Hankins. Said land was sold 12 April 1844. (Pp. 34-35)

MARY A. HILL Guardian. 13 January 1846. Guardian for James, Asaph, C. C., and Henry H. Hill, her minor children. Before the death of their father, he made a deed of gift to these four sons. (P. 40)

DAVID PHILIPS Guardian. Guardian of John Philips, insane. (P. 42)

ROBERT L. MILLS Guardian. 10 January 1846. Guardian of Sally, Mary, and Archebald Frith, the minor heirs of Archibald Frith. (P. 46)

JAMES N. CARTWRIGHT Guardian. Guardian of the minor heirs of Edward W. Cartwright, to wit, Sarah E., Samuel T., and Delila Ann Cartwright. Recorded 17 September 1846. (P. 57)

ROBERT L. MILLS Administrator. Administrator of Mary Frith deceased and Meredith G. Ward as administrator of Sarah Ward, his wife, and an administrator of Meredith F. Ward, his son. The said M. G. Ward is entitled to one third of the estate. Mrs. Dickerson who was entitled to two thirds of said estate has conveyed her interest to Archibald Frith and Meredith F. Ward. Recorded 15 July 1846. (Pp. 58-59)

B. R. OWEN Guardian. Guardian of John D. Owen. Recorded 15 July 1846. (P. 60)

RIAL C. JENNINGS Guardian. Guardian of Henrietta Bumpass, a minor heir of Robert H. Bumpass. (P. 61)

ARCHIBALD RHEA Guardian. Guardian of Louisa Rhea, a minor heir. Recorded 17 September 1846. (P. 62)

HOPE H. HANCOCK Guardian. Guardian of Matilda Johnson, a minor heir of Robert Johnson. Recorded 24 September 1846. (P. 63)

SIMON HANCOCK Guardian. Guardian of John Newby, a minor heir of John Newby. Recorded 3 November 1846. (P. 67)

JOHN M. WILEY Guardian. Guardian of Mary C. Henderson and David A. Walsh, minor heirs of Elizabeth Henderson and Mary Walsh. These minor children are entitled in right of their mother who was heir of Hugh Wiley. Recorded 7 November 1846. (P. 70)

ANDREW J. McDONALD Guardian. 6 July 1846. Guardian of Elizabeth Jane, Celia F., and Mary C. Walker, the minor heirs of Elisha Walker. (Pp. 76-77)

WILLIAM HATCHER Guardian. 4 April 1846. Guardian of Thomas E. Payne, now deceased, who was an idiot. (P. 79)

J. L. BOYD Guardian. Guardian of Thompson A. and Daniel L. Boyd, the minor heirs of William and Fathy Boyd. Recorded 10 November 1846. (P. 82)

NELSON D. HANCOCK Guardian. Guardian of Druritha Hicks, formerly Druritha Hancock. Recorded 11 November 1846. (P. 87)

SHELAH WATERS Guardian. Guardian of Elizabeth Sherrill, an old lady incompetent to transact her own business. Recorded 11 November 1846. (Pp. 88-89)

JOSEPH WILLIAMS. Guardian of James Payne, a minor heir of Joseph Payne. The widow's part was one-third. Recorded 12 November 1846. (P. 89)

THOMAS TURNER Guardian. 7 May 1846. Guardian of the minor heirs of Ebenezer Hearn, to wit, Alfred G., Orren D., Granderson L., Martha A., Susan T., and Robert E. Hearn. (P. 96)

MOSES M. CURREY Guardian. Guardian of Isaac N. Currey,

a minor heir of Isaac Newton Currey. Recorded 18 November 1846. (P. 102)

JONATHAN BAILEY Guardian. Guardian of James A. and Nancy Jane Donnell, the minor heirs of Allen Donnell. The mother of said heirs received an equal amount. Recorded 18 November 1846. (P. 103)

WILLIAM PHIPPS Guardian. 1 December 1846. Guardian of Phereby F. Walker, formerly Phereby F. Smith, and Daniel E. Smith. (P. 104)

ALEXANDER SIMMONS. Administrator. Administrator of the Estate of William Cluck. There are ten distributees, five of whom are minors. The minor heirs are John, Henry, Jack, Frank, and Caroline Cluck. Other heirs are Elizabeth Cluck who is the wife of Charles Carnes and Phebe Cluck, the widow. Recorded 17 January 1846. (P. 106)

SILAS TARVER Guardian. Guardian of Benjamin F. and Silas N. Hobson, the minor heirs of Henry Hobson. These heirs are called earlier Benjamin F. and Silas N. Tarver. Recorded 10 February 1847. (P. 114)

MOSES ELLIS Guardian. 1 January 1847. Guardian of E. E. B. and Pamelia Ellis, the minor heirs of James and Rebecca Ellis. (P. 121)

PRICE CURD Guardian. Guardian of the minor heirs of Richard Curd, to wit, John H., Josephine, Andrew P., and Richard D. Curd. Recorded 2 March 1847. (P. 128)

JOHN E. DICKINSON Administrator. Administrator of Elizabeth T. Sims. Her noncupative will divided her estate among her brothers and sisters. Recorded 25 August 1847. (P. 131)

EDWARD SWEATT Guardian. Guardian of Martha Sweatt. The following legacies are bequeathed in money to Rachel Spradley, Sally Siles, Emily and Sarah Jane Lash, and Martha Spradley, and (   ). Recorded 25 August 1847. (P. 132)

MATHEW C. HANKINS Guardian. 30 March 1847. Guardian of Pettes W., Finis Ewing, and Samuel M. Ragland, the minor heirs of Pettes Ragland. (P. 138)

WILLIAM BENTLEY Guardian. Guardian of James Millington Blaylock, the minor heir of Charles Blaylock deceased. The mother of this ward has also died. Recorded 28 August 1847. (P. 157)

HOPE H. HANCOCK Guardian. 24 July 1847. Guardian of Matilda Johnson, now Matilda Baird. (P. 160)

JOSEPH H. KENNEDY Guardian. 6 September 1847. Guardian of the minor heirs of William B. Kennedy, to wit, B. L., Elizabeth, Drucilla, and John Kennedy. The guardian has in his hands for six minors, the oldest, Benjamin F. Kennedy, is now of age. Another, Margaret Ann Kennedy, has lately died. The distributees of said Margaret Ann Kennedy are her mother and eight brothers and sisters. (P. 163)

ILA DOUGLAS Guardian. Guardian of Ralph and Agness Calhoun, the minor heirs of A. M. Calhoun. These heirs had a guardian appointed in Fayette County, Tennessee. Recorded 2 December 1847. (P. 172)

BERRY COX Guardian. Guardian of Louisa B. Graves, the minor heir of Susan Graves. Recorded 13 December 1847. (P. 178)

ROBERT L. WILBURN Guardian. Guardian of Francis G. Wilburn, a minor heir of Robert Wilburn. The ward is nearly of age. Recorded 13 December 1847. (P. 179)

SAMUEL SMITH Guardian. Guardian of his daughter, Caroline Smith. He has moved his guardianship to Rutherford County, Tennessee. Received one dollar of William Johns. Recorded 13 December 1847. (P. 179)

LAWRENCE SYPERT Guardian. Guardian of the minor heirs of Sarah Legan, to wit, Martha Jane, Nancy Piety, Richard, and Leonidas Marion Legan. The guardian was appointed in place of Richard Legan. The guardian reports that he received of John H. Legan, the administrator of the grandfather of these minor children. Recorded 13 January 1848. (P. 182)

HENRY P. BONE Guardian. Guardian of Lucinda Doughty, an idiot. Said guardian received the distributive share of Robert Doughty's estate due to said Lucinda as daughter of the deceased. Recorded 13 January 1848. (P. 183)

THOMAS NORMAN Guardian. Guardian of Martha Ann O. Atkinson. Recorded 21 November 1848. (P. 184)

EDWARD CRAWFORD Guardian. Guardian of Martha Jane Young who has married Ransom Tucker and the other minor heirs of Gilbert Young. Recorded 21 November 1848. (P. 186)

WILLIAM B. JENNINGS Guardian. 28 January 1848. Guardian of Thomas A. Hill, the minor heir of Isaac P. Hill. The former guardian, Thomas L. Hill, is now dead. (P. 195)

LAMONT LOYD Guardian. Guardian of Sally Clifton and Johnson, an idiot. Recorded 5 December 1848. (P. 202)

HENDERSON HALEY Guardian. 29 March 1848. Guardian of Samuel Shaw, a minor heir of Jesse W. Shaw. (P. 206)

JOHN WORD Guardian. Guardian of Sarah T., James T., Francis Ann, Eliza Jane, Mary Ann, and America W. Word, the minor heirs of James Word who left a widow and three children besides these. Two of these were of age, to wit, William H. and Martha Word. The share of John H. and the widow is one-fourth. Recorded 11 December 1848. (Pp. 209-212)

EDWARD CLEMMONS Guardian. Guardian of his daughter,

Mary J. Clemmons, who had a small legacy in the hands of William Woodrum, executor of Jacob Woodrum. The said Mary J. Clemmons has married James A. Clemmons. Recorded 12 December 1848. (P. 214)

SILAS TARVER Guardian. 9 February 1848. Guardian of William Atkinson, a minor heir of Joseph Atkinson. (P. 216)

ELIHU CARAWAY Guardian. Guardian of Daniel A. Richmond, a minor heir of Alexander P. Richmond. Recorded 13 December 1848. (P. 217)

Z. W. FRAZER Guardian. Guardian for Henry L. and Elizabeth C. Frazer, the minor heirs of Alexander Frazer. The deceased possessed a small tract of land in Kentucky which has since been sold. Recorded 13 December 1848. (P. 218)

ALFRED McCLAIN Guardian. 5 June 1848. Guardian of the minor heirs of Isaac T. Stevenson, to wit, Josiah, Francis Elizabeth, and Washington Moore Stevenson. Washington Moore Stevenson has died. The mother is Mrs. Manerva Arnold. (Pp. 224-230)

ILA DOUGLAS Guardian. Guardian for the minor heirs of A. M. Calhoun. William Wills married the widow. Recorded 14 December 1848. (Pp. 233-235)

PHILIP FISHER Guardian. Guardian of Mary Wheeler, John Wheeler, Elvira Coonrod, and Newton Coonrod, the minor heirs of Mrs. Coonrod who was a daughter of Robert Doughty. Recorded 14 December 1848. (P. 236)

LEVIN WOOLEN Guardian. 2 October 1846. Guardian of his children, to wit, Patsy E., Elizabeth Jane, Harriet C., Mary Charlotte, and Nancy Emily Woolen. Said children are minor heirs of Micajah Peacock. (P. 238)

ROBERT W. RUTHERFORD Guardian. Guardian of John A., Mary J., and Cheseldon Rutherford who are the minor heirs of Griffith W. Rutherford. Recorded 14 December 1848. (P. 239)

MILNER WALKER Guardian. 25 April 1848. Guardian of James Henry, Clinton, and William H. Walker who are the minor heirs of William L. Walker. (P. 240)

SAMUEL W. DONNELL Guardian. Guardian of Martha Jane Donnell, a minor heir of William Donnell deceased. The deceased willed that his wife and daughters Mary Donnell and Elizabeth Moore and the said Martha Jane Donnell shall equally share the use of the servants. Recorded 15 December 1848. (P. 249)

ISAIAH COE Guardian. Guardian for his two daughters Rhoda and Lelethia Coe, the minor heirs of Patsy Coe. Recorded 15 December 1848. (P. 253)

ISAIAH COE Guardian. Guardian of William Compton. The executor, James Wrather, had before his death left property to Patsy Coe after the death of Liza Wrather, the mother of said Patsy and widow of said James Wrather. The said Patsy, having died before her mother, the property was divided among her six children and two grand children of whom the said William was one and his half sister the other, their mother having also died before their 'great mother.' Recorded 15 December 1848. (Pp. 263-264)

HENRY D. LESTER Guardian. Guardian for Rebecca, Malinda, and Mary E. Jones. Recorded 18 December 1848. (P. 264)

JOEL SULLIVAN Guardian. Guardian of the minor heirs of Judy Williams. Recorded 18 December 1848. (P. 265)

ANDREW GWYNN Guardian. Guardian of William Hughs Eskew and Eliza Jane Eskew, the minor heirs of James and Eliza Eskew. Recorded 18 December 1848. (Pp. 268-269)

THOMAS E. BONNER Guardian. Guardian of James T. Edwards. Recorded 18 December 1848. (P. 271)

JOHN D. TAYLOR Guardian. 29 September 1848. Guardian of Mary Taylor, an idiot, and legatee of John Taylor. (P. 273)

JAMES L. HARRIS Guardian. Guardian of the minor heirs of Amelia Dearing, to wit, Elias H. C., Abner W., Willis B., Robert J., and Amelia Dearing. Amelia Dearing was a daughter of John Lawrence. Recorded 19 December 1848. (P. 274)

JAMES M. HUNT Guardian. Guardian of the minor orphans of Thomas Babb, to wit, Pamelia, Mary Jane, and Elizabeth Babb. Recorded 19 December 1848. (P. 274)

THOMAS B. ( ) Guardian. Guardian of Asa H. Blankenship, a minor heir of Daniel Blankenship. Recorded 19 December 1848. (P. 275)

ELIZA VANCE Guardian. Guardian of her children. Recorded 19 December 1848. (P. 275)

JOHN N. ROACH Guardian. 15 June 1847. Guardian for his children, Herschel C. and Newsom R. Roach. The guardian reports that he received from Thomas Kirkpatrick his children's part of the estate of Narcissa Robbins. (P. 276)

JOHN W. ALEXANDER Guardian. Guardian of Cordelia Nettles, a daughter of John A. Nettles. Recorded 19 December 1848. (P. 277)

CHARLES L. HARRIS Guardian. Guardian of Edith L., Frances W., Tacitus E., Joseph H., and America E. Harris, the minor heirs of Edward Harris. Recorded 19 December 1848. (P. 278)

JOHN M. HEARN Guardian. Guardian of Maria C. and William Hicks. Recorded 19 December 1848. (P. 279)

JOHN A. BROGAN Guardian. Guardian of Pamelia Brogan,

GUARDIAN SETTLEMENTS 1845-1851

A. H. MOSER Guardian. Guardian of the minor heirs of Benjamin P. Estes, to wit, Luritha, James, Mary, Amanda, Martha B., and Sarah B. Estes. Recorded 20 December 1848. (P. 281)

ISAAC G. COLES Guardian. Guardian of the minor heirs of Matthew Brown, to wit, William, Mary, James, and Martha Jane Brown. Recorded 21 December 1848. (P. 288)

JOHN ORGAN Guardian. Guardian of the minor heirs of John W. Beauchamp, to wit, Martha Jane, Annistasia, and John Beauchamp. (William Beauchamp was incorrectly listed according to the Clerk) Recorded 20 December 1848. (Pp. 289-290)

ELIZABETH McHENRY Guardian. 28 December 1848. Guardian for her children. Her daughter, Eliza, married Joel Fouch. The other daughter, Frances, is of age. Her youngest son, Thomas Carroll, is the only one still at home. Recorded 19 February 1849. (P. 302)

RUSSELL J. EVANS Guardian. 26 December 1848. Guardian for Ann E., Nancy B., William L., Caroline J., Benjamin B., John B., Harriet J., and Martha M. Ferrell, the minor heirs of William W. Ferrell. The widow's dower has been laid off. There are nine children. (P. 303)

JOHN MARKS Guardian. Guardian of Lucy Wilson, now Lucy Swann. Recorded 19 February 1849. (P. 305)

THOMAS MARKS Guardian. 29 December 1848. Guardian of George Marks. The guardian reports that a negro girl was willed to her guardian's wife. The legacy was received from John Lannom, grandfather of the said George Marks. Said grandfather died in Roan County, Tennessee. (P. 306)

JOHN EDWARDS Guardian. 28 December 1848. Guardian of his children, to wit, Mary Ann, Nancy, and Eliza Jane Edwards, the minor heirs of James Richmond, their grandfather. There were six children of the said John Edwards. (P. 307)

LUCY DAVIS Guardian. Guardian of John W. and James H. Davis, her children and minor heirs of William Davis. Recorded 20 February 1849. (P. 308)

WOOD H. SHEARIN Guardian. 23 January 1849. Guardian of his children, to wit, Robert G., Marion, Martha E., Andrew Jackson, and Albert Shearin. (P. 313)

JOHN J. HOOPER Guardian. 4 January 1849. Guardian of his daughter, Virginia G. Hooper, who had a legacy left her by Kiziah Donoho, her grandmother, late of North Carolina, now deceased. (P. 314)

WILLIAM BETTES Guardian. Guardian of the minor heirs of James L. Chapman, to wit, William, Elizabeth, and John Chapman. The mother of these children has since died. The grandfather of these children is the guardian. Recorded

24 February 1849. (P. 321)

WILBON R. WINTERS Guardian. Guardian of Charles G.
Carter, a minor heir of N. G. Carter. Recorded 26
February 1849. (P. 324)

WILBON R. WINTERS Guardian. Guardian for Thomas,
Robert, and William Willis, the minor heirs of James M.
Willis. Recorded 26 February 1849. (P. 326)

Z. TOLLIVER Guardian. 11 June 1849. Guardian of
Elizabeth L. Pitts, formerly Elizabeth L. Andrews, now
the wife of Richard W. Pitts. (P. 330)

JOHN KELLY Guardian. Guardian for Rebecca P. Payne,
Jr. and Mary K. Payne, the minor heirs of Alfred B.
Payne. Recorded 27 November 1849. (P. 331)

MILES L. AYRES Guardian. Guardian of Rufus B.
Ayres, a minor heir of Alfred M. Ayres. Recorded 27
November 1849. (P. 335)

JONATHAN HOOK Guardian. Guardian for the heirs of
Thomas Jones. Recorded 27 November 1849. (P. 335)

HENRY R. COX Guardian. Guardian of Elizabeth, John,
and Jordan Cox, the minor heirs of John Cox and distributees of William Cox, their grandfather. The said William
Cox died on the 27th day of November 1847. The children
of John Cox were seven in number. Recorded 28 November
1849. (P. 340)

ANDERSON JENNINGS Guardian. Guardian of Tennessee
C. Taylor, a minor orphan of Solomon Taylor deceased and
legatee of John Taylor. Recorded 29 November 1849. (P.
244)

BENJAMIN TARVER Guardian. Guardian of the minor
heirs of Isham Kitrell, to wit, Isabella, John B., George
M., Edmund J., and Isham Kitrell. Recorded 27 November
1849. (P. 346)

GEORGE WILLIAMSON Guardian. 23 March 1849. Guardian of Charles and (Levisa) P. Prim, the minor heirs of
Kizzie Prim. (P. 347)

DAWSON HANCOCK Guardian. Guardian of Houston Hancock, a minor heir of James Hancock. Recorded 30 November 1849. (P. 348)

THOMAS TELFORD Guardian. Guardian of John R. Mark-
ham, heir of Pleasant M. Markham. The said Pleasant M.
Markham left a widow and two children one of which died.
Recorded 30 November 1849. (P. 349)

CALVIN KELLY Guardian. 19 May 1849. Guardian of
William C. and America Ann Davis, the minor heirs of
William Davis. (P. 350)

WILLIAM HANCOCK Guardian. Guardian of Elizabeth,
Aseneth, Nancy A. Jane, Frances B., and Harriet F. Davis,
the heirs of David and Martha Davis, late of Lincoln Coun-

39

ty, Tennessee. The grandmother gave an uncle of these children a negro. Recorded 11 December 1849. (P. 353)

MARY L. HILL Guardian. 7 April 1849. Guardian of her children, to wit, Samuel, Asaph, C. C., and H. H. Hill, the minor heirs of Samuel Hill. (P. 354)

JONATHAN SHORES Guardian. Guardian of Elizabeth McMillon. Recorded 11 December 1849. (P. 354)

ALJOURNAL BRYAN Guardian. Guardian of John, Aljornal, and Tennessee Bryan, the minor heirs of John B. Bryan. Recorded 11 December 1849. (P. 355)

NATHAN OAKLEY Guardian. Guardian of Elizabeth and Jane Oakley, the minor heirs of William Oakley. Recorded 11 December 1849. (P. 356)

ZARA HARALSON Guardian. Guardian of Mary Haralson, an insane woman who has since died. Recorded 15 December 1849. (P. 370)

JOHN DONNELL Guardian. Guardian of Eli D. and Mary A. E. Sellars, the minor heirs of Andrew J. Sellars. Recorded 14 December 1849. (P. 372)

SOLOMON DAVIS Guardian. Guardian of the minor heirs of James B. Taylor, to wit, Armstead J., Hester A., Martha, and Elizabeth Taylor. Recorded 14 December 1849. (P. 373)

ROBERT L. MILLS Guardian. Guardian of Archibald Frith, a minor heir of Archibald Frith deceased. M. G. Ward married a sister of the said Archibald, Jr. who died leaving one child. A single sister also died in whose estate their mother also had a share which she relinquished. Recorded 6 January 1850. (Pp. 382-384)

THOMAS C. ANDERSON Guardian. Guardian of David M. Donnell who is now of age, Andrew K. Donnell who is now dead, Aceneth Donnell, James Mitchell Donnell, and George Donnell, the minor heirs of George Donnell. Recorded 6 January 1850. (Pp. 384-386)

COLEMAN JACKSON Guardian. Guardian of William R. and Mary Jane Jackson, the minor heirs of Robert Jackson. The guardian reports that he received from the grandfather of these children on the 9th February last. Recorded 6 February 1850. (P. 387)

HENRY TRUETT Guardian. Guardian of Mary and Jackey Vivrett, the minor heirs of William D. and Nancy Vivrett. The guardian received from the administrator of Snowden Hickman who was their grandfather. Recorded 11 February 1850. (P. 391)

MARION B. KITRELL Guardian. Guardian of William Hicks. Recorded 14 February 1850. (P. 401)

BRITTON ODUM Guardian. Guardian of William Britton, Dumpsey, A. W., Sarah F., Edward, M. V., and Mary Odum, the minor heirs of Lucy Odum. William is of age. These

40

minors reside in the State of Illinois and their father,
Moses Odum, has been appointed their guardian. The
legacy was left by William Lawrence deceased. He left
to each of the daughters of his of whom the said Lucy
was one. William Lawrence, Jr. was the executor of
William Lawrence, Sr. Recorded 14 February 1850. (P.
410)

LOUISA CHAPMAN Guardian. Guardian of her children,
William G. and James M., who are the minor heirs of Robert
Hill. Division was between the widow and seven children.
Recorded 13 Nov. 1850. (P. 411)

RICHARD ROUTON Guardian. Guardian of Polly Routon,
an idiot. Recorded 13 March 1850. (P. 412)

ALLEN BELL Guardian. Guardian of Jonathan Duncan
Estes, a minor heir of Fanny Estes. Recorded 25 November
1850. (P. 414)

ISHAM F. DAVIS Guardian. Guardian of Eli Cherry,
a minor heir of Eli Cherry. The estate of said deceased
is in Davidson County. Recorded 25 November 1850. (P.
415)

JOHN H. DONNELL Guardian. Guardian of James A.
Donnell, an idiot, and heir of Adnah Donnell. The guardian reported that he received from Josiah Donnell, executor of William Donnell his grandfather. Recorded 25
November 1850. (P. 416)

ISAIAH COE Guardian. Guardian of Rhoda and Taletha
Coe, his daughters. Recorded 4 December 1850. (P. 427)

NATHAN CARTMELL Guardian. 27 June 1850. Guardian
of Simon Reeves. (P. 428)

P. K. WILLIAMSON Guardian. Guardian of John M.,
Robert T., Preston Y., Cyrus H., and Armstead Hill. Recorded 7 December 1850. (Pp. 433-434)

LAWRENCE SYPERT Guardian. Guardian of Martha Jane,
Nancy Piety, Richard, and Leonidas M. Ligon, the minor
heirs of Sarah Ligon. Recorded 10 December 1850.
(P. 437)

JOHN A. CLOPTON Guardian. Guardian of Eliza Ann and
John A. Clopton, Jr., the minor heirs of William Clopton.
Recorded 11 December 1850. (P. 443)

JONATHAN HOOKER Guardian. Guardian of the minor
heirs of Thomas Jones, to wit, Joseph, Ignatius, and Lucinda Jones. Recorded 11 December 1850. (P. 443)

ANSWORTH HARRISON Guardian. Guardian of Peyton P.
Carver, Rhoda Carver, and Mary Jane Carver, the minor
heirs of Samuel Carver. Recorded 12 December 1850. (Pp.
447-448)

WESLEY HANCOCK Guardian. Guardian of Samuel, Julius,
Sarah J., and Mary N. Gilbert, the minor heirs at law of
John Hancock. A guardian also has been appointed in

GUARDIAN SETTLEMENTS 1845-1851

North Carolina. Recorded 12 December 1850. (P. 452)

JOHN C. JOHNSON Guardian. Guardian of Nancy Johnson, now Nancy Jennings, having married C. P. Jennings. A settlement of her father's estate. Recorded 12 December 1850. (P. 453)

WILLIAM C. BRANCH Guardian. 27 September 1850. Guardian of William C. Branch, a minor heir of William C. Branch. (P. 454)

JAMES C. TAYLOR Guardian. Guardian of Mortimore W. and Elizabeth S. Taylor, the minor heirs of Josiah Taylor. There are four distributees. Recorded 16 December 1850. (P: 455)

ANDREW W. PARTAIN Guardian. Guardian of Martha Partain, a minor heir of James and Dovy Partain. Recorded 18 December 1850. (P. 464)

ELIJAH WAMMACK Guardian. Guardian of Martha and George Fulton Donnell, the minor heirs of John W. Donnell. A settlement has been made with Agness Donnell, the mother. Recorded 18 December 1850. (P. 465)

THOMAS EARHEART Guardian. 10 January 1851. Guardian of Nancy J. C. and Margaret E. V. Thompson, the minor heirs of Henry Russell Thompson. (P. 466)

LUCINDA HOLT Guardian. Guardian for her children who are minor heirs of Jesse Holt. Recorded 17 February 1851. (P. 469)

WILLIAM JACKSON Guardian. 14 January 1851. Guardian of his children, to wit, Mary D., R. C., W. F., and Henry C. Jackson, the minor heirs of Sally Jackson. (P. 471)

COLEMAN JACKSON Guardian. Guardian of William R. and Mary Jane Jackson, the minor heirs of Robert Jackson. Recorded 20 February 1851. (P. 473)

ROBERT JOHNS Guardian. 7 December 1850. Guardian of Thomas Terrell, an idiot. Anthony Terrell was first appointed guardian of the idiot. Richard Terrell who has since died was next appointed guardian. The idiot is a distributee of William Terrell. (P. 474)

ELIZA VANCE Guardian. Guardian for her children, to wit, Thomas J., Sarah, John H., Martha Ann, and Daniel B. Vance who are the minor heirs of Daniel Vance. These children are all small. Recorded 20 February 1851. (P. 475)

MOSES ELLIS Guardian. Guardian of Susan, Nathan, and William Walker who are the minor heirs of Milner Walker. Caroline Walker is the mother of these children. Recorded 20 February 1851. (P. 477)

E. C. JENNINGS Guardian. Guardian of Nancy Webb, an insane old lady. Recorded 25 February 1851. (P. 478)

42

GUARDIAN SETTLEMENTS 1845-1851

THOMAS CHAMBERS Guardian. 5 February 1844. Guardian of Nancy D., Elizabeth M., Henry C., and Martha L. Hobson, the minor heirs of Benjamin Hobson. (P. 483)

J. G. ALLEN Guardian. Guardian of Frances Medlin, a minor heir of John Medlin. Recorded 12 November 1851. (P. 487)

H. RAGLAND Guardian. Guardian of Lucy Jones, a minor heir of William F. Jones. He is also guardian for William Burchett. Recorded 17 November 1851. (P. 487)

WILLIAM BOND Administrator. 15 March 1851. Administrator of Lewis Bond. (P. 496)

ROBERT GWYNN Guardian. 25 November 1851. Guardian of J. A. Gwynn, a minor heir of Ransom Gwynn. (Pp. 504-505)

WILLIAM BENTLEY Guardian. 1 January 1851. Guardian of James Milligan Blalock, a minor heir of James Blalock. (P. 507)

JOHN GRISSIM Guardian. Guardian of Martha Reed, a minor heir of William Reed. Recorded 13 December 1851. (P. 510)

WILLIAM WOODRUM Guardian. Guardian of the minor heirs of Alfred S. Hughley, to wit, Alfred W., John, Fountain, E. P., Samuel, Terza Ann, and Belotty Hughley. The mother received her share. (P. 514)

WILLIAM SWANN Guardian. Guardian of John L. Swann, a minor heir of Thomas Swann. The guardian received from the Pension Board a part of a five year pension due on account of his father's service and death in the Army of the United States. Recorded 17 December 1851. (P. 518)

ZARA HARALSON Guardian. Guardian of James H., Ephraim L., and Elizabeth W. Haralson, the minor heirs of Vincent L. Haralson. Recorded 17 December 1851. (P. 519)

BENJAMIN D. MOTTLEY Guardian. Guardian of Ann and Cornelia Mottley, the minor heirs of Benjamin T. Mottley. Recorded 19 December 1851. (Pp. 527-528)

JAMES CLEMMONS Guardian. Guardian of (Lazarus) G. Castleman, a minor heir of Jacob and Ann Castleman. Recorded 19 December 1851. (P. 529)

GUARDIAN SETTLEMENTS 1851-1856

BENJAMIN L. WOOD Guardian. 11 September 1851. Guardian of Sarah, Docea, Ann, and Martha J. Cowan who are the minor heirs of James and Nancy Cowan. (Pp. 4-5)

JOHN ORRAND Guardian. Guardian of Ann Eliza Tatum, formerly Ann Eliza McAdow. Recorded 22 December 1851. (P. 6)

W. T. CARTWRIGHT Guardian. 22 August 1851. Guardian of George M. and Sarah E. Lash, the minor heirs of John C. Lash. Since the marriage of the widow, the property has been divided between her and her two children. (P. 7)

DUNCAN JOHNSON Guardian. Guardian of William Neal, now deceased. Death of the said William probably took place about the 1st March last. Recorded 22 December 1851. (P. 10)

GEORGE W. JENNINGS Guardian. Guardian of the minor children of Ashel Jennings, to wit, Nancy M., Christian S., Ann Eliza, Frances M., and Ashel A. Jennings. Recorded 22 December 1851. (P. 10)

B. D. HA   ) Guardian. Guardian of James O., Thomas B., M. A. V., C. O., and S. M. Hicks, the minor heirs of Lucy H. Hicks. Recorded 22 December 1851. (Pp. 12-13)

ROBERT P. HATCHER Guardian. Guardian of Thomas W., Elizabeth, John, and Sarah Hatcher, the minor heirs of William Hatcher. Thomas W. Hatcher is now of age. Recorded 22 December 1851. (P. 14)

JOSEPH H. BARKLEY Guardian. Guardian for his children, to wit, Lucinda and Lydia Ann Barkley, the minor heirs of Martha Barkley. These children are entitled to a distributive share of their grandfather, William F. Jones, the father of their mother who is dead. Recorded 23 December 1851. (P. 15)

GEORGE J. WOOD Guardian. Guardian of (Vanilea), Josiah, Jefferson, George, and Avaline M. Motheral, the minor heirs of William Motheral. The said William Motheral died intestate in Gibson County, Tennessee. Recorded 13 February 1852. (P. 22)

WILLIAM C. ROBBINS Guardian. 27 January 1852. Guardian of John, Ruth, and Ann Robbins, the minor heirs of H. M. Robbins. (P. 25)

WILLIAM L. CLEMMONS Guardian. 30 January 1852. Guardian of Thomas Wray, an old insane man. (P. 26)

BENJAMIN A. LATIMER Guardian. Guardian of Mary Lutitia Latimer. Recorded 19 February 1852. (P. 27)

LARKIN ALLEN Guardian. Guardian of William C. McDonald, a minor child of Narcissa McDonald and an heir of William Allen. Recorded 21 February 1852. (P. 30)

JOHN KELLY Guardian. Guardian of Fanny, (Littie), and Benjamin R. Davis, the minor heirs of Dr. Benjamin R. Davis. Recorded 12 March 1852. (P. 38)

GUARDIAN SETTLEMENTS 1851-1856

E. C. JENNINGS Guardian. 5 February 1852. Guardian of Mrs. Nancy Webb who was insane and is dead. (P. 40)

JOHN KELLY Guardian. 1 March 1851. Guardian of the minor heirs of M. T. Cartwright, to wit, Elizabeth D., Martha, and John A. Cartwright. (Pp. 42-43)

W. T. CARTWRIGHT Guardian. Guardian of Josaphine Frances Ann Judson and John Foster Lash who are the minor heirs of George W. Lash. Recorded 6 May 1852. (P. 46)

COLEMAN JOHNSON Guardian. 2 April 1852. Guardian of Samuel Haynes (now dead), Manerva Johnson (wife of S. E. Johnson), Moody P. Haynes, and Harriet Haynes who are the minor heirs of Moody P. Haynes. (P. 48)

ROBERT JENNINGS Guardian. Guardian of Hannah E. Jennings, a minor heir of John A. Jennings. Said guardian was also appointed guardian of Robert B. Jennings who arrived at full age before the division of the estate. Recorded 8 May 1852. (P. 50)

WILLIAM BROWN Guardian. 25 March 1852. Guardian for Elizabeth, Munroe, William, Josaphine, and Sarah J. Smith, the minor heirs of Jesse Smith deceased on the 28th March 1851. There are eight distributees (seven children and the widow). (P. 51)

WILLIAM P. F. BABB Guardian. Guardian for his child, Sintha Thomas Babb, a minor heir of Daniel Moser. Recorded 10 May 1852. (P. 52

JOHN EPPERSON Guardian. Guardian of (Kittarah) Gregory who was incapable of managing her affairs. Recorded 12 May 1852. (P. 56)

B. H. BELL Guardian. Guardian of Catherine Lindsey, an idiot. Recorded 14 May 1852. (P. 60)

CAROLINE WALKER Guardian. Guardian of her daughter, Josaphine C. Walker, a minor heir of Milner Walker. Said guardian was formerly Mrs. Mooningham. Recorded 14 May 1852. (P. 61)

WILLIAM GREEN Guardian. 27 May 1852. Guardian for Sarah Ann, John, William, Martha, Eli, Susan, Mary, James, Thomas, Josaphine, and Jane Green who are the minor heirs of Anderson Green. Their mother is entitled to a child's part which is one twelfth. (P. 70)

JAMES H. PEYTON Guardian. Guardian of William, Nancy, and Elizabeth Cabell. William is of age. Recorded 29 June 1852. (P. 73)

ZEBULUM BAIRD Guardian. Guardian of William C. Baird, a minor heir of James H. Baird. The money was divided between the two children. Recorded 1 July 1852. (P. 76)

W. L. HOLMAN Executor. Executor of Robert M. Holman. Recorded 9 July 1852. (P. 84)

ARMSTEAD BROGAN Guardian. 18 June 1852. Guardian of William A. Whitlock, a minor heir of Nancy Whitlock. (P. 85)

JOHN CHAMBERS Guardian. Guardian of Sarah Ann Bell, a minor heir of Jefferson Bell. She married Henry Walker and is now a widow. The ward was one of the distributees of James Johnson. Recorded 14 July 1852. (P. 88)

SAMUEL COLES Guardian. Guardian of Martha Walker who is insane. Said Martha is a distributee of James D. Walker. Recorded 21 July 1852. (P. 90)

JOHN F. HANCOCK Guardian. Guardian of Green H. Hancock who is insane. Recorded 11 November 1852. (P. 102)

MOSES ELLIS Guardian. Guardian of Elizabeth Trout, formerly Elizabeth Chappell, a minor heir of Thomas B. Chappell. Recorded 11 November 1852. (P. 104)

GEORGE HARSH Guardian. 26 September 1852. Guardian of Josaphine W. Guthrie, a minor heir of Thomas Guthrie. (P. 109)

CHARLES WRIGHT Guardian. 28 October 1852. Guardian of Jane, Levi, James, William, and Martha Wright, the minor heirs of William Wright, heir of Hollis Wright. (P. 109)

JOHN BRIDGES Guardian. Guardian for his children, to wit, William B., David, Alexander, and Jonathan Bridges, the minor heirs of Milly Bridges who was a daughter of Jonathan Aldridge who died in Missouri. Recorded 20 December 1852. (P. 110)

E. K. HARRISON Guardian. 20 November 1852. Guardian of Martha, Ann, Willis, Charles, and Virginia Hankins who are the minor heirs of Willis N. Hankins. (P. 113)

BIRD DEBOW Guardian. 11 November 1852. Guardian of Richard Jarratt, a minor heir of John Jarratt. (P. 114)

CELEA LOUISA WALKER Guardian. Guardian of her children, to wit, Washington B. H. and William C. Walker who are minor heirs of James D. Walker. Recorded 11 February 1853. (P. 116)

JOHN ORGAN Guardian. 18 December 1852. Guardian of Martha, Julia, and George Billings, the minor heirs of Sally Billings deceased. These minors are grandchildren of Ennis Organ deceased. (P. 119)

ARCHIBALD ALLEN Guardian. 15 December 1852. Guardian of Elizabeth J., John G., Mary M., and Martha M. Allen. He bought a certificate from the Clerk of Smith County. Recorded in Guardian Book KK, page 480. Elizabeth J. lives in Kentucky and has married a man named Tanner. The guardian has received lately from the administrator of Christopher Smith, an uncle of said minors who died without family. (P. 120)

JOHN A. CRISWELL Guardian. 23 December 1852. Guardian for his minor son, John A. Criswell, Jr. The guardian has received from the estate of James Mays. (Pp. 121-122)

46

GUARDIAN SETTLEMENTS 1851-1856

JOHN W. TATE Guardian. 8 January 1853. Guardian of Mary, Maria, and John A. Eatherly, the minor heirs of Andrew R. Eatherly. (P. 122)

WILSON L. WATERS Guardian. 18 January 1853. Guardian of Richard R. L., Thomas L., Labetha Jane, John R., and Jasper N. Compton, the minor heirs of Nancy Compton deceased and heir of George Hearn who was their grandfather and guardian of George P. Hancock, an idiot, and also a grandchild and an heir of George Hearn. Labetha Jane Compton is now Labetha Jane Grandstaff. (P. 123)

JOHN KELLY Guardian. 4 February 1853. Guardian of Elizabeth B. Drake, a minor heir of N. F. M. Drake and Martha Drake. (Pp. 129-130)

GUY T. GLEAVES Guardian. 20 January 1853. Guardian of his daughters, Catharine and Margaret, the legatees of William Hardy. (P. 130)

JOHN KELLY Guardian. 22 January 1853. Guardian of Fanny, Elizabeth, and Benjamin R. Owen, the minor heirs of Dr. B. R. Owen deceased. (Pp. 131-133)

MOSES ELLIS Guardian. 24 January 1853. Guardian of Susan D. Webb, formerly Susan D. Walker. (Pp. 138-140)

JAMES P. PORTER Guardian. 11 January 1853. Guardian for his children, to wit, George L. and Benjamin F. Porter, heirs of Elizabeth A. Porter. (P. 142)

JOAB P. CAWTHON Guardian. 20 January 1853. Guardian of John N. Davis, insane, and a son and legatee of Nathaniel Davis. Robert A. Davis was the executor until his removal from the county. (Pp. 144-145)

WILLIAM DUNCAN Guardian. Guardian for Louisa, William, America, Lavice, and Ann Page, the minor heirs of John S. Page. He died in Smith County. Recorded 24 February 1853. (Pp. 146-147)

WILLIAM SIMS Guardian. 14 January 1853. Guardian of Elizabeth Mary Chastain, formerly Elizabeth Mary Bingham. Also guardian for Matthew Jackson, James Thomas, Sarah, and Jane F. Bingham, the minor heirs of John A. Bingham. Elizabeth married E. E. Chastain who is of age. (P. 147)

THOMAS R. CASTLEMAN Guardian. 10 January 1853. Guardian of Margaret Castleman, a minor heir of Jacob Castleman. (P. 148)

AARON GIBSON Guardian. 4 March 1853. Guardian of Charlotte L., Robert H., Martha A., Susan, Mary E., and Amand S. Medlin, the minor heirs of R. S. Medlin. (P. 156)

WILLIAM B. BYRN Guardian. 1 June 1853. Late guardian of Rebecca Ann Luck, the wife of H. A. Baxter. Also late guardian of Nancy A. Luck, the wife of B. F. Knox. (P. 159)

47

SUSAN F. HARRIS Guardian. 23 February 1853. Guardian for her children, to wit, Nathan, J. C. and Richard F. Allen. Martha Ann Harris also is a daughter. Said children are legatees of John Jarratt. (P. 161)

ROBERT GWYNN Guardian. 17 February 1853. Guardian of William J. A. Gwynn and the heirs of Ransom Gwynn. (P. 162)

JOHN A. CLOPTON Guardian. 30 March 1853. Guardian of Eliza Ann McNamer, formerly Eliza Ann Clopton. She has married M. H. McNamer. (P. 164)

JOSEPH BELL Guardian. 2 April 1853. Guardian of William Joseph Bell, a minor heir of Robert B. Bell. (P. 170)

NERI LOWE Guardian. 30 April 1853. Guardian of the minor heirs of James D. Moore, to wit, Mary Ann, Andrew K., and John Moore. (Pp. 174-175)

WILLIAM C. DENTON Guardian. 25 February 1853. Guardian for his children, to wit, Ann Eliza, Temperance, John Edwards, Eleanor W., Mary Elizabeth, and William W. Denton, the legatees of Edward Denton. (Pp. 175-176)

JOHN S. HALEY Guardian. 28 April 1853. Guardian of Joseph B. Haley, now of age. Said John S. is an heir of J. Haley. (P. 176)

HARDIN RAGLAND Guardian. 23 April 1853. Guardian of James W. Sayle, a minor heir of Dr. William P. Sayle, late of Mississippi. (P. 177)

JOHN H. JOHNSON Guardian. 30 May 1853. Guardian for John and James Bryant, the minor heirs of Richardson Bryant. (P. 186)

RUSSELL J. EVANS Guardian. 2 May 1853. Guardian for William W. Ferrell, a minor heir of William W. Ferrell. William W. was previously omitted on the mistaken belief that he was of age. (P. 188)

LARKIN STEWART Guardian. Guardian of John S., George C., Mary, Martha, and Susan Webb. The guardian reports that he has received from the executor of Ann Stewart, late of the State of Virginia now deceased, who was the grandmother of said minors, to wit, received in April 1852 for the children of (Mickie) Webb of whom there were nine. Recorded 11 August 1853. (P. 191)

W. R. WINTER Guardian. 6 July 1853. Guardian of Thomas R. and James M. White. (P. 196)

STERLING B. HARDY Guardian. 20 May 1853. Guardian of Margaret H., Elizabeth S., William H., and Henry B. Mattock, the minor heirs of Amzy Mattock deceased and legatee of James Hardy. These minors were to receive an equal share with three others. Mrs. Hardy, their grandmother, keeps the children. (Pp. 196-197)

GUARDIAN SETTLEMENTS 1851-1856

SAMUEL H. PORTERFIELD Guardian. 27 May 1853. Guardian of John W. and Margaret Francis Collier, the minor heirs of Mark Collier. The guardian received a land warrant in which the mother and the wards were equally entitled for the said Mark Collier's service as a soldier in the Mexican War. (P. 198)

WOOD H. SHEARIN Guardian. 11 June 1853. Guardian of Benjamin L., Henry, James M., Amanda, Fredonia E., (Donnel), and Lavina Rigan, the minor heirs of Samuel A. and Martha A. Rigan. The guardian received of the estate of Francis Rigan who was the grandmother of the children. (Pp. 202-204)

JOHNATHAN BAILEY Guardian. Guardian of James and Nancy Jane Donnell, the minor heirs of Adlai Donnell. Recorded 18 August 1853. (P. 208)

HARRISON LESTER Guardian. 3 September 1853. Guardian of Amos J. Patterson, a minor heir of Philfin Patterson and an heir at law of Robert Jarmon. The two children of Philfin Patterson were entitled to a distributive share. One of the children has since died and his share paid to his father. (P. 214)

DAVID W. QUARLES Guardian. Guardian of William W., James F., Nancy Ann, Littleberry Jackson, James P., and Harriet B. Quarles, the minor heirs of William J. H. Quarles. Recorded 14 September 1853. (P. 220)

JAMES H. YANDELL Guardian. Guardian of James Yandell who was insane, but is now dead. Recorded 26 December 1853. (P. 223)

JACOB B. LASATER Guardian. Guardian of Elizabeth F. and George A. Bone, the minor heirs of Adnah Bone. Recorded 26 December 1853. (P. 226)

CALVIN W. JACKSON Guardian. Guardian of Andrew (Gallatin), Sarah E., and (William) D. Martin, the minor heirs of Sarah Martin and heirs at law of Andrew (Greer). The guardian received the proceeds from land sold in Lincoln County. Recorded 26 December 1853. (P. 227)

CALVIN W. JACKSON Guardian. Guardian of Charles P., John Thomas, Benjamin F., and Jordan L. Shavers, the minor heirs of William Shavers. Recorded 27 December 1853. (P. 233)

JOHN W. RYE Guardian. Guardian of William and James Rye, the minor heirs of Henry Rye. Also guardians of Martha, Sarah, and Louisa Griffin who are heirs of Henry Rye's deceased daughter. Recorded 20 January 1854. (P. 234)

GEORGE W. DALE Guardian. Guardian of his children, to wit, James K. P., William R., and George W. Dale who are distributees of Richard Pruett. The guardian received from the Administrator, William Pruett. Recorded 20 January 1854. (P. 234)

WILLIAM E. DENTON Guardian. Guardian for his children who have been previously named. There have been two children born since the last report, to wit, Emily Rebecca and Albert Young Denton. Recorded 30 March 1854. (P. 247)

HENRY TRUETT Guardian. Guardian of Jacky Ann Vivrett, a minor heir of Drewry Vivrett. Recorded 5 April 1854. (P. 259)

WILLIAM BROWN Guardian. Guardian of the minor heirs of Jordan Robertson, to wit, Andrew J., Luke L., James M., William C., and Thomas J. Robertson. Recorded 6 April 1854. (P. 261)

HARRISON LESTER Executor. Executor of Frances Puckett. Recorded 12 April 1854. (Pp. 269-270)

JOHN LEGAN Executor. Executor of Geraldus Bolton. The testator left a widow and made her his only legatee. Recorded 13 April 1854. (Pp. 271-272)

WILLIAM D. GRINDSTAFF Administrator. Administrator of David Grindstaff. Recorded 13 April 1854. (P. 273)

SILAS M. DONNELL Executor. 4 January 1854. Executor of the will of James Donnell. Heirs: wife; children Amanda D. Spears, Alfred E. Donnell, William H. Donnell, Samuel H. Donnell, James E. Donnell, John A. Donnell, and Elizabeth S. Thompson. The widow is to have the farm which at her death is to go to the youngest son-- Silas M. Donnell. (P. 279)

SOLOMON R. SHAW Administrator. Administrator of Alsy Shaw. There are six distributees. The eight Allen heirs have one eighth share each. Recorded 17 April 1854. (P. 280)

WILLIAM H. GRIMMETT Guardian. Guardian of James Puckett, a minor heir of Frances Puckett. Recorded 18 April 1854. (P. 283)

JOHN W. MARSHALL Guardian. Guardian of Charles, George, and Marilda Hutchinson, the minor heirs of Bacley Hutchinson. Recorded 19 April 1854. (P. 285)

WILLIAM LILLARD Guardian. Guardian of Elizabeth, Thomas, Sinthea, and Susan Bartholomew. Recorded 19 April 1854. (P. 286)

JAMES F. PUCKETT Guardian. Guardian of Lucy E. Puckett, a minor heir of Washington Puckett deceased and legatee of Frances Puckett. Recorded 19 April 1854. (P. 288)

ANSWORTH HARRISON Guardian. Guardian for his children, to wit, Clack S., Margaret S., James P., and Henry A. Harrison. They are legatees of Edward Denton. Recorded 3 August 1854. (P. 313)

THOMAS P. MOORE Guardian. Guardian for Thomas Wilson. The guardian received from David Burres who is the administrator of his ward's mother. Recorded 3 August 1854. (P. 316)

MOSES McMILLEN Guardian. Guardian of Charles and James McMillen, the minor heirs of John McMillen. The guardian received from Zadoc McMillen their share of John McMillen's estate. Recorded 4 August 1854. (P. 318)

SILAS TARVER Guardian. Guardian of Harriet, Mary, and Alexander Bandy, the minor heirs of Epperson Bandy who was a legatee of Edward Denton. Recorded 4 August 1854. (Pp. 318-319)

WILLIAM A. MAHEN Guardian. Guardian of Sarah J., Peter R., and Susan C. Mahen. Sarah J. Mahen is now Sarah J. Burton. Recorded 4 August 1854. (Pp. 320-321)

JONATHAN SHORES Guardian. Guardian of Elizabeth Rainey, formerly Elizabeth McMillen, who has married John Rainey. She is an heir of Andrew McMillen. Recorded 4 August 1854. (P. 322)

GEORGE K. ROBERTSON Administrator. Administrator of Alfred McClain. Recorded 9 August 1854. (P. 329)

RIAL C. JENNINGS Guardian. 13 August 1854. Guardian of Henrietta Bumpass who is married to Padget. Recorded in Book SS. (P. 330)

GEORGE R. WARD Guardian. Guardian for his child, Mary Ann Elizabeth Ward, an heir of her mother, Mary A. Ward. He received of James Ward who is the grandfather of said child. Recorded 13 August 1854. (P. 330)

JAMES RICE Guardian. Guardian of Sallie Ann, John Wesley, James Harvey, and William Pitts Rice, the minor heirs of Patricia Rice who was a daughter of John Baird. Wilson Baird, the administrator of John Baird. Recorded 18 September 1854. (P. 333)

B. G. W. WINFORD Guardian. Guardian of Augustus A., Martha Jane, and Don D. Atwell, the minor heirs of Don D. Atwell deceased. The guardian has received their distributive share of the estate of the grandfather, late of Virginia. Recorded 19 September 1854. (P. 336)

WILLIAM W. CARTER Guardian. 30 August 1854. Guardian of Cornelia and Sophronia B. Bell, the minor heirs of Robert D. Bell. (Pp. 340-341)

JAMES F. PUCKETT Guardian. 1 November 1854. Guardian of Lucy E. Mathews, formerly Lucy E. Puckett. (P. 347)

JAMES BRADLEY Guardian. Guardian of George Bradley, insane. Recorded 21 February 1855. (P. 359)

ALEXANDER POSEY Guardian. Guardian of his children, to wit, Mary, Elizabeth, Jane, Thomas, and Jemima Posey, legatees of Silas Chapman who was their grandfather. Re-.

corded 26 February 1855. (P. 359)

ISAAC G. COLES Guardian. 20 October 1851. Guardian of Isaac A. Williams, a minor heir of William B. Williams. (P. 356)

MARTIN SKEEN Guardian. Guardian of Luraney, Elizabeth, Mary, Lucinda, Joseph Thomas, Robert Wilson, James Shelby, and Littleberry W. Wier, the minor heirs at law of Lucius P. Wier. Recorded 26 February 1855. (P. 360)

GEORGE NEAL Guardian. 10 January 1855. Guardian of George, Martha Jane, and James A. Marks, the minor heirs of Lewis Marks. The widow keeps the negroes. (P. 364)

THOMAS B. CHAPMAN Guardian. Guardian of (Elvirenda) and Mary Snow as well as the other heirs of Augustine Snow. Recorded 2 March 1855. (P. 372)

B. A. LATIMER Guardian. Guardian of Mary Letha Latimer, his minor daughter who has a family of negroes from her grandfather James Stratton. Recorded 2 March 1855. (P. 373)

ELIJAH B. DRAKE Guardian. Guardian of John, Joseph, Dorcus, Kiziah, and Mary Jane Nettles, the minor heirs of Zachariah Nettles. Recorded 2 March 1855. (Pp. 375-376)

JOSEPH G. BELL Guardian. Guardian of William Joseph Bell, a minor heir of Robert D. Bell, Jr. Recorded 27 October 1855. (P. 378)

BENJAMIN TUCKER Guardian. Guardian of Elizabeth Kidwell, a minor heir of Solomon Kidwell. The guardian applied for a land warrant for this minor on account of the service rendered by her father in United States service. Recorded 27 October 1855. (Pp. 378-379)

BENJAMIN TUCKER Guardian. Guardian of Benjamin, Celia Jane, Mary Ann, Byrd, Marion H., and Martha Maria Bloodworth, the minor heirs of Jesse Bloodworth. The guardian applied for a land warrant for the minor on account of the service rendered by their father in the service of the United States. Recorded 27 October 1855. (P. 379)

JOHN W. RYE Guardian. Guardian of James Rye. Also of Martha, Sarah, and Louisa Griffin, the children of Elizabeth Griffin and grandchildren of Henry Rye. William Rye, another of the said Henry Rye's children has since arrived at full age. Recorded 10 February 1855. (Pp. 385-386)

JOHN S. CHAPMAN Guardian. Guardian of William, Elizabeth, and James Chapman, the minor heirs of James L. Chapman and legatee of Silas Chapman. Recorded 29 October 1855. (P. 388)

LOVET DIES Guardian. Guardian of James S. Dies. The guardian received from George W. Walker and David Dies, administrators of the estate of his grandfather.

GUARDIAN SETTLEMENTS 1851-1856

Recorded 30 October 1855. (Pp. 388-389)

PATTERSON TAYLOR Guardian. Guardian of Josaphine Taylor, a minor heir of Josiah Taylor, late of the County of Davidson. Recorded 30 October 1855. (P. 389)

COLEMAN S. PUCKETT Guardian. Guardian of Lucind S., a minor of Joseph and Elizabeth Cleveland, late of Smith County. Recorded 6 November 1855. (Pp. 397-398)

JAMES C. OWEN Guardian. 5 May 1855. Guardian of Josaphine, Caledonia, and Theodora Owen, the minor heirs of Stephen W. Owen. The distributees are a widow and three children. (P. 403)

JOHN J. CRITTENDEN Guardian. Late guardian of Maria, Philip W., Willis A., and A. C. B. Jones, the minor heirs of William B. Jones. Recorded 17 November 1855. (Pp. 414-416)

ROBERT W. WHITLOCK Guardian. Guardian of Sarah and Susan Wood, the minor heirs of James Wood. Recorded 19 November 1855. (Pp. 416-417)

F. S. ANDERSON Guardian. Guardian of his children, to wit, James Stephen, Sarah, and Nancy Anderson, heirs of James Robertson who is their grandfather. Recorded 26 November 1855. (Pp. 424-425)

JOHN F. HARKREADER Guardian. Guardian of George G. Harkreader, an heir of John Harkreader. Recorded 28 November 1855. (Pp. 426-427)

T. M. EDWARDS Guardian. Guardian of Sarah Jane, Martha, and Albert J. Edwards, the minor heirs of James Edwards. Recorded 22 December 1855. (P. 428)

WOOD H. SHEARIN Guardian. Guardian of the minor heirs of Samuel and Martha Rigan. Benjamin E. Rigan is of age. Amanda Rigan married Richard Gill. The other heirs are minors. Recorded 25 December 1855. (Pp. 437-439)

JAMES B. RUTLAND Guardian. Guardian of Augustine Rutland, a minor heir of Isaac Rutland and his mother, Emily Rutland. Recorded 25 December 1855. (P. 439)

P. H. VIVRETT Guardian. Guardian of (Lucrecy) Vivrett who is a daughter of Henry Vivrett. Recorded 25 December 1855. (P. 440)

COLEMAN TALLY Guardian. Guardian of Rufus D., Brunetta, and Susan Hearn, the minor heirs of William F. Hearn. Recorded 25 December 1855. (P. 441)

NATHAN GREEN Guardian. Guardian of Eliza D. Martin, a minor. Recorded 22 December 1855. (P. 452)

E. D. JOHNSON Guardian. Guardian of Laura Hankins, an heir of Albert Hankins. Recorded 29 January 1856. (P. 461)

CHLOE PARTLOW Guardian. 28 November 1855. Guardian

53

of her children, to wit, Robert D., Rebecca Frances, and Sarah Jane Partlow, the minor heirs of Thomas Partlow deceased. (P. 462)

J. D. MARTIN Guardian. 30 January 1856. Guardian of Martha E., Amanda J., and John C. Martin, the minor heirs of James L. Martin. (P. 465)

WILLIAM W. SEAY Guardian. Guardian of Lelia V. and Erastus C. Harris, the minor heirs of E. A. R. and Mary S. Harris, and also legatees of Elizabeth Hearn. Recorded 30 January 1856. (P. 466)

THOMPSON EATHERLY Guardian. Guardian of Robert J., Alexander, John W., Emery M., and William J. Eatherly, the minor heirs of Rufus Eatherly. There are five children and the widow. Recorded 27 March 1856. (Pp. 482-483)

HENRY JACKSON Guardian. Guardian of John Mitchell. Recorded 29 May 1856. (P. 491)

LOUISA CARSON Guardian. Guardian of her children. She was formerly Louisa Chapman. Recorded 29 May 1856. (P. 492)

JOHN H. JOHNSON Guardian. Guardian of Mary Jane McDearmon, now Mary Jane Puckett having intermarried with C. W. Puckett. Recorded 20 May 1856. (P. 498)

E. B. MARTIN Guardian. 13 March 1856. Guardian of Elizabeth E., John H. H., and Robert W. Martin, the minor heirs of James Martin. (P. 505)

EDWARD WILLIS Guardian. Guardian of Robert and Pleasant C. Burton, the minor heirs of Edmund Burton. Recorded 6 June 1856. (Pp. 508-509)

RICHARD H. LIGON Guardian. Guardian of Leonidas M. Ligon, a minor. Recorded 7 June 1856. (P. 511)

JOHN H. JOHNSON Guardian. Guardian of James and Caswell Bryant, the minor heirs of Richard Bryant. Recorded 9 June 1856. (P. 516)

GUARDIAN SETTLEMENTS 1856-1862

HENRY B. GRINDSTAFF Guardian. Guardian of Levi, Martha, Wilson, Samuel A., and Shelah Grindstaff, the minor heirs of David Grindstaff. Recorded 24 August 1856. (Pp. 3-4)

WILLIAM J. BAIRD Guardian. 28 April 1856. Guardian of Andrew Baird, the minor heir of William Baird. (P. 5)

G. W. THOMPSON Guardian. Guardian of Ann and Robert Baird, the minor heirs of William Baird. Recorded 19 May 1856. (Pp. 9-10)

HOSEA JOLLY Guardian. Guardian of Henry J., William H., and Micajah Vivrett, the minor heirs of Henry Vivrett. Recorded 22 November 1856. (P. 38)

J. S. PATTERSON Guardian. 18 September 1856. Guardian of Isaac and William D. Ricketts who are minor heirs of Isaac Ricketts. Also, heirs of William Ricketts. (P. 39)

JOHN W. MARSHALL Guardian. 10 September 1856. Guardian of Marilda F., Sarah J., and James C. Jones, the minor heirs of Isaiah Jones. (P. 41)

JOHN ORGAN Guardian. 28 October 1856. Guardian of Theodrick Donnell, an heir of Bernard Carter who is his grandfather. His mother is dead. (P. 54)

JOHN ORGAN Guardian. Guardian of Azariah, Elisha, and Benjamin Chastain, the minor heirs of Elisha Chastain. Recorded 24 December 1856. (Pp. 53-54)

JOHN DIAS Guardian. Guardian of Ruth Jane Dias who has married James Rankin. Recorded 30 December 1856. (P. 56)

THOMAS BASS Guardian. Guardian of Thomas Philips, the minor heir of Bethel Philips. Recorded 31 December 1856. (P. 57)

CHLOE PARTLOW Guardian. 1 December 1856. Guardian for her children, to wit, Robert D., Rebecca Frances, and Sarah Jane Partlow who are the minor heirs of Thomas Partlow. Robert D. Partlow is now dead. (P. 62)

AMELIA HARRIS Guardian. Guardian of her children, Harriet F. and Susan E. Harris, the minor heirs of Richard W. Harris. Recorded 24 April 1857. (Pp. 62-63)

WILLIAM HANCOCK Guardian. Guardian of Acenith, Frances, and Harriet Davis. Acenith Davis is now of age. Frances Davis has married Clemmons. Recorded 16 December 1856. (Pp. 66-68)

MARTHA SULLIVAN Guardian. Guardian of Flavius, Josephus, Eliza J. P., Edmond L., and John A. Sullivan, the minor heirs of Edmund S. Sullivan. Eliza J. P. Sullivan is now Eliza J. P. Wilkinson. Recorded 27 April 1857. (P. 69)

ROBERT TAYLOR Guardian. Guardian for Mary Taylor,

his idiot sister, and legatee of John Taylor. She has
the benefit of 138 acres in the First District of Wilson
County. The said Mary Taylor is not only an idiot, but
entirely helpless. Can only 'set' up by being confined
in a chair. She is 24 or 25 years old. Recorded 29
April 1857. (P. 73)

FINIS E. SHANNON Guardian. Guardian of Mary Wilson
Henry, a minor. Recorded 29 April 1857. (P. 75)

J. W. EDWARDS Guardian. Guardian for Hiram C.,
Elijah C., and Martha Edwards, the minor heirs of G. B.
Edwards. Also, guardian for Pollony C., Annis, (Herty),
and Emily Edwards, the minor heirs of Stokes Edwards.
They are heirs of Sarah Edwards. Recorded 29 April 1857.
(P. 79)

JOHN CHAMBERS Guardian. Guardian of Alexander and
Isabella Duncan, the minor heirs of William L. Duncan.
Recorded 2 May 1857. (P. 82)

RIAL C. JENNINGS Guardian. Guardian of Henrietta
Bumpass who moved to Mississippi and married a man by the
name of Padgett. It is said that she has died leaving
one child. Recorded 2 May 1857. (P. 83)

HENRY TRUETT Guardian. Guardian of Thomas McCart-
ney, a minor heir of Andrew McCartney who was a son of
Mary Randolph, formerly Mary McCartney, now deceased.
Recorded 11 May 1857. (P. 83)

J. W. HEWGLEY Guardian. Guardian of Harrison Spic-
ard, a minor heir of Harrison Spickard and an heir of
John Spickard who was the grandfather of said minor.
Recorded 11 May 1857. (P. 84)

JOHN A. McCLAIN Guardian. Guardian of Alfred and
James McClain, the minor heirs of Alfred McClain. ReO
corded 12 May 1857. (Pp. 88-90)

WILLIAM SIMS Guardian. Guardian of Elizabeth Chastain, formerly Elizabeth Bingham. Also, guardian of
James L., Mathew F., and Sarah Bingham. They are all
minor heirs of John A. Bingham. Recorded 12 May 1857.
(P. 91)

ROWLAND G. ANDREWS Guardian. Guardian of Anderson
P., Joseph W., Martha J., and Saraphine Loyd, the minor
heirs of Anderson Loyd. Recorded 14 May 1857. (P. 95)

MARION B. KITTRELL Guardian. 30 October 1854.
Guardian of Julia, James, William, and Henry Capliner,
the minor heirs of Samuel Capliner. William Capliner is
executor of said Samuel Capliner and of Lavinia Capliner
who was a sister of these minors. (P. 102)

WESLEY HANCOCK Guardian. Guardian of Samuel S.,
Julius H., and Milly M. Gilbert, the minor heirs of James
L. Gilbert. Recorded 9 June 1857. (P. 107)

THOMAS B. CHAPMAN Guardian. Guardian of William,
Elizabeth, and John Chapman, ·the minor heirs of William

Bettes, their grandfather. They are children of James S. Chapman. Recorded 10 June 1857. (P. 108)

THOMAS H. RUTHERFORD Guardian. 10 March 1857. Guardian of Julia Ann, John W., and Nancy Catherine Rutherford, the minor heirs of John R. Rutherford and legatees of Steth Hightower. (P. 110)

ROBERT P. SWEATT Guardian. Guardian for his children, to wit, Margaret T. and Ellen M. Sweatt, the heirs of Hugh L. Sherrill who was their half brother. Recorded 29 June 1857. (P. 118)

PRESTON HENDERSON Guardian. Guardian of Martha Blankenship, a minor heir of David Blankenship. Jane Blankenship, another of the heirs, has married. Recorded 29 June 1857. (P. 119)

JAMES A. BLANKENSHIP Guardian. Guardian of Martha, Haley, and Phebe Bond, the minor heirs of Green Bond and legatee of Reverend James Bond deceased. Recorded 30 June 1857. (P. 120)

JAMES RICE Guardian. Guardian of his children, the minor heirs of Patricia Rice who was a daughter of John Baird. Recorded 1 July 1857. (P. 121)

GUY T. GLEAVES Guardian. 20 May 1857. Guardian of Margaret, Pamelia C., and Robert Crudup, the minor heirs of Josiah and Louisa Crudup. The children are small, the youngest was but a few days old when his mother died. The grandmother, Mrs. Wright, has charge of them. (P. 122)

WILLIAM BAIRD Guardian. 7 May 1857. Guardian of Jerome R. Baird, the minor heir of William Baird. (P. 125)

WILLIAM B. DUNN Guardian. 1 April 1857. Guardian of Mary Ann, Sarah Jane, John E., and James W. Hass, the minor heirs of Phillip Hass and heir of John Hass who was their grandfather. There were nine children and the widow. (P. 130)

WILLIAM L. CLEMMONS Guardian. Guardian of John C. and Andrew Eskew, the minor heirs of Dr. Andrew Eskew. Recorded 19 September 1857. (P. 148)

BENJAMIN W. WARREN Guardian. Guardian of Lafayette Eskew, the minor heir of Dr. Andrew Eskew. Recorded 14 October 1857. (P. 149)

THOMAS WATERS Guardian. Guardian of Julia A., Agness, Timothy, Sarah, and Isaac J. Dodson, the minor heirs of Isaac J. Dodson and heirs of Timothy Dodson who is their grandfather. Recorded 14 October 1857. (Pp. 152-153)

JOHN K. CARTWRIGHT Guardian. 18 April 1857. Guardian of Amanda S. Neely, a minor heir of William B. Neely and an heir of William Neely late of Smith County. Nathan T. Neely was executor of William Neely. (P. 155)

JESSE A. GRIGG Guardian. Guardian of Abner and Ellen Eskew, the minor heirs of Andrew Eskew. Recorded 19 October

1857. (P. 157)

M. T. BENNETT Guardian. 15 August 1857. Guardian
of Sophronia Tarver, the minor heir of William Tarver.
(P. 158)

JOHN ORGAN Guardian. 10 September 1857. Guardian
of Martha and Julia Billings, the minor heirs of Sally
and George Billings. Julia Billings is now Julia Trice.
(P. 166)

CARY ANN KITTRELL Guardian. 17 September 1857.
Guardian of the minor heirs of Isham Kittrell. (Pp. 167-
168)

ISAAC N. SWANN Guardian. Guardian of Barbary Swann,
the minor heir of John Swann. Recorded 10 November 1857.
(P. 168)

ELIJAH WILLIAMS Guardian. 28 January 1858. Guardian of Elijah Carroll and William Caswell McDearmon,
the minor heirs of William McDearmon. (P. 178)

THOMAS C. TELFORD Guardian. Guardian of John R.
Markham. Thomas Telford, the former guardian, is now
dead. (P. 181)

MATHEW SKEEN Guardian. Guardian of Edward, Frances,
Ruth Hannah, America Ann, Mary, and John James Skeen, the
minor heirs of Hope H. Skeen. Recorded 29 March 1858.
(P. 189)

H. A. GOODALL Guardian. Guardian of John G. Goodall,
Jr. and Nancy A. Champ, who are heirs of Thomas Tuggle
who died in Smith County. Recorded 30 March 1858. (P.
194)

JAMES S. CLUCK Guardian. Guardian of Sarah A., James
L., and Caladonia Burke who are the minor heirs of
Fielding Burke. Sarah A. Burke is now Sarah A. Lanum.
Recorded 11 May 1858. (P. 213)

N. H. ROBERTSON Guardian. 6 March 1858. Guardian of
John S. Barbee, a minor heir of Sarah H. Barbee. (P. 216)

JOHN WHITED Guardian. Guardian of Matilda Roper,
formerly Matilda Whited, and a minor heir of James and
Matilda Whited. She has moved with her uncle to Illinois
and married James Roper. Neither of them are of age. Recorded 11 May 1858. (P. 216)

JOHN D. COMPTON Guardian. 23 March 1858. Guardian
of Jasper N. Compton, a minor heir of Charles Compton.
Richard P. Compton was the former guardian. (Pp. 217-
218)

MILES T. AYRES Guardian. 5 April 1858. Guardian of
Mitchel H. Thompson, a minor heir of James Thompson. (P.
220)

THOMAS DUNN Guardian. 29 March 1858. Guardian of
the minor heirs of John Hass, the grandfather, to wit,

GUARDIAN SETTLEMENTS 1856-1862

Mary Ann, Sarah Jane, John E., and William H. Hass who are minor heirs of Philip Hass deceased; William D., Louisa, Nancy F., Mary Jane, Thomas H., Luise Anne, John, and Joshua Hass who are minor heirs of Albert G. Hass; and Luisa Jane, George W., Mary E., and John H. Coleman who are minor heirs of Elizabeth Coleman deceased. Louisa Jane has intermarried with Harrison Cavender. (Pp. 220-221)

WILLIAM D. GRINDSTAFF Guardian. Guardian of Sally Jane, Tabitha, Margaret Ann, and John William Barbee, the minor heirs of John Barbee. Recorded 7 August 1858. (P. 229)

JAMES S. HARRIS Guardian. 8 March 1858. Guardian of Josaphine Rebecca Litchford, formerly Josaphine Rebecca Sherrell, and Dolphus Sherrell who are the heirs of Hugh Sherrell. (Pp. 233-234)

JOHN D. TAYLOR Guardian. 8 June 1858. Guardian of John and William Arnold, the minor heirs at law of their half brother, Samuel H. Stevenson. (P. 242)

JOHN D. BONE Guardian. 28 May 1858. Guardian of Robert C. and Martha N. Bone, the minor heirs of Henry P. Bone. (P. 245)

F. R. COSSETT Guardian. Guardian of Alice A. Fisher, a minor heir. Recorded 24 August 1858. (P. 260)

STEPHEN L. PRESTON Guardian. Guardian of John C., Joshua E., and James C. Preston, the minor heirs of John Preston. Recorded 22 February 1859. (P. 268)

JOHN THOMPSON Guardian. Guardian of Martha Jane Thompson, a minor heir of Andrew J. Thompson. Recorded 1 March 1859. (P. 278)

GEORGE D. YOUNG Guardian. Guardian of Andrew J. Thompson, a minor heir of James Thompson. Recorded 1 March 1859. (P. 276)

JOHN GAY Guardian. Guardian of his children, John M. and James N. Gay who are of age. His other children, Mary L. S., Maria P., John H. C., Zachez T., and Tabitha C. Gay are heirs of Archer Clay. Recorded 14 March 1859. (Pp. 280-281)

JOHN PRICHETT Guardian. Guardian of Catharine, Elizabeth, William Thomas, and James Prichett, the minor children of William Prichett and heirs of George Prichett. Recorded 14 March 1859. (P. 288)

HOUSTON THORNTON Guardian. Guardian of John, Houston, Nancy, Susan, and Doshea Thornton, the minor heirs of Joseph and Nancy Thornton. Recorded 15 March 1859. (P. 291)

J. M. HEDGEPETH Guardian. Guardian of Sarah Ann Foster, formerly Sarah Ann Dobson. She has married James Foster. Recorded 15 March 1859. (P. 291)

59

A. H. SANDERS Guardian. Guardian of Alfred W., Fountain E., and Belotty Hewgley, the minor heirs of Alfred L. Hewgley. Recorded 11 April 1859. (Pp. 304-305)

JOHN B. COX Guardian. Guardian of Laura Hawkins, the minor heir of Albert G. Hawkins. Baker W. Harris was the former guardian. Recorded 13 April 1859. (Pp. 315-316)

A. W. VICK Guardian. Guardian of Synthea, Jane, Martha B., Nancy, Amanda, and Sarah B. Estes who are the minor heirs of Benjamin B. Estes. Recorded 14 April 1859. (Pp. 319-320)

ELIZABETH MARKS Guardian. Guardian of George Marks, the minor heir of Thomas Marks. Recorded 4 May 1859. (P. 329)

WILLIAM RALSTONE Guardian. Guardian of James D. Hamilton, a minor heir of John V. Hamilton, late of Sumner County. Recorded 5 May 1859. (P. 334)

SUTTON E. BELCHER Guardian. Guardian of John Belcher and ( ) Belcher, the minor heirs of James E. Belcher. Recorded 5 May 1859. (P. 335)

SILAS TARVER Guardian. Guardian of Mary Crutcher, formerly Mary Bandy, a legatee of Edward Denton. Recorded 5 May 1859. (P. 337)

BENJAMIN J. TARVER Guardian. Guardian of George L. and Benjamin F. Porter, the minor heirs of Elizabeth A. Porter. James L. Porter, their father, has removed with his children to Texas. Recorded 7 July 1859. (P. 349)

HENRY D. LESTER Guardian. Guardian of George H. Holleman, a son of Caroline Holleman deceased who was a daughter of George H. Bullard deceased. Recorded 12 July 1859. (P. 349)

ANDERSON S. WILLIAMS Guardian. Guardian of the minor heirs of A. A. Massey, to wit, Nancy M., Mary, and Matthew Massey. Recorded 13 July 1859. (Pp. 356-357)

JAMES HOLMES Guardian. Guardian of Edward L. and Delila L. Bradley, the minor heirs of George Bradley. Recorded 14 July 1859. (Pp. 360-361)

ISAAC G. COLE Guardian. Guardian of Katarah Gregory, now (compres menter). Recorded 21 July 1859. (Pp. 364-365)

ELY MASSEY Guardian. Guardian of Etheldred P. and Albert W. H. H. Massey, the minor heirs of A. A. Massey. Recorded 15 August 1859. (P. 371)

ELIZABETH C. SCRUGGS Guardian. Guardian for her children, to wit, Elizabeth Penny, Samuel (Grass), James C., Martha B., Margaret Ann, and Demaascus H. Scruggs, the minor heirs of D. H. Scruggs. Recorded 15 August 1859. (Pp. 372-373)

GUARDIAN SETTLEMENTS 1856-1862

G. W. THOMPSON Guardian. Guardian of Ann and Robert Baird, the minor heirs of William Baird. Ann Baird is now deceased. Recorded 15 September 1859. (P. 374)

R. G. ANDREWS Guardian. Guardian of Martha Jane and Mary Caroline Andrews, the heirs of Emiline Andrews deceased who died in the State of Missouri. Thomas Davis of Missouri is the administrator. Martha Jane is now Martha Jane Bass. Recorded 15 September 1859. (P. 375)

ALEY DUNCAN Guardian. Guardian of her children, to wit, Martha, Elizabeth, Amanda, Polk Etta, and Alice Duncan, the minor heirs of Edwin Duncan. Recorded 15 September 1859. (Pp. 376-377)

FRANCIS ANDERSON Guardian. Guardian of Hannah E. and Josephine E. Bogle, the minor heirs of Joseph Bugle. Recorded 15 September 1859. (P. 378)

B. W. WARREN Guardian. Guardian of Lafayette Eskew, the minor heir of Dr. Andrew Eskew. The guardian received of the grandfather, John McFarland deceased. Recorded 17 September 1859. (P. 381)

LEWIS W. ROBERTSON Guardian. Guardian of Nancy Link who is a minor heir of James A. Link. Recorded 20 September 1859. (P. 385)

WILLIAM M. KNIGHT Guardian. Guardian of William H., Sally Jane, Hiram G., and John W. Bennett, the minor heirs of John Bennett. Recorded 20 September 1859. (P. 386)

EMANUEL S. THOMPSON Guardian. Guardian of Elizabeth M. Thompson, the minor heir of William A. Thompson. Recorded 20 September 1859. (P. 387)

MILES A. THOMPSON Guardian. Guardian of Henry F. Thompson, a minor heir of William A. Thompson. Recorded 20 September 1859. (P. 388)

JOHN WORD Guardian. Guardian of Moses L. H., Martha L., William B., and James P. Taylor, the minor heirs of James A. Taylor. Recorded 20 September 1859. (P. 389)

BAILEY PHILIPS Guardian. Guardian of L. D., Livisa, William R., Brown, and Persevius Philips, the minor children of Seth Philips and heirs of Thomas Harlin. Recorded 31 October 1859. (P. 392)

WILLIAM S. WOODRUM Guardian. Guardian of John, Mary, and Frances (Lenam), the minor heirs of George L. (Lenam). Recorded 31 October 1859. (P. 393)

ZARA HARALSON Guardian. Guardian of Ephraim L. Haralson, a minor heir of Vincent Haralson deceased and an heir of Levi Haralson. There are two children of age, to wit, James H. and Elizabeth M. Haralson. Elizabeth M. Haralson is married to Carroll Commons. Recorded 2 November 1859. (P. 396)

R. R. BOGLE Guardian. Guardian of Thomas Bogle, the minor heir of Joseph Bogle. Recorded 3 November 1859. (P. 398.

61

JOHN ORGAN Guardian. 18 October 1859. Guardian of Sally Clifford, an idiot. (P. 408)

JOHN ORGAN Guardian. Guardian of Crawford E. Bass, a minor heir of Elias Bass. Recorded 3 December 1859. (P. 408)

JAMES M. CALHOUN Guardian. Guardian of the minor heirs of William W. Calhoun, to wit, Fannie, William, Thomas, Emily, and Hezekiah Calhoun. Recorded 21 December 1859. (Pp. 410-412)

GEORGE W. C. BOND Guardian. Guardian of Augustus Lain, an idiot, who is very old, and entirely helpless, requires the attention of a child. Has to be helped up, fed, etc. Recorded 30 January 1860. (P. 417)

J. F. CLEMMONS Guardian. Guardian of the minor heirs of Edwin Clemmons, to wit, Rufus P., William E., Joseph, and Robert Clemmons. The guardian received from the estate of John Clemmons deceased. Recorded 31 January 1860. (P. 424)

RICHARD B. JONES Guardian. Guardian of his daughter, Mary F. Jones who is an heir of John Clemmons. Recorded 29 February 1860. (P. 426)

ANDERSON WILLIAMS Guardian. Guardian of Mary Massey who has now married Charles L. Baird. Recorded 12 March 1860. (P. 431)

JOHN D. TAYLOR Guardian. Guardian of John and William Arnold, the minor heirs of their half mother, Genie H. Stevenson. Recorded 12 March 1860. (P. 432)

JAMES N. CARTWRIGHT Guardian. Guardian of Martha and John Cartwright, the minor heirs of Martha T. Cartwright. Their sister is Mrs. Turner. Recorded 12 March 1860. (Pp. 434-435)

JOHN H. JOHNSON Guardian. Guardian of Mary James McDearmon who married C. W. Puckett from whom she has been divorced. Recorded 26 March 1860. (P. 436)

WILLIAM L. HOLMAN Guardian. Guardian of Mary C., Marcia Ann, William R., and Sarah C. Holman who are grandchildren and heirs at law of William Robb, late of Rutherford County, Tennessee. Recorded 26 March 1860. (P. 440)

GEORGE H. CAMPBELL Guardian. Guardian for Hugh and Adelaid Wills, the minor heirs of Stephen R. Wills. The administration was in Smith County. Recorded 11 August 1860. (P. 443)

JACOB THOMASON Guardian. Guardian of James Marks, insane. Recorded 15 November 1857. (P. 456)

SAMUEL E. ESTES Guardian. Guardian of Pamelia F. Freeman, a minor heir of Dorrell Freeman. Recorded 22 November 1860. (P. 465)

GUARDIAN SETTLEMENTS 1856-1862

WILLIAM BRADLEY Guardian. Guardian of William T. and Mary E. Bradley, the minor heirs of Everett Bradley. Recorded 28 November 1860. (P. 472)

NANCY VANHOOK Guardian. Guardian for her children, to wit, Mary Elizabeth, Eliza, John, and Frederick Vanhooser who are the minor heirs of Ackson Vanhooser. Recorded 12 December 1860. (P. 478)

ALEXANDER BRETT Guardian. Guardian for John and William A. Murphey who are children of W. H. E. Murphey and heirs of Rutherford Rutland. Recorded 15 December 1860. (P. 483)

MATTHEW SKEEN Guardian. Guardian of the minor heirs of Hope H. Skeen. Their mother is Winney Skeen. Recorded 13 December 1860. (Pp. 484-485)

E. L. ROSS Guardian. Guardian of Charles, George, Brown, and Nancy Hill, the minor heirs of E. C. Hill. Recorded 17 December 1860. (P. 491)

NATHAN OAKLEY Guardian. Guardian of James H. Davis, a minor heir of William H. Davis. Recorded 17 December 1860. (P. 492)

JOHN ORGAN Guardian. Guardian for William W. Wynne, a minor heir of John W. Wynne. Recorded 2 January 1861. (P. 499)

GEORGE SANDERS Guardian. Guardian of Ann Eliza Sanders, a minor heir of Stephen Sanders deceased, and an heir at law of John Johnson, her grandfather, late of Davidson County, Tennessee. Recorded 3 January 1861. (P. 500)

JONATHAN F. HOOKER Guardian. Guardian of Alexander J. Hamilton, a minor heir of George Hamilton. Recorded 3 January 1861. (P. 501)

WILLIAM S. CHAPMAN Guardian. Guardian of Elizabeth and John Chapman, the minor heirs of James L. Chapman. The previous guardian was Thomas B. Chapman. Recorded 4 January 1861. (P. 502)

HOUSTON ANDREWS Guardian. Guardian of William M. Andrews who was a lunatic, but is now dead. Recorded 16 January 1861. (P. 508)

MILBREY H. ANDREWS Guardian. Guardian of John Houston Andrews who is now of age. Recorded 17 January 1861. (P. 513)

J. S. WAMMACK Guardian. Guardian of his minor child, Erixon E. Wammack who was an heir of Erixon E. Wammack. Recorded 18 January 1861. (P. 513)

THOMAS A. PARTLOW Guardian. Guardian of Jonathan N. and Mary E. Partlow, the minor heirs of Thomas Partlow deceased. The distributees were a widow and ten children. Recorded 18 January 1861. (P. 517)

JOHN ORGAN Guardian. Guardian of Louisa D. Thompson, a minor heir of James G. Thompson. Recorded 18 January 1861. (P. 519)

ISAAC G. COLE Guardian. Guardian of Mary B. and Martha L. McDaniel, minors. These minors received a portion of their mother's estate. Recorded 23 January 1861. (P. 527)

ISAAC G. COLE Guardian. Guardian of Isaac N. Williams, a minor heir of William B. Williams. Recorded 23 January 1861. (Pp. 529-531)

WILLIAM B. PURSLEY Guardian. Guardian of Mrs. Elizabeth Rutherford who is insane. Recorded 29 January 1861. (P. 546)

JOHN EATHERLY Guardian. Guardian of Nancy J. Terry, formerly Nancy J. Wilson, a minor heir of John R. Wilson. She is also an heir of James Donalson. Recorded 30 January 1861. (Pp. 552-553)

WILLIAM P. SULLIVAN Guardian. Guardian of John H., Thomas A., and Mary T. Clemmons, the minor heirs of Samuel T. Clemmons. Recorded 31 January 1861. (P. 556)

EDWARD ROBINSON Guardian. Guardian of Eliza Ann Jennings, a minor heir of Joel Jennings. Recorded 31 January 1861. (P. 561)

JOHN T. SIMPSON Guardian. Guardian for Virginia Hill, a minor who has intermarried with John Quarles who is also a minor. Recorded 31 January 1861. (P. 561)

ANDREW J. CLIMER Guardian. Guardian of his minor children, to wit, John A. and (Ferbis) B. Climer who are heirs of their mother, Rachel Climer, who was a (brother) and heir of Samuel Marrs. Recorded 31 January 1861. (P. 562)

THOMAS WATERS Guardian. Guardian of Elizabeth, John A., Robert A., Martha A., Thomas, and Benjamin Hankins, the minor heirs of John Hankins. Recorded 28 November 1861. (P. 567)

JOHN G. LIGAN Guardian. Guardian for his daughters, Nancy E. and Mary E. Ligan, who are heirs of Edward Sweatt, their grandfather, and of Alexander C. Sweatt, their uncle. Recorded 28 November 1861. (P. 569)

JOHN S. HALEY Guardian. Guardian of Nancy Elizabeth, John, Mary Edward, Sarah, James, Benjamin, and Parthenia Corder, the minor heirs of Margaret Corder. Recorded 26 November 1861. (P. 573)

THOMAS E. WILLIAMSON Guardian. Guardian of John P. McFarland, a son of John B. McFarland, and a grandson of James McFarland. Recorded 28 November 1861. (Pp. 578-579)

PETER G. DUFFER Guardian. Guardian of Sally M. Belcher who was formerly Sally M. Lester. Also, guardian for

GUARDIAN SETTLEMENTS 1856-1862

Joshua, and James L. Lester. Recorded 28 November 1861.
(P. 580)

JAMES M. BROWN Guardian. Guardian of Lucy and Julia
Jackson, the minor heirs of Mark Jackson. Recorded 2
December 1861. (Pp. 583-584)

WILLIAM L. HOLMAN Guardian. Guardian of Susan E.
Harris, one of the children of W. and Amelia Harris, deceased. Recorded 3 December 1861. (P. 585)

DAVID W. QUARLES Guardian. Guardian of James T.,
Mary A. S., Littleberry J., Jesse P., and Harriet B.
Quarles who are heirs of William J. A. Quarles. James T.
Quarles is now of age. Mary A. S. Quarles is now married.
Jesse P. Quarles has died. Recorded 11 December 1861.
(Pp. 594-596)

JOSEPH MOTTLEY Guardian. Guardian of Theophilus,
Augustus, James, Delea, and Martha Peace. The guardian
reported that he received from Louisiana a portion of
the estate of James Peace. Recorded 20 February 1861.
(P. 597)

ED. R. PENNEBAKER Guardian. Guardian of James
McCausland, a minor heir of James McCausland. Recorded
12 December 1861. (P. 598)

JOHN G. BURKE Guardian. Guardian of Nancy and Tarl-
ton Lavender, the minor heirs of William Lavender. Recorded 12 December 1861. (P. 599)

JOHN EATHERLY Guardian. Guardian of Hugh P. and
Thomas R. Wilson, the heirs of James Donalson deceased in
1854 and as heirs of John R. Wilson deceased 1856. Recorded 12 December 1861. (Pp. 608-609)

MATTHEW HILL Guardian. Guardian of James R. M.,
Frances J., David R. M. N., Elijah H., Mary E., and Susan
D. Etcherson. The guardian received for his wards in the
State of Georgia. Recorded 13 December 1861. (Pp. 610-
612)

WILLIAM P. BANDY Guardian. Guardian of Flemming G.,
Henry H., and William L. Scruggs, the minor heirs of C. C.
Scruggs. Their mother was first appointed guardian. Re-
corded 20 December 1861. (Pp. 619-620)

JAMES B. THOMAS Guardian. 20 May 1861. Guardian
of George A. Bogle, an heir of Joseph H. Bogle who died
in Canon County. (Pp. 624-625)

GEORGE SANDERS Guardian. Guardian of Ann Eliza Sanders, an heir of John Johnson who was her grandfather.
The guardian reported that he received from the executor
of her uncle Albert Johnson. Recorded 21 December 1861.
(P. 630)

JEFFERSON LUCK Guardian. Guardian of William L.,
Margaret, Mahaley, Joseph, and Alice Massey, the minor
heirs of Henry Y. Massey. Recorded 21 December 1861.
(P. 630)

GUARDIAN SETTLEMENTS 1856-1862

SAMUEL S. AYRES Guardian. Guardian of Thomas Buchanan James, a minor heir of Rachel J. James. Recorded 23 December 1861. (P. 638)

RUSSELL ESKEW Guardian. Guardian of Lucy F., Rhoda Ann, Bird, Albert, and Margaret Guill, the minor heirs of their grandfather, Alexander Eskew. Their mother was entitled to dower. Recorded 23 December 1861. (Pp. 639-640)

WILLIAM F. ROBERTSON Guardian. Guardian of the minor heirs of Mark Collier. Samuel H. Porterfield was first appointed guardian, but has moved from this state. Recorded 24 December 1861. (P. 644)

JANE TURNEY Guardian. Guardian of Rachel, Joseph, Catharine, Rebecca, Jasper, John A., Isaac G., and James T. Turney, her children and minor heirs of William Turney. Recorded 19 November 1862. (P. 647)

WILLIAM S. RHODES Guardian. Guardian of Quicksanna, William, James E., (Phelps) B. who are minor heirs of J. G. Allen. Recorded 27 December 1861. (Pp. 648-649)

JOHN A. CLARK Guardian. Guardian of Mary Reese who is old and unable to tend to her own business. Recorded 27 December 1861. (Pp. 651-652)

L. J. TRIBBLE Guardian. Guardian of Patience Tribble who is insane. Recorded 15 January 1862. (P. 660)

JAMES W. WRIGHT Guardian. Guardian of John G. Puckett who is unable to tend to his own business. Recorded 12 February 1862. (P. 668)

JAMES WRIGHT Guardian. Guardian of Charles Puckett who is unable to tend to his own business. Recorded 12 February 1862. (P. 669)

AUGUSTUS L. REDMAN Guardian. Guardian of Harvey W. Robinson, a minor heir of A. W. Robinson. Recorded 18 November 1862. (P. 678)

W. R. WINTER Guardian. Guardian of Bettie Castleman. He received a small part of her estate from the executor of William White deceased. Recorded 19 November 1862. (P. 684)

JACOB B. LASATER Guardian. Guardian of Kiziah Lasater who is an idiot. Recorded 19 November 1862. (P. 688)

WILLIAM H. SMITH Guardian. Guardian of Henry F. Smith who is now dead. The deceased in his last days was palsied. Recorded 19 November 1862. (Pp. 689-690)

ANDERSON L. WILLIAMS Guardian. Guardian of Nancy M. Baird, formerly Nancy M. Massey. She has married R. A. Baird. Recorded 20 November 1862. (P. 692)

JOHN CHAMBERS Guardian. Guardian of Alexander and Isabella Duncan, the minor heirs of William S. and Eliza Duncan. Recorded 22 November 1862. (P. 703)

HANNAH SMITHWICK Guardian. Guardian of (Mattie) Smith. Recorded 27 June 1865. (P. 1)

ROBERT L. CARUTHERS Guardian. Uncle and former guardian of Mary Cahal. Recorded 19 September 1865. (P. 1)

H. A. GOODALL Guardian. Guardian of Etha and Jonnie F. Waters, the minor heirs of John F. Waters. Recorded 19 December 1863. (P. 5)

GREEN HOBBS Guardian. Guardian of Emely B. Hobbs. Recorded 16 December 1863. (P. 6)

JOHN KELLY Guardian. Guardian of the children of Jacob Horn, to wit, Mary and Viola P. Horn. Recorded 4 February 1864. (P. 9)

GEORGE J. WOOD Guardian. Guardian of the minor heirs of William Motheral, to wit, Josiah P., Jefferson, George W., and Rosaline M. Motheral. Josiah P. Motheral is supposed to be dead. Recorded 12 August 1864. (Pp. 21-22)

J. H. ALLEN Guardian. Guardian of the children of Larkin G. Allen, to wit, Angeline who has married John Morris, and Richard, William, and Ann Elizabeth Allen who are heirs of Richard W. Harris. Recorded 17 February 1864. (Pp. 25-26)

E. W. JARRALL Guardian. Guardian of Thomas Davis who is of age. He has received from the administrator of his mother. Recorded 24 February 1865. (P. 32)

BERYM. L. RUCKER Guardian. Guardian of Jonathan H., David, Sarah Ann, and Marriet M. Rucker, the minor heirs of Berym. Rucker deceased. Also, appointed guardian of (Laurum) B. Rucker who is of age. Harriet M. Rucker has died. Recorded 24 July 1865. (P. 35)

ELIAS BARBEE Guardian. Guardian of America Donnell, a granddaughter and heir of Adlai Donnell. Recorded 4 August 1865. (P. 39)

J. L. CLUCK Guardian. Guardian of Caladonia T. Flowers. She is now Caladonia T. Lannom. She is a daughter of Fielding Burk. She has been twice married. She was divorced from her first husband. Recorded 4 August 1865. (P. 44)

W. W. MOORE Guardian. Guardian of George Lavender who is of age. Recorded 16 October 1865. (P. 50)

WILLIAM BROWN Guardian. Guardian of the heirs of Jordan Robinson, to wit, Luke S., Andrew J., James M., William C., and Thomas J. Robinson. Recorded 16 October 1865. (P. 52)

MRS. M. L. KELLY Executrix. Executrix of John Kelly deceased. Recorded 17 October 1865. (Pp. 54-55)

MATHIAS MONNET Guardian. Guardian of Mary Francis, Louisa Jane, and Susan Elizabeth Bond, the minor heirs of H. H. Bond. Recorded 18 October 1865. (P. 60)

J. WILKERSON Guardian. Guardian of the children of William S. Holman deceased. They are heirs of their grandfather, William Robb, of Rutherford County. Recorded 24 October 1865. (P. 68)

SAMUEL AYRES Guardian. Guardian of Thomas B. James, a minor heir of Rachel J. James. He is entitled to a share of the estate of Buchanan James. Recorded 24 October 1865. (P. 70)

J. W. ANDERSON Guardian. Guardian of Clinton, Frank, Caladonia, and Larkin Anderson, the minor heirs of Mary Anderson. Also, heirs of Cader Bass, Also, of J. W. Anderson. Recorded 25 October 1865. (P. 70)

JOHN T. THARP Guardian. Guardian of Henry C. Puckett who is of age. Recorded 25 October 1865. (Pp. 73-74)

JOSEPH M. ANDERSON Guardian. Guardian of Priscilla Chandler, a daughter of Ekellia M. Chandler. Recorded 26 October 1865. (P. 75)

MEDES P. ANDERSON Guardian. Guardian of his children, F. F., Cader B., and Nancy J. Anderson. Said children are minor heirs of Martha Anderson and heirs of Cader Bass. Recorded 27 October 1865. (P. 81)

ROBERT TAYLOR Guardian. Guardian of his idiot sister, Mary Taylor, who died in the Spring of 1862. Recorded 10 November 1865. (P. 84)

CAROLINE A. BRYAN Guardian. Guardian of her children, Henry Jefferson and John A. Tally, the minor heirs of John C. Tally. After her appointment as guardian, she married Nelson Bryan. Recorded 10 November 1865. (P. 85)

L. J. GRAVES Guardian. Guardian of (Melessark), John, and Stokes Donalson, the minor heirs of John Donalson. Recorded 16 February 1866. (P. 95)

ANDERSON P. LOYD Guardian. Guardian of Saraphine Loyd, now Saraphine Porterfield. Recorded 10 May 1866. (P. 107)

WILLIAM H. ORR Guardian. Guardian of William E. T. Bonner, a minor heir of Ed R. Bonner. Recorded 18 May 1866. (P. 113)

WILLIAM L. BENNETT Guardian. Guardian of Sophrona Hight, formerly Sophrona Tarver, a minor heir of William Tarver. Recorded 18 May 1866. (P. 114)

SAMUEL H. HARRIS Guardian. 2 April 1866. Guardian of Elizabeth F., Lucy J., John F., Arthur P., Samuel L., and Nancy A. Harris, the minor heirs of Elizabeth Harris. (P. 115)

JOHN A. McCLAIN Guardian. Guardian of Josie, Mary S., and Kittie R. Ross, the minor heirs of Samuel N. Ross. Recorded 20 May 1866. (Pp. 116-117)

NANCY GAINES Guardian. Guardian of her children,

Margaret, Elizabeth, Gideon, Tennessee, Agness, Melberry, Frances, Riley, and Thomas Gaines. Recorded 17 June 1866. (P. 125)

JOHN CRUDUP Guardian. Guardian of Louisa, John B., Byron, and Polly B. Graves, the minor heirs of G. B. Graves. Recorded 20 June 1866. (Pp. 127-128)

JOHN H. JOHNSON Guardian. Guardian of James Bryant and Caswell Bryant, the minor heirs of Richard Bryant. Recorded 21 August 1866. (P. 131)

GEORGE W. WHITE Guardian. Guardian of Bettie Manning, formerly Bettie Castleman, and an heir of William H. White. Recorded 21 October 1866. (P. 141)

THOMAS J. BRATTON Guardian. Guardian of Uriah Neal, a minor heir of William Neal. Recorded 15 November 1866. (P. 143)

JOHN T. SIMPSON Guardian. Guardian of Virginia Quarles, formerly Virginia Hill. She is now the wife of L. B. J. Quarles. Recorded 15 December 1866. (P. 148)

W. D. VIVRETT Guardian. Guardian of Caladonia and Elizabeth Anderson, minors. Recorded 15 December 1866. (P. 149)

JONATHAN F. HOOKER Guardian. Guardian of Nancy J., George W., and Virginia L. Dodson, the minor heirs of Benjamin Dodson. Recorded 10 January 1867. (P. 151)

JOHN A. LESTER Guardian. Guardian of Sophia and Margaret Burdine, the minor heirs of Jefferson Burdine. Recorded 10 January 1867. (P. 153)

JOHN ORGAN Guardian. Guardian of Sarah P., Frances P., Wrepps, and Ann R. Wammack, the minor heirs of Richard Wammack. Recorded 10 January 1867. (P. 154)

E. W. NEAL Guardian. Guardian of Samuel L. Neal, a minor heir of John H. Neal. Recorded 4 March 1867. (P. 165)

JOHN T. GLEAVES Guardian. Guardian for the minor heirs of Drury Tharp. Recorded 4 March 1867. (P. 169)

SPENCER B. TALLY Guardian. Guardian of Robertson and James Johnson, the minor heirs of James M. Johnson. Recorded 10 April 1867. (P. 173)

DAVID CLARK Guardian. Guardian of William A. and Isabella Duncan. Said Isabella Duncan is now married to Samuel Johnson. Recorded 2 April 1867. (P. 177)

EZEKIEL BASS Guardian. Guardian of his children, Tabitha B., Tennessee, and Wilson T. Bass, the minor heirs of Daniel Barbee. Recorded 21 May 1867. (P. 181)

JAMES PEMBERTON Guardian. Guardian for his five minor children who are heirs of (Jonas) Bradley. Recorded 21 May 1867. (P. 183)

C. STONE Guardian. Guardian of Mary Jane, Maria, Adaline, William, and Susan Martin, the minor heirs of Wesley Martin. Recorded 5 June 1867. (P. 186)

W. A. D. JONES Guardian. Guardian of William H. Steed, the minor heir of Martin H. Steed a grandson and heir of Ezekiel Holloway. Recorded 5 June 1867. (P. 189)

JAMES A. WILLIAMS Guardian. Guardian of William A., Margaret A., Julius, Martha Jane, John H., James R., and Sarah R. Philips, the minor heirs of John Philips. The mother has since died. Recorded 10 July 1867. (P. 190)

NANCY PATTON Guardian. 4 July 1864. Guardian of Charles Patton, a minor heir of T. M. Patton. (P. 193)

WILLIAM C. RICE Guardian. Guardian of Lucinda E. and Nancy G. Gates, the minor heirs of Elizabeth Gates. Recorded 20 September 1867. (P. 194)

PETER THOMPSON Guardian. Guardian of Milly N. Gilbert, a minor heir of James G. Gilbert. Sarah J. Gilbert was another heir of James G. Gilbert. She married George E. Donnell. Recorded 20 September 1867. (P. 200)

TILMAN W. LANNOM Guardian. Guardian of Nancy, Malissa, Mary E., and Elmira Jane Bond, the minor heirs of Robert Bond. Recorded 10 October 1867. (P. 203)

I. J. WILKERSON Guardian. 9 November 1867. Guardian of William R. Holman and Sarah C. Holman, the minor heirs of William L. Holman. William R. Holman has departed this life. (P. 208)

WILLIAM D. HAMBLIN Guardian. Guardian of Patrick and Polena Donalson, the minor heirs of Robert Donalson, Jr. Recorded 31 December 1867. (Pp. 213-214)

GEORGE E. DONNELL Guardian. Guardian of Milly N. Pierce, formerly Milly N. Gilbert. Recorded 31 December 1867. (P. 216)

WILLIAM M. SANDERS Guardian. Guardian of Mary E. L. Martin, the minor heir of Lindsey C. Martin. Recorded 31 December 1867. (P. 217)

L. J. TRIBBLE Guardian. Guardian of Patience Tribble who died in 1862. Recorded 20 January 1868. (Pp. 223-224)

THOMAS YOUNG Guardian. Guardian of Marshall Carter who is of age. A settlement was made with the administrator of the father of this young man on the 15th of March 1866 which shows that he had received from the estate of John G. Carter. Marshall Carter is the only living child. Marshall Carter (X) made his mark. Recorded 20 January 1868. (P. 225)

ROBERT COX Guardian. Guardian of J. T. and Polena Hankins, the minor heirs of Susan Hankins. Recorded 12 March 1868. (P. 226)

GUARDIAN SETTLEMENTS 1863-1875

JOHN ORGAN Guardian. Guardian of Sarah E. Dodson who is now married to Dr. W. H. Bennett. Recorded 12 March 1868. (P. 229)

JONATHAN F. HOOKER Guardian. Guardian of Nancy J. and Virginia T. Dobson, the minor heirs of Benjamin Dobson. Recorded 12 March 1868. (P. 231)

S. B. F. C. BARR Guardian. Guardian of James Johnson, a minor heir of G. B. Johnson. Recorded 12 March 1868. (P. 232)

F. M. SHERON Guardian. Guardian of Corrie A., John, and Harvey D. Peyton, the minor heirs of Sterling B. Peyton. Recorded 12 March 1868. (P. 233)

JONATHAN F. HOOKER Guardian. Guardian of William A., Hansel, and Susan Kirkpatrick. Recorded 12 March 1868. (P. 234)

STEPHEN ROBINSON Guardian. Guardian of Leander Chumley, a minor heir of Pleasant Chumley. Recorded 12 March 1868. (P. 236)

JONATHAN F. HOOKER Guardian. Guardian of the minor heirs of Joseph Morris, to wit, Mary Ann, Thomas, and Benjamin Morris. Recorded 12 March 1868. (P. 237)

D. J. CARNEY Guardian. 25 February 1868. Guardian of A. C. Carney. Note held on S. W. Stubblefield. (P. 241)

LOVICK DIES Guardian. 4 February 1868. Guardian of Gilla and Mary E. Tomlinson, the minor heirs of Allen Tomlinson. (P. 243)

W. B. CAMPBELL Guardian. Guardian for Fannie A., Joseph A., John B., and Lemuel R. Campbell. Money was received from the estate of Gov. David Campbell. The record then states that it was received from the estate of Governor William B. Campbell. Recorded 10 May 1868. (P. 247)

ANDY DAVIS Guardian. Guardian of Robert, Kittie, and Morgan Davis, the minor heirs of Morgan Davis. Recorded 10 May 1868. (P. 251)

GEORGE W. COWAN Guardian. Guardian of Robert C., Joseph M., Henry, Fathey A., and Dabney Lawrence, and Mary Holt, the minor heirs of Robert Lawrence. Mary Holt is now dead. Recorded 10 May 1868. (Pp. 252-254)

D. F. PAYNE Guardian. Guardian of his daughter, Laura Elizabeth Payne, a granddaughter of James F. Hamblin. Recorded 10 May 1868. (P. 261)

BAXTER HILL Guardian. Guardian of James, Jackey, and Saphronia Caroline Carr, a minor heir of John Carr. Recorded 10 May 1868. (Pp. 261-262)

JAMES M. BROWN Guardian. Guardian of Julia Jackson, a minor heir of Mark Jackson. Recorded 10 May 1868. (Pp. 262-263)

GUARDIAN SETTLEMENTS 1863-1875

JAMES ARRINGTON Guardian. Guardian of Nancy W. Walker, a minor heir of James H. and Frances W. Walker. Recorded 10 May 1868. (P. 265)

ALEX W. VICK Guardian. Guardian of C. H. Figures who is now of age. Recorded 10 June 1868. (P. 266)

WILLIAM HAGAN Guardian. Guardian of George W., William A., James, Maud, and John P. Cowgill, minor heirs of James P. Cowgill. Recorded 10 June 1868. (Pp. 267-268)

C. L. MURPHY Guardian. Guardian of Francis P. Murphy, a minor heir of Francis Palmer. Recorded 10 June 1868. (Pp. 269-270)

WILLIAM J. WOOD Guardian. Guardian of his son, William T. Wood, a minor heir of L. Y. Neal. Recorded 10 July 1868. (Pp. 272-273)

C. H. COOK Guardian. Guardian of James F. and Martha Lain. The guardian received from the estate of their grandfather, Levi Holloway. Martha Lain married William S. Goodman. Recorded 8 June 1868. (Pp. 273-274)

GEORGE W. YOUNG Guardian. Guardian of Maria E., Henry F., and Malissa M. Young, the minor heirs of Mary F. Young. Recorded 10 October 1868. (Pp. 275-276)

A. S. YOUNG Guardian. Guardian of Samuel S., Louisa, Margaret, and Nancy Young, the minor heirs of Samuel M. Young. Recorded 10 October 1868. (Pp. 276-277)

JOHN PHILIPS Guardian. Guardian of Lycurgus and John T. Bass, the minor heirs of (Amzi) Bass. Recorded 19 October 1868. (Pp. 277-278)

W. H. AUST Guardian. Guardian of (Millie) L. Bowen, a minor heir of John W. Bowen and an heir of her grandfather, John Gordon. Recorded 19 October 1868. (Pp. 279-280)

HENRY DAUGHTRY Guardian. Guardian of Henry D. and Mary M. Hays, the minor heirs of Sampson Hays. The guardian received from Samuel Hays who was the administrator of James T. Hays. Mary M. Hays is now Mary M. Clifford. Recorded 19 October 1868. (P. 283)

H. M. GREEN Guardian. Guardian of the minor heirs of Harris H. Simmons, to wit, Alex, William B., and Harris H. Simmons. Recorded 19 October 1868. (Pp. 284-285)

C. H. COOK Guardian. Guardian of Henry and Rebecca Castleman, the minor heirs of Burwell P. Castleman. Recorded 19 October 1868. (Pp. 286-287)

W. M. KNIGHT Guardian. Guardian of the children of James C. Clemmons, to wit, George, Oby, Dred, Francis, and (Brissew) Clemmons. Recorded 19 October 1868. (Pp. 287-288)

C. R. PUCKETT Guardian. Guardian of Indy, Elizabeth,

and James Puckett, the minor children of Smith Puckett, deceased. They are heirs of (Coleman) Puckett. Recorded 15 October 1868. (Pp. 288-289)

ROBERT D. REED Guardian. Guardian of Lucinda, James, and Mary Patterson, the minor heirs of H. G. Patterson who died in the State of Missouri. They received from the administrator of their grandfather. Recorded 9 December 1869. (Pp. 291-292)

JONATHAN F. HOOKER Guardian. Guardian of William H., Hansel, and Susan Kirkpatrick, heirs of their great grandfather, Hugh Kirkpatrick. Recorded 12 December 1868. (Pp. 292-293)

JAMES S. CARTMELL Guardian. Guardian of A. E. and N. G. Cook, the minor heirs of Nathaniel Cartmell. There are six heirs. Recorded 20 December 1868. (P. 296)

BERRY W. COX Guardian. Guardian of Berry W. Wier, a minor. The guardian received from the estate of Thomas V. Wier. Recorded 19 December 1868. (P. 297)

ELIJAH C. HUNT Guardian. Guardian of George and M. J. Hunt, minor heirs of Dolphus Hunt. Also, heirs of Jesse Hunt. Recorded 7 January 1869. (P. 300)

FINIS E. SHANNON Guardian. Guardian of his children, to wit, Finis E., Texanna, V. T., and Lousanna M. D. Shannon, heirs at law of Samuel Hunt late of Rutherford County. Recorded 7 January 1868. (P. 302)

L. L. PRESTON Guardian. Guardian of Ann C. Alsup, a minor heir of William L. M. Alsup. Recorded 4 January 1869. (P. 306)

L. L. PRESTON Guardian. Guardian of Kate Clemmons, a minor heir of Robert Clemmons. Recorded 7 January 1869. (P. 306)

JONATHAN F. HOOKER Guardian. Guardian of Lucinda E. and Nancy G. Gates, the minor heirs of William and Elizabeth Gates. Also, heirs of Benjamin Rice. The previous guardian, William C. Rice, resigned. Recorded 17 February 1869. (P. 309)

JOHN CRUDUP Guardian. Guardian of the minor heirs of Archibald Carver, to wit, Martha E., Pamelia E., Samuel S., and Lucy A. Carver. Martha E. Carver has now married George W. Cantrell. Recorded 20 January 1869. (P. 316)

GEORGE W. WARD Guardian. Guardian for his minor child, Mary E. Ward. Recorded 5 April 1869. (P. 317)

T. B. EATHERLY Guardian. Guardian of Louiza C. and Dolly C. Young, the minor heirs of P. B. Young. Recorded 8 April 1869. (P. 320)

JOHN WORD Guardian. Guardian of James D. Taylor, the minor heir of James A. Taylor. Also, heir of Bennett Babb. Recorded 8 April 1869. (P. 321)

GUARDIAN SETTLEMENTS 1863-1875

WILLIAM M. CARTMELL Guardian. Guardian of Mary E. and Henry T. Cartmell, the minor heirs of Henry T. Cartmell. Also, heirs of Nathaniel Cartmell. Recorded 12 April 1869. (P. 325)

PURNAL LAIN Guardian. Guardian of his daughter, Ann Elizabeth, who has married Newton Ricketts. She is a granddaughter of Absolum Laster who was a brother of Kiziah Laster whose estate she inherited. Recorded 12 April 1869. (P. 327)

W. J. ROGERS Guardian. Guardian of James, Malissa, William, and Jackson Shannon, the minor heirs of G. W. B. Shannon, and James Shannon. Recorded 12 April 1869. (P. 329)

A. M. OAKLEY Guardian. Guardian of Zachariah T., Leeman W., Burrell, and Rebecca Spears, the minor children of James Spears. Zachariah T. Spears is now of age. Recorded 12 April 1869. (P. 330)

SAMUEL S. AYRES Guardian. Guardian of T. B. James, a minor. He has an interest in the estate of his grandmother, Margaret James. Recorded 12 April 1869. (P. 332)

J. C. ESKEW Guardian. Guardian of Jonas N. Carver, a minor heir of John W. Carver. Recorded 25 May 1869. (P. 333)

A. S. YOUNG Guardian. Guardian of Nancy, Virginia, and Tennessee Measles, the minor heirs of James Measles deceased and Susan Measles deceased. The guardian received from Jacob Measles, the administrator of these wards' grandmother. There were three shares. Recorded 25 July 1869. (Pp. 338-339)

D. CUNNINGHAM Guardian. Guardian of Sophia C., Sarah F., James T., and Martha T. Scarborough, the minor heirs of Sarah J. Scarborough. Recorded 25 July 1869. (P. 339)

L. M. EDWARDS Guardian. Guardian of Ellen Bobo, formerly Ellen Sweatt, who is now of age. Recorded 1 July 1869. (P. 342)

A. J. PATTERSON Guardian. Guardian of James Moser who was a son of Henry Moser, Jr. Recorded 25 September 1869. (P. 346)

M. T. BENNETT Guardian. Guardian of his two sons, William H. and C. O. Bennett, the minor heirs of Frank Palmer and William Palmer. Recorded 26 September 1869. (P. 347)

C. C. H. BURTON Guardian. Guardian of Louiza C. and Dolly C. Young, minor heirs of P. B. Young and heirs of Dr. J. C. Eatherly. Recorded 13 October 1869. (Pp. 348-349)

LEWIS LINDSEY Guardian. Guardian of Thomas Barkley,

a minor heir of Jane Barkley. Recorded 18 October 1869.
(P. 349)

P. N. LAWRENCE Guardian. Guardian of his minor chil-
dren, to wit, Joseph T., Delila, Harden R., Turner M.,
George W., and B. R. Lawrence who are heirs of John Taylor.
Recorded 10 November 1869. (P. 353)

JOHN H. SMITH Guardian. Guardian of James W. Conyers,
an heir of his grandfather, William Conyers deceased.
Braxton Hill served as administrator of Agness Conyers
and executor of William Conyers. Recorded 10 November
1869. (P. 354)

L. P. ROSE Guardian. Guardian of Zacry T. and Mary
L. Rose, the minor child of Mary Rose and heir of Azariah
Corder. Recorded 22 December 1869. (P. 359)

SYNTHIA ( ) Guardian. Guardian of John R. O'Rian,
a minor. Recorded 13 January 1870. (P. 367)

JAMES T. PATTON Guardian. Guardian of Lavina Thompson, a minor child of M. H. Thompson. Recorded 10 February 1870. (Pp. 370-371)

JOHN B. VIVRETT Guardian. Guardian of Beady Brown,
James Brown, Nancy Brown, and Nancy Green. They are all
persons of unsound mind. The guardian reported that he
was administrator for Elisha Brown. Recorded 10 February
1870. (P. 373)

R. C. BONE Guardian. Guardian of William, Callie,
and Sallie Bone, the minor heirs of Alfred Bone. They
have a farm in DeKalb County. Recorded 10 February 1870.
(Pp. 376-377)

A. E. GREEN Guardian. Guardian of John, Lucy, Rufus,
and Martha Green, the minor heirs of John G. Green. Recorded 14 March 1870. (Pp. 379-380)

ISAAC MULLINAX Guardian. Guardian of Catharine,
Samuel, Joseph, and Lucinda Moore, the minor children
of Cynthia Moore and heirs of J. H. Gatton. Recorded 14
March 1870. (Pp. 382-383)

GEORGE C. BOND Guardian. Guardian of Joseph, Landy,
and Patience Lain who are all persons of unsound mind.
The guardian is now dead. Augustus Lain was the father
of these idiots. Recorded 21 April 1870. (Pp. 389-390)

ROBERT REAVES Guardian. Guardian of Harvey H.,
Doctor, George W., and Mitty Whitlock, the minor heirs of
Thomas K. Whitlock. Recorded 21 April 1870. (P. 390)

D. F. WHITLOCK Guardian. Guardian of James W., L. E.,
and Parthy T. Whitlock, the minor heirs of Thomas K. Whitlock. The guardian lives in the upper end of the county.
Recorded 21 April 1870. (Pp. 390-391)

JOHN ORGAN Guardian. Guardian of Edward, Susan,
Laura, and William Tompkins, the minor children and heirs
of E. H. Tompkins. Also, heirs of James T. Tompkins. Re-

corded 21 April 1870. (Pp. 396-397)

PETER THOMPSON Guardian. Guardian of Henry and
Elizabeth Moser. Recorded 12 May 1870. (Pp. 402-403)

JOHN BRUCE Guardian. Guardian of the minor heirs of
James Barkley, to wit, George, James, Nicey, and Martha
Barkley. Recorded 12 May 1870. (Pp. 406-407)

SARAH CRISMAN Guardian. Guardian of her children, to
wit, William D., Mary C., and Louisa J. Irving. Recorded
29 June 1870. (P. 409)

JOHN L. PATTON Guardian. Guardian of the minor heirs
of W. W. Washburn, to wit, Vesparia, Catherine, William,
and Ada Washburn. There is a tract of land in Smith County. Recorded 10 June 1870. (P. 415)

L. M. EDWARDS Guardian. Guardian of Amanda Hunt,
an heir of A. M. Hunt. Recorded 29 July 1870. (P. 418)

HENRY J. ROGERS Guardian. Guardian of Mary K. White,
a minor heir of Joseph W. White. The estate was settled
in Cheatham County. Recorded 24 August 1870. (P. 419)

A. A. BEADLE Guardian. Guardian of Eli, Martha F.,
Abram L., Wilson H., and Hardin R. Beadle, the minor heirs
of Wilson Beadle and heirs of Robert and Margaret Reed.
Recorded 14 September 1870. (P. 421)

MARTHA W. LESTER Guardian. Guardian for her children, Hiram W. and Sarah W. Lester, the heirs of Manson B.
Lester. Hiram W. Lester is now of age. Sarah W. Lester
is married to E. W. Moody. Recorded 14 September 1870.
(P. 423)

ISAAC L. THOMPSON Guardian. Guardian of Eli W., Wm.,
Allie F., and Diantha Thompson, the minor heirs of W. L.
Thompson. Recorded 20 September 1870. (P. 427)

R. W. HUDSON Guardian. 5 November 1870. Guardian
of Thomas B. (about 20), Martha Ann (about 18), Rosaline
(about 15), and Magie (about 12), the minor children and
heirs of Robert Johns. (P. 428)

Z. McMILLEN Guardian. Guardian of George and Delia
C. Adamson, the minor heirs of (Lamun) Adamson. Recorded
9 December 1870. (P. 429)

JAMES R. JOHNSON Guardian. Guardian of Francis M.
and George L. Johnson, the minor children and heirs of
Joseph C. Johnson. Also, heirs of Samuel Johnson. Recorded 9 December 1870. (P. 430)

WILLIAM GREEN Guardian. Guardian of William C.,
Elizabeth, Nancy L., Eliza, and Susan Green, the minor
heirs of James R. Green. Elizabeth Green is now Mrs. Cox.
Nancy L. Green is now Mrs. Carter. Recorded 9 December
1870. (Pp. 431-433)

WILLIAM PHILLIPS Guardian. Guardian of Berry and
Wilson Phillips, the minor heirs of Josiah Phillips. Re-

corded 23 January 1871. (P. 435)

WILLIAM R. DOBSON Administrator. Administrator of John M. Bland. C. C. Robbins received the share to which his wife, Sarah E. Bland, was entitled. Recorded 23 January 1871. (Pp. 440-441)

W. W. TAYLOR Guardian. Guardian of Zachariah P. Bland, a minor child of John M. Bland. Recorded 23 January 1871. (Pp. 440-441)

P. G. OZMENT Guardian. Guardian of P. C. Goodman and Robert Crudup, the minor heirs of Josiah Crudup. P. C. Goodman was formerly P. C. Hester. Recorded 14 February 1871. (Pp. 445-446)

D. F. PAYNE Guardian. Guardian of his children, Henrietta and Hubbard Payne, legatees of William Duke. Another daughter, Laura Payne, is now Mrs. Capart. Recorded 14 February 1871. (P. 446)

P. S. CARVER Guardian. Guardian of S. E. Carver, one of the minor heirs of Henry Carver. She is now the wife of A. H. Ellis. Recorded 14 February 1871. (Pp. 451-452)

JAMES M. JOHNSON Guardian. Guardian of a minor child of James Lemmons. The name is not known. Recorded 14 February 1871. (Pp. 457-458)

URIAH JENNINGS Guardian. Guardian of Samuel T. Ayers, a minor heir of Lowery Ayers. Recorded 14 February 1871. (P. 460)

JOHN D. CHAMBERS Guardian. Guardian of David and Mattie Chambers, the minor heirs of John Chambers. T. M. Chambers is now of age. Recorded 14 February 1871. (P. 461)

SAMUEL MOTTLEY Guardian. Guardian of Mary B., Henry M., and Bettie Donaho, the minor heirs of Dr. Ed Donaho. Recorded 14 March 1871. (Pp. 463-464)

L. M. EDWARDS Guardian. Guardian of Matilda C., James M., and John Hunt, the minor heirs of James M. Hunt. Recorded 14 March 1871. (Pp. 467-468)

J. H. ALLEN Guardian. Guardian of Eliza Ellis. He was appointed in the will of Moses Ellis. Recorded 14 June 1871. (P. 472)

CAROLINE JOHNSON Guardian. Guardian of her children, to wit, Luella, Penelope, James, and Josie Johnson, the minor heirs of Archie Johnson. Recorded 14 June 1871. (P. 473)

W. D. HAMBLIN Guardian. Guardian of John and Stokeley Donalson, the minor heirs of John Donalson. Recorded 14 June 1871. (Pp. 473-474)

J. B. MARKS Guardian. Guardian of Jackson and Nicholas Vantrease, the minor heirs of Washington Vantrease. Recorded 14 June 1871. (P. 485)

E. F. TUCKER Guardian. Guardian of Robert F. and Julia Chambers, the minor heirs of James Chambers. Recorded 14 August 1871. (Pp. 495-496)

P. L. CARVER Guardian. Guardian of James H., Isaac H., Nicey E., and (Tiphena) E. Carver, the minor heirs of Henry Carver. Recorded 14 October 1871. (Pp. 497-500)

JOHN ORGAN Guardian. Guardian of Mary E., George W., W. J., and Sarah Alexander, the minor heirs of W. L. Alexander. Recorded 14 October 1871. (Pp. 501-502)

R. CANTRELL Guardian. Guardian of Mary E. Stewart, a minor child of Charles P. Stewart. Recorded 14 October 1871. (Pp. 502-503)

A. CUMMINS Guardian. Guardian of Sarah A. Rideout, daughter of Mary Rideout. Also, guardian of Martha Ann, James K. Polk, Joseph, and Araminta Cummins, the children of James W. Cummins. Recorded 14 October 1871. (P. 504)

Z. S. PATTERSON Guardian. Guardian of Lucinda, James, and Mary Patterson, the minor heirs of Nathaniel G. Patterson and heirs of John T. Patterson. Recorded 14 November 1871. (P. 511)

R. BROWN Guardian. Guardian of Humphrey M., Henry C., and Elizabeth Underwood, the minor heirs of Thomas Underwood. Recorded 14 November 1871. (P. 511)

JOHN ORGAN Guardian. Guardian of Dosia Ann and Henry C. Smith, the minor heirs of James C. Smith. Recorded 20 January 1871. (Pp. 515-516)

Z. S. PHILLIPS Guardian. Guardian of Locky and Sally Davis, the minor heirs of E. A. Davis. Recorded 24 January 1872. (Pp. 522-523)

J. L. TRICE Guardian. Guardian of Mary J. Holloway, a minor child of L. D. Holloway deceased. Recorded 24 January 1872. (P. 523)

N. OAKLEY Guardian. Guardian of Gideon P., Joseph, John R., and Jasper Marler, the minor heirs of Anthony Marler. Recorded 14 February 1872. (P. 524)

J. H. CARTWRIGHT Guardian. Guardian of W. B. Cartwright, a minor. J. C. W. Jones of Woodruff County, Arkansas was the former guardian. He is dead. Recorded 14 February 1872. (Pp. 525-526)

J. B. DAVID Guardian. Guardian of ?. K., Mary S., Martha J., and Victoria F. David who are his minor children. Recorded 7 February 1872. (P. 540)

JOHN C. ESKEW Guardian. Guardian of Jonas N. Carver, a minor heir of John W. Carver. Recorded 7 February 1872. (P. 540)

W. L. WATERS Guardian. Guardian of Thomas, Joseph, Lila, Ezra, and Charles Smith, the minor heirs of C. C.

Smith. Recorded 9 March 1872. (P. 546)

W. C. DAVIS Guardian. Guardian of J. Harvey Davis
who is non compas mentis. Recorded 9 March 1872. (Pp.
546-547)

GIDEON M. ALSUP Administrator. Administrator of
Asaph Bond. The administrator on 28 February 1872 omit-
ted one share viz. Sarah Bond. Recorded 10 April 1872.
(P. 552)

ALMON ROLLINS Guardian. Guardian of (ve, Robert
H., Martha J., and Albert Neal, the minor children of
Robert Neal deceased and heirs of Robert and Frances
Branch. Recorded 10 April 1872. (P. 554)

W. L. PATEY Guardian. Guardian of Nannie E. Briggs,
a minor child of G. W. Briggs. Recorded 9 May 1872. (P.
556)

R. J. WALTON Guardian. Guardian of James Johnson,
a minor child of G. B. Johnson. Recorded 9 May 1872.
(Pp. 559-560)

W. H. WETMORE Guardian. Guardian of my children, to
wit, C. W. L., L. E. F., and C. A. W. Wetmore. I received
for them in Davidson County. Recorded 9 May 1872. (P.
560)

SARAH L. DOUGHERTY Guardian. Guardian of Dick,
Media, J. C., Mary, and Augustus W. Dougherty, her minor
heirs and heirs of Mark Dougherty. Recorded 6 June 1872.
(P. 562)

H. H. DELAY Guardian. Guardian of Jonas L., Susan
W., Nancy D., and Mary C. Delay, the minor heirs of Nancy
Delay and heirs of John A. and Susannah Jennings. Re-
corded 6 June 1872. (P. 503)

JOHN B. TARVER Guardian. Guardian of Nannie and
Charley Westbrooks, the minor heirs of Jane Westbrooks and
heirs of J. H. Peyton. Recorded 6 June 1872. (P. 564)

JACK THOMPSON Guardian. Guardian of John P., Sarah,
James B., and Margaret Cook, the minor heirs of Eliza
Cook. They have an interest in the estate of their
grandfather, Osborne Thompson. Recorded 6 June 1872.
(P. 565)

CATHERINE NEAL Guardian. Guardian of her children,
Isaac S. and Henry G. Neal, heirs of Nancy Neal. Recorded
10 July 1872. (P. 566)

J. A. BETTES Guardian. Guardian of Joseph and
Robert Clemmons, the minor heirs of Cowen Clemmons. Recorded 10 July 1872. (P. 568)

SAMUEL H. HARRIS Guardian. Guardian of Mary E.,
Robert J., and Thomas W. Harris, the minor heirs of Hannah
Harris and heirs of John A. and Susannah Jennings. Recorded
10 July 1872. (P. 569)

79

GUARDIAN SETTLEMENTS 1863-1875

WILLIAM BRADLEY Guardian. Guardian of Robert J., Richard, Francis P., George A., and William H. Bradley, the minor heirs of Julia Ann Bradley and heirs of R. P. Sweatt. Recorded 10 August 1872. (Pp. 571-572)

Z. H. BAIRD Guardian. Guardian of Mattie, William M., Estella, and Margaret Bond, the minor heirs of John Bond and heirs of Hicksey Shaw. Recorded 10 September 1872. (Pp. 574-575)

S. J. BASS Guardian. Guardian of Roxie Bass, a minor heir of Richard Bass. Recorded 10 September 1872. (Pp. 575-576)

SAMUEL HARLAN Guardian. Guardian of Paralee, Rueben, Francina, Ella Martha, and James Hobbs who are minor children of Robert Harlan deceased. Paralee, Rueben, and Ella Hobbs are now dead. Recorded 10 September 1872. (Pp. 578-582)

R. C. SCOBEY Guardian. Guardian of W. L. Scobey, a minor heir of Amanda Scobey. Recorded 10 September 1872. (P. 588)

J. H. JACKSON Guardian. Guardian of W. A. and Marcus Jackson, the minor heirs of Henry Jackson. Recorded 10 September 1872. (P. 589)

W. J. GRANNIS Guardian. Guardian of Mary W. Grannis, a minor. Recorded 10 October 1872. (P. 593)

W. R. PALMER Guardian. Guardian of J. W. Andrews, a minor heir of J. B. Andrews. Recorded 10 October 1872. (P. 594)

ISAAC MULLINAX Guardian. Guardian of Joel, William, and John Adamson, the minor heirs of Simeon Adamson. Recorded 10 October 1872. (Pp. 597-598)

J. W. McFARLAND Guardian. Guardian of Mattie E. McFarland, a minor legatee of Dr. J. H. McFarland. Recorded 5 October 1872. (Pp. 598-599)

LEWIS GRAVES Guardian. Guardian of William L., Daniel A., Nancy Ann, and John A. Graves, his minor children and heirs of their grandfather, John Edwards. Recorded 10 December 1872. (Pp. 602-603)

ANVOLINE HUGHES Guardian. Guardian of his children, to wit, Mary G. and George B. Hughes. Recorded 10 December 1872. (P. 604)

GEORGE H. CAMPBELL Guardian. Guardian of Adelaid Wills, now Mrs. M. A. Wright. Recorded 10 December 1872. (P. 604)

WILLIAM G. BASS Guardian. Guardian of Andrew N., Laura, Thomas, and John Barr, the minor heirs of John L. Barr. The dower has been assigned. Recorded 10 December 1872. (P. 607)

B. D. HAGAR Guardian. Guardian of Robert Vantrease, heir of John Vantrease. Recorded 10 December 1872. (pp.

GUARDIAN SETTLEMENTS 1863-1875

608-609)

J. B. MARKS Guardian. Guardian of the minor children of Washington Vantrease. Said children are heirs of Britton Odum. Recorded 5 February 1873. (Pp. 617-618)

JAMES P. HARRISON Guardian. Guardian of Walter, Maggie, Samuel, and Sarah Davis, the children of James E. Davis deceased and Samuel Davis deceased. Recorded 25 January 1873. (P. 618-619)

A. B. WHITLOCK Guardian. Guardian of Dicey E. and Menerva C. Whitlock, the minor heirs of Stanhope Whitlock and heirs of Thomas K. Whitlock. Recorded 6 February 1873. (P. 622)

WILLIAM LANIUS Guardian. Guardian of Nancy Jackson, a minor heir of John J. Jackson and an heir of Asa Jackson. Recorded 6 February 1873. (P. 622)

JOHN ORGAN Guardian. Guardian of James, Hezekiah, Mattie, John, and Lennie Wood, the minor heirs of J. L. Wood. Recorded 11 February 1873. (P. 637)

J. A. BLANKENSHIP Guardian. Guardian of John Bass, a minor heir of John B. and Susan Bass. Recorded 10 March 1873. (P. 639)

R. K. WILLIAMSON Guardian. Guardian of the children of Ann Jones whose names are unknown. They are supposed to be seven in number. They are heirs of George Graves - Mildred Graves - Benjamin Graves, Jr. Recorded 10 March 1873. (P. 641)

J. W. PHILLIPS Guardian. Guardian of Sallie K. Howard, a minor heir of John K. Howard. The guardian made a trip to Minnesota to see about the ward's lands. Recorded 10 March 1873. (P. 642)

J. K. PHILLIPS Guardian. Guardian of Jane Edwards, a minor heir of Gilbert Edwards. The entire estate consists of a pension. Recorded 10 March 1873. (Pp. 643-644)

W. H. WETMORE Guardian. Guardian of his minor children who are heirs of Timothy Kizer. Recorded 14 April 1873. (Pp. 647-648)

S. B. TALLY Guardian. Guardian of the minor heirs of James M. Johnson and W. W. Harrison. Recorded 22 March 1873. (Pp. 655-656)

ELI FITE Guardian. Guardian of Margaret E. Witt. Recorded 12 May 1873. (P. 663)

WILLIAM B. BLOODWORTH Guardian. Guardian of Manerva, Mary Ann, Susan E., and Abram Green, the minor heirs of Nicholas Green. Recorded 12 May 1873. (P. 663)

M. E. S. FISHER Guardian. Guardian of Mattie S. B. and Mary E. C. Fisher, the minor heirs of R. W. Fisher and of Levi Fisher. Recorded 29 July 1873. (P. 677)

GUARDIAN SETTLEMENTS 1863-1875

T. M. TURNER Guardian. Guardian of Bettie J. Turner, a minor of E. A. Turner and of Thomas Turner. Recorded 29 November 1873. (Pp. 699-700)

T. B. VAUGHT Guardian. Guardian of his minor children, Samuel and G. H. Vaught. Recorded 13 December 1873. (P. 704)

WILSON COUNTY COURT MINUTES 1814-1829

THOMAS DONAHO Power of Attorney. 29 October 1805.
Thomas Donaho of Caswell County, North Carolina gave his
power of attorney to James Sanders of Sumner County,
Tennessee. Recorded 19 September 1814. (P. 1)

HULDA SHERRILL Agreement. 4 June 1814. Hulda Sherrill to Samuel Wilson Sherrill, John Brown, Ephraim Sherrill, Abel Sherrill, and Ambrose Sherrill all my personal
property. They in turn agree to pay their part to the
heirs of Jacob Sherrill. Witness: H. L. Douglas. Recorded 6 September 1814. (P. 2)

JAMES DAVIDSON Sale. 26 May 1814. Sheriff Thomas
Bradley publicly sold the personal property of James
Davidson to William Patterson. Recorded 6 September 1814.
(P. 3)

JAMES BATES Sale. 3 September 1814. James Bates to
John Brown a negro girl. Witnesses: William Walker and
Edmund Greenage. Recorded 27 October 1814. (P. 4)

LEWIS DANTERIDGE Deed of Gift. 10 September 1814.
Lewis Danteridge to my sister Milberry. Property included my draw from the United States for my service in
the Army. Witnesses: Micajah Vivrett, Edward Tisdale,
and Lancelot Vivrett. Recorded 26 October 1814. (P. 5)

WILLIAM BRYAN, SR. Deed of Gift. 21 September 1814.
William Bryan, Sr. to my son Willis Bryan a negro girl.
Witnesses: Daniel Parrott and Arving Parrott. (P. 6)

JOHN HARPOLE Quit Claim. 5 April 1814. John Har-
pole, Sr., Asa Dill, William Dill, and Thomas Dill re-
linquish their claims to a tract of land where Henry
Johnson now lives, the property of John Dill deceased.
Witnesses: George H. Bullard, William H. Peace, and
Adam Moser. Recorded 27 October 1814. (Pp. 7-8)

NEWT RAMSEY Deed of Sale. 9 September 1811. Newt
Ramsey of Rutherford County, Tennessee to Richard Ramsey
of Wilson County two negroes. Recorded 17 December 1814.
(P. 9)

JOSEPH MARTIN Sale. 8 December 1812. Joseph Martin to David Fields "the following property. . ." Witnesses: B. Howard and John Edwards. Recorded 15 February 1815. (P. 11)

JOHN PROVINE Power of Attorney. 22 November 1808.
John Provine, one of seven heirs of John Provine, granted
to Samuel Harris and Alexander Provine   power to sell
land to Jesse Maxwell of Davidson County. Recorded 15
February 1815. (Pp. 12-13)

JOHN HENDERSON Power of Attorney. 28 October 1808.
John Henderson of Garland County, Kentucky, husband of
Nancy Provine one of the heirs of John Provine, granted
to Samuel Harris and Alexander Provine power to sell land.
Also, to divide with Thomas Elliott and Samuel Hensley.
The seven Provine heirs are Frances Hall, Alexander Provine,

Samuel Harris, William Provine, Polly Provine, Rebecca
Provine, John Provine, and myself. Recorded 15 February
1815. (P. 14)

WILLIAM PROVINE AND OTHERS Power of Attorney. 4
October 1808. William, Polly, and Rebecca Provine, all
of Clark County, Indiana Territory, granted to Samuel
Harris and Alexander Provine the power to sell land on
the Harpeth River. Recorded 16 February 1815. (Pp. 15-
16)

EPHRAIM BEASLEY Deed of Gift. 11 March 1813.
Ephraim Beasley to my son, Benny Barbee Beasley, slaves.
I shall hold said negroes as long as my wife shall live.
Witnesses: Franklin Foster, Dillard Beasley, and Polly
G. Beasley. Recorded 16 February 1815. (Pp. 16-17)

THOMAS G. ELLIS Sale. 19 April 1813. Thomas G.
Ellis of Lunenburg County, Virginia loaned a negro girl
to Polly Warren who was the wife of Booth M. Warren.
Said Polly Warren paid $300 for the "loan." At her
death, the girl was to be divided between James, Richard
L., Polly W., Rebecca Ann, Ball E., and Robert B. Warren.
Witnesses: Richard Ha) and George Allen. Recorded
22 May 1815. (P. 17)

JOHN BELL Sale. 28 January 1814. John Bell to
William Steele a negro boy. Witnesses: Joseph Trout,
James Wier, Richard Hight, and John Travilian. Recorded
22 May 1815. (P. 18)

WILLIAM BABB Sale. 22 March 1814. William Babb
to Brittain Drake a negro slave. Witness: Patrick L.
Anderson. Recorded 22 May 1815. (P. 19)

THOMAS BEADLE Power of Attorney. 7 November 1814.
Thomas Beadle granted power of attorney to John Fisher
to receive the legal payments due me for serving in the
Militia under the command of Major General William Carroll. Witnesses: James Cross and James Williams. Recorded 22 May 1815. (P. 20)

JACOB MILDHAM Power of Attorney. 3 September 1810.
Jacob Mildham of Bedford County, Tennessee granted to
Archibald Simpson of the same County power to receive my
share of the estate of Joseph Branch of Halifax County,
North Carolina. Witnesses: John Currey and William
Simpson. Recorded 12 January 1815. (Pp. 21-22)

LEONARD H. SIMS Power of Attorney. 21 June 1815.
Leonard H. Sims of Wilson County appointed Jesse Jennings
to receive any money due me from my lawsuit in Green County, Georgia with Royaton and Zachariah Sims. Recorded 23
June 1815. (P. 23)

SOLOMON DELOACH Sale. 8 February 1810. Solomon Deloach to Jerusha Deloach a negro girl. Witnesses: Micajah Vivrett and Elizabeth Vivrett. Recorded 14 August
1815. (Pp. 25-26)

ROWLAND W. GRISSIM Sale. 12 September 1814. Bill of sale to Fergus S. Harris. Witnesses: James Wrather. Recorded 14 August 1815. (P. 27)

BONNER Bill of Sale. 1 October 1811. Bill of sale from John and Thomas Bonner to Milby Hearn. Witnesses: Ebenezer Hearn and William Bonner. Recorded 14 August 1815. (P. 28)

EPHRAIM BEASLEY Deed of Gift. 28 January 1813. Ephraim Beasley deed of gift to my loving son, Dillard Beasley. Witness: F. Foster. Recorded 14 August 1815. (P. 29)

SHERIFF THOMAS BRADLEY Bill of Sale. 17 June 1815. Execution of a decree from Smith County wherein James A. Hunter is the plaintiff and William Kavanaugh is the defendant. The sheriff publicly sold a negro man to John Brown. Recorded 14 August 1815. (P. 30)

WILLIAM BARRETT Bill of Sale. 9 May 1815. Bill of sale to John W. Lumkin. Witness: Willie Williford. Recorded 14 August 1815. (P. 31)

HORATIO (ARDON) and WILLIAM MORRISON Deed of Patent Right. 5 June 1814. Said (Ardon) and Morrison of Cincinatti, Hamilton County, Ohio to William Wilson of Wilson County, Tennessee. Witnesses: Alexander Beard and Robert Branch. Recorded 14 August 1815. (P. 32)

FREDERICK CARTER Bill of Sale. 13 February 1815. Bill of sale to William Stafford. Witnesses: William Donnell and Jesse Donnell. Recorded 14 August 1815. (P. 33)

ARON ROGERS Deed of Gift. 1 March 1815. Rogers of Wake County, North Carolina to my brother Solomon Rogers, his wife Rebecca Rogers, and his children, to wit, William and Patsy Rogers. Elizabeth Rogers is excepted because I have already given to her. Witness: Griffin (Bandle). Recorded 14 August 1815. (P. 34)

BONNER Bill of Sale. 20 June 1815. John and Thomas Bonner to John Knox. Witnesses: Samuel Hogg and John Fisher. Recorded 28 October 1815. (P. 35)

STRAYBORN and TABITHA NORTH Bill of Sale. 12 September 1815. Bill of Sale to Daniel Cherry. Recorded 28 October 1815. (P. 36)

BENJAMIN SPRINGS Bill of Sale. 25 July 1815. Bill of sale to Daniel Cherry. Witnesses: John Springs, Moses Springs, William Springs, and William Howard. Recorded 25 October 1815. (P. 37)

DANIEL (LEEGITT) Bill of Sale. 26 March 1810. Leegitt of Washington County, North Carolina to Daniel Cherry of Martin County, North Carolina. Witnesses: Jesse Cherry, Hardy Climer, and Henry Cooper. Recorded 28 October 1815. (P. 38)

CHARLES BRADLEY Bill of Sale. 16 August 1815. Bill of sale to Daniel Cherry. Witnesses: James W. Armstrong, William Hadly, and J. Anderson. Recorded 28 October 1815. (P. 39)

THOMAS CAWTHON Bill of Sale. 15 September 1815. Bill of sale to James H. Cawthon. Witnesses: John Martin and Zachariah Leak. Recorded 28 October 1815. (P. 40)

JOSHUA WOOLEN Power of Attorney. 20 September 1815. Woolen gave power of attorney to Jesse Rhodes of North Carolina "to conduct my business in that State." Witnesses: James Palmer and Edward Woolen. Recorded 28 October 1815. (P. 41)

JOHN MORTIMER Bill of Sale. 7 November 1815. Bill of sale to Jacob Dice. Witnesses: John Bonner and John Allcorn. Recorded 26 December 1815. (P. 42)

JOHN MORTIMER Bill of Sale. 7 November 1815. Bill of sale to Justice Ruleman. Witnesses: John Bonner and John Allcorn. Recorded 7 November 1815. (P. 42)

JOHN KORNEGGY Bill of Sale. 25 November 1815. Bill of sale to John and Bryan Ward of Smith County, Tennessee. Witnesses: John M. Phillips, Jeremiah Belote, and Samuel Gibson. Recorded 20 January 1816. (P. 45)

JOSEPH STACY Deed of Gift. 4 December 1815. Joseph Stacy deed of gift to his son, Joseph Stacy. Witness: Dabney Martin. Recorded 20 January 1816. (P. 45)

CONSTABLE WILLIAM SCOTT Bill of Sale. Public sale to Alexander P. Richmond. Slave had been the property of Theoderick Easley. Recorded 10 January 1816. (Pp. 46,48)

ABIJAH WRIGHT Power of Attorney. 19 December 1815. Abijah Wright, widow and relict of Isaac' Wright, and one of the heirs of John Somers, late of Caswell County, North Carolina, appoint my brother, James Somers of Wilson County, my true and lawful attorney. Recorded 6 March 1816. (Pp. 47-48)

JOHN LUMPKINS Bill of Sale. 10 January 1816. Bill of sale to Samuel Elliott. Witnesses: Thomas L. Green and John W. Nichols. Recorded 25 May 1816. (P. 49)

ELI ANDERSON Bill of Sale. 27 December 1814. Bill of sale to James Richmond. Witnesses: Charles L. and William K. Bennet. Recorded 25 May 1816. (P. 50)

WILLIAM SADLER Bill of Sale. 27 January 1816. Sadler of Jackson County, Tennessee to Samuel Elliott. Witnesses: Joseph and Nancy L. Johnson. Recorded 27 May 1816. (P. 51)

THWEATT HARRISON Bill of Sale. 20 January 1816. Bill of sale to Samuel Elliott. Witnesses: T. Bradley and P. Anderson. Recorded 25 May 1816. (P. 52)

BANDY Articles of Agreement. 20 January 1816. The

heirs of Richard Bandy, to wit, Jameson, Eperson, Solomon, Joseph, Wilcher, Peron, and Richard Bandy, James Cornelius, and Edward Brown agree to make a sale of the plantation. Witnesses: Henry Corke, Daniel Glenn, Edward W. Vaughn, and Will Parrish. Recorded 27 May 1816. (P. 53)

NELLY W. MADDOX Bill of Sale. 14 October 1807. Nelly W. Maddox of Jackson County, Georgia to Notty W. Maddox, Jr. of Wilson County. Witness: R. Atkins. Recorded 1 June 1816. (P. 54)

JOHN HALLUM Bill of Sale. 19 December 1815. Bill of sale to Samuel Elliott. Witness: H. L. Douglass. Recorded 1 June 1816. (P. 55)

NOTTY W. MADDOX, SR. Bill of Sale. 14 April 1810. Notty W. Maddox, Sr. of Wilson County to Notty W. Maddox, Jr. Witness: Simon Hancock. Recorded 1 June 1816. (P. 56)

JOHN BELL Bill of Sale. 30 October 1815. Bill of sale to William Steele. Witnesses: Simpson Organ, Phillip Ward, and Andrew Foster. Recorded 9 September 1816. (P. 57)

THOMAS WOOLDRIDGE Bill of Sale. 27 December 1815. Bill of sale to James Foster. Witness: William Woodward. Recorded 10 September 1816. (P. 58)

DELOACH Bill of Sale. 9 March 1816. Jerusha Deloach, widow and relict of Samuel Deloach late of Johnson County, North Carolina, and the children of said Samuel Deloach, to wit, Joseph, William (Speer) and his wife Lucretia, Samuel, and Shadrack Ingram and his wife Polly to Thomas Davis. Witnesses: Hickman Lewis and James H. Davis. Recorded 10 September 1816. (Pp. 59-60)

GEORGE HODGE and WILLIAM HANNAH Bill of Sale. 3 December 1813. Bill of sale to William Crawford. Witnesses: John R. Rice and Jesse Bloodworth. Recorded 10 September 1816. (P. 61)

EPHRAIM BEASLEY Deed of Gift. 12 September 1810. Deed of gift to my daughter, Sally W. Cunningham's heirs, to wit, Alexander, Sarah, and Prudence. Witnesses: Jesse Warren and Benny Beasley. Recorded 29 September 1816. (P. 62)

PLEASANT HARDY Bill of Sale. Commissioners appointed to divide the estate of Pleasant Hardy. Recorded 29 September 1816. (P. 63)

THOMAS HARRINGTON Bill of Sale. 16 January 1816. (P. 64)

LEONARD H. SIMS Bill of Sale. 18 July 1816. (P. 65)

EPHRAIM BEASLEY Deed of Gift. 7 September 1816. Deed of gift to my son, Josiah Beasley. Witnesses: John Allcorn and Samuel Elliott. Recorded 17 October 1816.

(66-67)

ELI HARRIS Power of Attorney. William, Samuel, and Abner Harris, heirs of Edward Harris, gave Eli Harris their power of attorney. Witnesses: John Adams and Fergus S. Harris. Recorded 5 December 1816. (Pp. 68-69)

JOHN P. SLAUGHTER Power of Attorney. 9 December 1816. John P. Slaughter of Campbell County, Virginia gave Mathew Martin power of attorney to conduct his business in Wilson County. Recorded 2 January 1817. (Pp. 70-71)

WILLIAM SEARCY Power of Attorney. 14 December 1807. William Searcy of Centerville, Livingston County, Kentucky gave Robert Searcy power of attorney to conduct his business in Wilson County. Recorded 1 January 1817. (P. 72)

JOHN W. LUMPKIN Bill of Sale. 25 November 1816. Bill of sale to Thomas Bradley. Recorded 11 March 1817. (Pp. 73-74)

JOHN WYNNE Deed of Gift. 16 December 1816. John Wynne for the love and affection which I have for my grandchildren, to wit, Robert, Betsy, John, Joel, William, and Polly Wynne who are children of Isham Wynne deceased. Recorded 12 March 1817. (P. 75)

JOHN MARTIN Bill of Sale. John Martin, executor of the estate of David Martin, to James Johnson. Witnesses: Isaiah Coe and Richard Hankins. Recorded 5 April 1817. (P. 76)

WILLIAM WOOLDRIDGE Deed of Gift. 6 December 1816. Deed of gift for the love and affection that I have for my daughter, Sally Coe. Witness: Thomas Wooldridge. Recorded 2 June 1817. (P. 77)

H. L. DOUGLASS Bill of Sale. 14 November 1815. H. L. Douglass, Edmund Crutcher, and Thomas Bradley to Leonard H. Sims. Witness: John Allcorn. Recorded 14 November 1817. (P. 78)

DENNIS DIAL and (SINNA) DIAL Bill of Sale. 10 February 1816. Bill of sale to James McFarland. Witnesses: James Henderson and Rubin Dial. Recorded 7 June 1817. (P. 79)

SAMUEL PATTERSON Division. 10 January 1817. Elijah Wammack given his share. Witnesses: William and Robert Patterson. Recorded 9 June 1817. (Pp. 80-81)

THOMAS MORTON Bill of Sale. 26 February 1817. Bill of sale to John Brown. Witness: Flowers McGrigor. Recorded 27 June 1817. (P. 83)

JOSEPH BISHOP Bill of Sale. 17 November 1808. Joseph Bishop of Smith County, Tennessee to Azariah Alexander of Jackson County, Tennessee. Witness: John Cage. Recorded 28 June 1817. (P. 85)

JAMES QUARLES Deed. 9 October 1815. Two platts of land transferred to Arthur Harris. Recorded 16 August

1817. (P. 86)

THOMAS RAY Deed of Gift. 9 May 1816. Deed of gift
to my children, to wit, James, William, Sally, and Jane
Ray. Witness: William Seawell. Recorded 29 June 1817.
(P. 87)

JOSEPH COLE Bill of Sale. 26 January 1814. Bill of
sale to Samuel Elliott. Witnesses: J. Charters, James
and Patrick Anderson. Recorded 2 September 1814. (P. 89)

HENRY GUSTON KERNEY Bill of Sale. 22 November 1816.
Henry Guston Kerney of Murray County, Tennessee to David
Marshall of Wilson County. Witnesses: J. Charters and
H. L. Douglass. Recorded 4 September 1817. (P. 90)

EZEKIEL BASS Deed of Gift. 23 September 1816. Deed
of gift to the children of Abraham Smith, to wit, John,
Elizabeth, Daley W., and Abraham Jr. Smith. I give the
children the property I bought at their father's sale.
Witness: Frederick A. Lane. Recorded 18 October 1817.
(P. 91)

THOMAS BRADLEY Bill of Sale. 2 January 1817. Bill
of Sale to Thomas Dooley. Witnesses: Samuel Hogg and
Thomas Wilson. Recorded 18 October 1817. (P. 92)

JOHN DUNN Power of Attorney. 27 August 1817. John
Dunn of Bullet County, Kentucky to Ransom King power of
attorney to conduct his business in Wilson County. Witnesses: Gabriel Barton and John Allcorn. Recorded 25
October 1817. (P. 93)

ROBERT CARTWRIGHT Relinquishment. January, 1813.
I sell my interest in my father's estate to Jesse Cartwright of Pa couper Parrish, Louisiana. I relinquish
all my rights to my brother, the above mentioned. My
mother has a life estate. Recorded 29 November 1817.
(P. 94)

JOEL ECKOLS, JR. Relinquishment. 25 December 1817.
I relinquish to my brother, Richard Eckols, all rights
I have in the estate of my mother, Elizabeth Eckols.
The slaves left by my father, Elkanah Eckols are to be
divided among the three children after my mother's death.
Witnesses: William Seawell and J. Charters. Recorded 27
February 1818. (P. 95)

JOHN BRADLEY, SR. Deed of Gift. 2 December 1817.
Deed of gift to Hugh Bradley. Said Hugh is hereafter to
have no claim as a legatee of the said John Bradley. The
slaves are reserved by John Bradley and his wife, Martha,
during their lifetimes. Witnesses: John Allcorn and
Stephen Barton. Recorded 27 February 1818. (P. 97)

DRENNAN Relinquishment. 20 September 1817. Thomas,
John, David, and James Drennan, John Arnold, and Henry
Miller relinquish any claim they might have to a slave,
named Nancy, to Thomas Partlow who is the son of their
sister, Anne Drennan. Said Anne received the slave from

89

their uncle, Matthew Bigger (of York County, South Carolina). Their father, John Drennan, had no claim to said slave whatsoever. Witnesses: Joseph Hamilton and Clabourn Goodman. Recorded 27 February 1818. (P. 98)

JOHN B. SEAWELL Bill of Sale. 9 July 1817. Bill of sale to Thomas Seawell. Witness: Benjamin Seawell. Recorded 28 February 1818. (P. 99)

DARRENY HANCOCK Dower. 26 January 1818. Darreny Hancock, widow of Samuel Hancock, given her dower. Recorded 5 March 1818. (P. 100)

TASWELL and EVERETT MITCHELL Bill of Sale. 19 January 1818. Bill of sale to John M. Jackson. Witnesses: James W. Locke and Thomas Parham. Recorded 12 June 1818. (P. 101)

PLEASANT HAILEY Bill of Sale. 5 May 1818. Bill of sale to George Roberts. Recorded June 1818. (P. 102)

SAMUEL QUARLES Guardian. 25 March 1818. Guardian for Sarah W. Quarles of Bedford County, Virginia. I appoint Dr. Alanson Trigg to receive any money due my ward from the estate of her father James Quarles deceased of Wilson County. Recorded 24 June 1818. (Pp. 103-104)

MARIA QUARLES Guardian. 1818. Maria Quarles of Bedford County, Virginia appointed Dr. Alanson Trigg her representative to receive all money coming to her from the estate of her father, James Quarles deceased. Recorded 24 June 1818. (Pp. 105-106)

WILLIAM WOOLDRIDGE Deed of Gift. 29 January 1816. Deed of gift to my daughter, Polly Edwards. Witnesses: H. L. Douglass, Job Bass, and Thomas Wooldridge. Recorded 7 October 1818. (P. 107)

JOHN WALKER Deed of Gift. 1 October 1817. John Walker deed of gift to the heirs of Robert H. Enox. Witnesses: Daniel C. Tradevill and Gray Anson. Transaction occurred in Davidson County, Tennessee. Recorded 7 October 1818. (P. 108)

MARY GRIFFIN Power of Attorney. John Henry given power of attorney by Mary Griffin to sell my land on Barton's Creek entered under the name of Mary Henry. Witness: Jesse Henry. Power of attorney given by said Mary Griffin in Shelby County, Kentucky. Recorded 26 March 1819. (P. 109)

JAMES HARRIS and MARGARET ROSEBOROUGH Power of Attorney. 6 February 1815. James Harris of Franklin County and Margaret Roseborough of Lincoln County, heirs of Edward Carne Esqr. late of Craven County, North Carolina gave power of attorney to Eli Harris of Wilson County. Recorded 14 November 1818. (P. 110)

HARRIS Power of Attorney. 19 February 1816. James McCallum and wife Mary, Thomas Stevenson and wife Lydia, all of Iredell County, North Carolina, and heirs of Edward

Harris. Witnesses: George Robinson and Alexander Terrence. Recorded 14 November 1818. (P. 111)

HARRIS Power of Attorney. 30 April 1816. Eli Harris given power of attorney for Andrew Provine and his wife Rebecca, Robert McCord and Permelia his wife of Madison County, Kentucky, heirs at law of Edward Harris of Craven County, North Carolina and Samuel P. Harris of the County and State aforesaid heirs at law of Andrew Harris of Williamson County, Tennessee. Recorded 21 November 1818. (P. 112)

WILLIAM ROBB, SR. Bill of Sale. 25 November 1816. Robb's slaves sold to Thomas Campbell of Bedford County, Tennessee. Said slaves are now in the hands of Robert Harris of Cabarris County, Carolina. Witnesses: William Robb, Jr. and Richard Ramsey. (P. 113)

HUGH CUMMINGS Deed of Gift. 7 May 1818. Deed of gift to his daughter, Ana Sarah Rhodes of Rutherford County, Tennessee. Witnesses: Charles and Charles W. Cummings, and James Gray. Recorded 12 January 1819. (P. 114)

MATHEW BROOK Articles of Agreement. 16 May 1807. Articles of agreement between Mathew Brook of Davidson County, Tennessee and Charles Braden of Robertson County, Tennessee. Witness: Will Wilson. Recorded 12 January 1819. (P. 115)

JEREMIAH BROWN Bill of Sale. 10 December. Bill of sale to Joseph Johnson. Witnesses: A. H. Wynne and E. A. White. Recorded 4 March 1819. (P. 117)

JOHN HALLUM, SR. Deed of Gift. 15 September 1818. Deed of gift to my son George Hallum. Slaves reserved during the lifetime of John Hallum, Sr. and his wife, Sally. Witness: Thomas Bradley. Recorded 3 March 1819. (Pp. 118-119)

HANNAH SHELBY Guardian. Guardian of her sister, Martha J. Brown, who received a legacy from Henry Shelby. Witnesses: Thomas Brevard and William Stitt. Recorded 5 March 1819. (Pp. 120-121)

HENRY SHELBY Will. 7 November 1818. Heir: Jordan Brown, his brother in law, the youngest surviving son of Jeremiah Brown. Recorded 10 March 1819. (Pp. 121-122)

LANDON HARRISON Bill of Sale. 27 February 1817. Bill of Sale to Shelah Waters. Witnesses: Sterling Harrison and George Waters. Recorded 10 March 1819. (P. 123)

ROBERT JOHNSON Power of Attorney. 3 October 1817. Robert Johnson of Harden County, Kentucky granted power of attorney to Elijah Truett. Witnesses: Allen Bagwell, Henry Truett, and Thomas L. Green. Recorded 12 March 1819. (Pp. 124-125)

TASWELL and EVERETT MITCHELL Deed of Sale. Deed to Thomas Milton. Recorded 24 March 1819. (P. 126)

SAMUEL HARRIS Power of Attorney. 1 August 1818.
Samuel Harris of Crawford County, Illinois Territory gave
Elie Harris of Wilson County his power of attorney to con-
vey a deed to Daniel Benthall. Recorded 5 August 1818.
(Pp. 127-128)

WILLIAM DONNELL Will. 16 November 1818. Heirs:
widow Mary Donnell; children Hugh Morrison and wife Mary,
William Donnell, Robert Donnell, Alexander Marrs and wife
Martha, Robert Wilson and wife Jane, John Gwin and wife
Sarah, and David Foster, executor of Samuel Donnell who
was one of the heirs. Witnesses: James Foster and Alexander Foster. Recorded 23 April 1819. (Pp. 129-130)

JAMES H. DAVIS Bill of Sale. 2 April 1819. Bill of
sale to James Frazer. Witnesses: John L. Wynne and
Deveraux Wynne. Recorded 11 May 1819. (P. 132)

HENRY YARBOROUGH Bill of Sale. 10 April 1819. Henry
Yarborough of Franklin County, North Carolina to John
Brown. Witnesses: John C. Brown and William McGrigor.
Recorded 11 May 1819. (P. 133)

ELIZABETH DAVIS Deed of Gift. 4 October 1816. Deed
of gift to my dear children, to wit, Nathaniel, Isham F.,
and John Davis. (Pp. 135-318)

SWINDLE Power of Attorney. 20 July 1819. John J.
S. Ruffin of Raleigh, North Carolina given power of attorney by Barbary and Thomas Swindle. Said Swindles, heirs
of William Harrison, were seeking military land warrants
due Harrison for his service as a soldier in the Revolutionary War, having served in the North Carolina Continental Line. Witnesses: Abner Wasan and Bernard P.
Brown. Recorded 9 November 1819. (P. 139)

BENJAMIN TURNER Power of Attorney. 19 October 1819.
Benjamin Turner of White County, Tennessee, the legal
heir of John Turner, granted to John J. S. Ruffin his
power of attorney to receive a military land warrant due
the said John Turner. Turner served as a soldier in
Captain Brown's Company in the First Regiment of the Continental Line of North Carolina. Witnesses: Bernard P.
Brown and Woodson Webb. The foregoing power of attorney
is also recorded in the Register's Office in Book D, page
140. (P. 140)

JOHN HALLUM Bill of Sale. 3 September 1819. Mary-
ville. Bill of Sale to William N. Haskins. Witnesses:
William Hallum and John Stone. Recorded 15 December
1819. (P. 141)

DELPHA DRENNAN Bill of Sale. 26 October 1819. Bill
of sale to William Robertson of Rutherford County. Witnesses: William Arnold and William McCutty. Recorded
27 December 1819. (P. 143)

BETSY TALLY Deed of Gift. 6 September 1819. Deed
of gift to my children, to wit, Hannah, William W., Betty,
Coleman, and Frances Tally. Witness: Boaz Southern. Re-

corded 20 January 1820. (P. 144)

EDWARD BURKE Bill of Sale. 20 January 1820. Bill of sale to Thomas Edwards. Witness: William Matthews. Recorded 26 February 1820. (P. 145)

WILLIAM CARLIN Bill of Sale. 3 August 1818. Bill of sale to Martin Tally. Witnesses: E. Cross and Samuel Elliott. Recorded 13 April 1820. (P. 146)

AUSTEN CORLEY Bill of Sale. 1 December 1819. Bill of sale to John M. Jackson. Witnesses: Henry Jackson and Jesse Jackson. Recorded 13 April 1820. (P. 147)

RICHARD BROWN Deed of Gift. 3 January 1820. Deed of gift to my son, John Brown, of Cairo, Sumner County, Tennessee. Witness: James Guild. Recorded 14 April 1820. (P. 148)

SARAH STEPHENSON Deed of Gift. 20 January 1820. Deed of gift to my son, Isaac T. Stephenson. Witnesses: Micajah Estes and Clem Jennings. Recorded 17 April 1820. (P. 149)

THOMAS CHAMBERLAIN Bill of Sale. 4 January 1820. Bill of Sale to Jeremiah Johnson. Witnesses: William Carlin and Samuel Chamberlain. Recorded 17 April 1820. (P. 150)

THOMAS GRIFFIN Bill of Sale. 9 December 1819. Bill of sale to James Crosser. Witnesses: Thomas Cox and John Cartwright. Recorded 19 April 1820. (P. 151)

JOSEPH JONES Bill of Sale. 22 June 1819. Bill of sale to Robert Alexander. Witnesses: John W. Peyton and Lucy Jones. Recorded 20 March 1820. (Pp. 152-153)

WILLIAM E. MATTHEWS Power of Attorney. 1 March 1820. Power of attorney granted to Thomas Edwards. Recorded 27 May 1820. (P. 153)

CHARLES GOLSTON Bill of Sale. 15 April 1820. Bill of Sale to Daniel Cherry. Witness: Nancy Barnet. Recorded 2 June 1820. (P. 154)

WILLIAM H. WILLIAMS Bill of Sale. 19 October 1820. William H. Williams of Martin County, North Carolina to Daniel Cherry of Wilson County. Witnesses: Darling Cherry, Willie Byrd, and William Anderson. Recorded 2 June 1820. (P. 155)

J. K. EASON Bill of Sale. 24 July 1817. Bill of Sale to John W. Nichols. Recorded 2 June 1820. (P. 157)

THOMAS VAUGHN Bill of Sale. 27 December 1819. Bill of sale to George Pierce of Sumner County. Witness: Elisha Vaughn. Recorded 2 June 1820. (P. 158)

MOSES ECKOLS Bill of Sale. 5 September 1809. Bill of Sale to Daniel Cherry. The land was formerly purchased from Samuel Barton, Sr. Witnesses: Cornelius Buck and Frances Woodward. Recorded 3 June 1820. (P. 159)

JOSEPH L. WILSON Bill of Sale. Bill of sale to my mother, Martha Wilson. These slaves belonged to the estate of my father, Joseph Wilson deceased. Witnesses: James Frazer and Simpson Organ. Recorded 3 June 1820. (Pp. 159-160)

JAMES MILTON Bill of Sale. 8 November 1819. Bill of sale to Thomas Milton. Recorded 3 June 1820. (P. 161)

ARCHER S. WOOD Deed of Gift. 10 February 1820. Deed of gift to my son, Larkin Wood. Recorded 5 June 1820. (P. 162)

JOEL ECKOLS, JR. Bill of Sale. 15 February 1820. Bill of sale to Deveraux Wynne. Witnesses: William R. Phepps and John F. Brown. Recorded 6 June 1820. (Pp. 163-165)

LEONARD H. SIMS Bill of Sale. 21 February 1820. Bill of sale to William E. Matthews. Recorded 6 June 1820. (P. 156)

JOEL BOLTON Bill of Sale. 5 April 1820. Bill of sale to Geraldus Bolton. Witnesses: John Dobson and John H. Pasley. Recorded 17 July 1820. (P. 167)

SARAH CERBY Deed of Gift. 20 March 1820. Deed of gift to my children, to wit, Nancy, William B., John M., Elias R., and Susan Ann Cerby. Witnesses: Joshua Kelly and Paul P. Kelly. Recorded 17 July 1820. (P. 168)

LUCRETIA ESPY Power of Attorney. 2 May 1820. Power of attorney to William Bloodworth. Recorded 18 July 1820. (P. 170)

JAMES W. LEWIS Bill of Sale. 8 May 1820. James W. Lewis of Franklin County, Tennessee to Matthew Figures who is the trustee for Martha H. Lewis. Recorded 21 August 1820. (P. 171)

JESSE WARREN Bill of Sale. 19 February 1820. Bill of sale to John M. Jackson. Recorded 21 August 1820. (P. 172)

BROGAN Power of Attorney. John Brogan and Betsy his wife gave their power of attorney to Woodson Webb to receive from the estate of Joseph Owen and his wife Phebe in Halifax County, Virginia. Witnesses: George L. Smith, Robert Smith, and Bernard P. Brown. Recorded 21 August 1820. (P. 173)

EDWARD KING Bill of Sale. 10 April 1820. Bill of sale to Lewis Bond. Witness: N. Craddock. Recorded 21 August 1820. (P. 174)

COR. N. LEWIS Bill of Sale. 2 February 1820. Bill of sale to Matthew Figures. Witnesses: A. Roan and Robert Dellis. Recorded 21 August 1820. (P. 175)

BENJAMIN MOORE Deed of Gift. 13 July 1820. Deed of gift to Abner Moore. Witnesses: James Odum, Nelson Bryan, and James Michie. Recorded 22 August 1820. (P. 176)

KELLY Power of Attorney. William and John Kelly, legal heirs of James Kelly deceased gave ( ) their power of attorney to receive the military land warrants to which James Kelly was entitled as a soldier in the Revolutionary War. Witnesses: George S. Cain and John Meador. Recorded 23 August 1820. (P. 177)

HUGH CAMPBELL Power of Attorney. 5 August 1820. Hugh Campbell, heir at law of William Campbell, gave ( ) power of attorney to claim the military land warrants in North Carolina due to said William Campbell as a soldier in Captain Donoho's Company of the Sixth Regiment of the North Carolina Continental Line. Witnesses: Felix W. Henry and Bernard P. Brown. Recorded 25 August 1820. (P. 178)

THOMAS HENRY Mortgage. 1 July 1820. Mortgage by Thomas Henry to Ephraim Sherrell. Recorded 5 November 1820. (P. 179)

JOHN BELL Bill of Sale. 10 July 1820. Bill of sale to Coleman Jackson. Recorded 5 November 1820. (P. 180)

MICHAEL MONTGOMERY Settlement. Caswell County, North Carolina. 11 October 1820. Heirs: widow Jennett Montgomery; children James Montgomery, Mary Elizabeth Howard Montgomery, Alexander Montgomery, and Thomas Gunn and wife Anne. Recorded 13 November 1820. (Pp. 181-182)

WILLIAM WEBB Deed of Gift. 8 September 1820. Deed of gift to my (niece) Hannah Tally, the daughter of Spencer Tally. Witnesses: Betsy Tally and William Tally. Recorded 30 December 1820. (P. 183)

JOHN HALLUM Bill of Sale. 24 March 1820. Bill of sale to Robert Hallum. Recorded 10 January 1821. (P. 184)

GEORGE COOPER Bill of Sale. 4 March 1820. Bill of sale to John Telford. Recorded 11 January 1820. (P. 185)

A. ROAN Bill of Sale. 8 January 1821. Deputy Sherriff A. Roan publicly sold to Robertson Johnson. Recorded 15 January 1821. (P. 186)

LUCY CLARK Bill of Sale. 31 October 1820. Bill of sale to William H. Blackburn. Recorded 25 January 1821. (P. 187)

CHARLES BARNES Bond. 21 January 1821. Charles Barnes of Hardin County, Tennessee bound to Henry Carson of Wilson County. Witnesses: J. McNeely and David Bradshaw. Recorded 29 January 1821. (P. 188)

BENJAMIN TURNER Power of Attorney. 2 December 1820. Josiah Hall of Smith County given power of attorney by Benjamin Turner, legal heir at law of Adam Turner and attorney of John and William Turner the other heirs. Said Hall to receive the military land warrants to which Adam Turner was entitled as a soldier in Captain Majors' Company of North Carolina Line in the Revolutionary War, a part of the Tenth Regiment. Recorded 14 February 1821. (P. 189)

BENJAMIN H. GARRELL Bounty Transfer. 23 November 1818. Benjamin H. Garrell of Camden, North Carolina, the only heir to my uncle Stratton Garrell, to Daniel Cherry of Wilson County. Said Stratton Garrell served in the Continental Line of North Carolina. Recorded 3 April 1821. (P. 192)

RICHARD WATKINS Bill of Sale. 30 January 1821. Bill of sale to Edward Ward of Davidson County. Recorded 3 April 1821. (P. 193)

WILLIAM CROSS Bill of Sale. 6 March 1820. Bill of sale from William Cross of Bedford County to James Cross. Witnesses: Uriah Cross and William R. Cross. Recorded 4 April 1821. (P. 194)

JOHN BROWN Power of Attorney. 22 April 1820. Power of attorney given by John Brown of Frankfort, Kentucky to Edmund Crutcher of Wilson County. Recorded 4 April 1821. (P. 195)

DARLING CHERRY Bill of Sale. 30 January 1821. Bill of sale by Darling Cherry of Martin County, North Carolina to John Gleaves of Wilson County. Recorded 4 April 1821. (P. 196)

DARLING CHERRY Power of Attorney. 24 April 1816. Power of attorney to my friend, Daniel Cherry, to represent me in the division of Wilie Cherry and land warrants of my own. Recorded 4 April 1821. (P. 197)

FRANCIS PALMER Bill of Sale. 26 August 1820. Bill of sale to James Wier. Recorded 4 April 1821. (P. 199)

CLACK STONE Bill of Sale. 17 January 1821. Bill of sale to Solomon Hartsfield. Recorded 4 April 1821. (P. 199)

JOEL FOSTER Power of Attorney. 31 March 1821. Joel Foster of Union District, South Carolina gave his power of attorney to Edmund Foster who was to represent him in the settlement of the estate of Thomas Foster in Wilson County. Recorded 7 May 1821. (P. 200)

HOWEL LEWIS Bill of Sale. 2 May 1821. Howel Lewis of Sumner County to Benjamin Wright. Recorded 15 May 1821. (P. 201)

WILLIAM C. MORGAN Bill of Sale. 2 May 1821. Bill of sale to Jeremiah Brown. Recorded 28 May 1821. (P. 203)

JAMES WILLIAMS Bill of Sale. 3 May 1821. Bill of sale to Joshua Harrison. Recorded 28 May 1821. (P. 204)

JAMES WILLIAMS Bill of Sale. 3 May 1821. Sheriff James Williams to Joshua Harrison. Recorded 30 May 1821. (P. 205)

THOMAS PARHAM Bill of Sale. 17 March 1821. Bill of sale to Spencer W. Tally. Recorded 30 May 1821. (P. 206)

PRIM Mortgage. 15 March 1821. William W. Prim and Kinzie Prim, merchants and partners) are indebted to Isaac Gollady and Michael Yerger. Witnesses: William Robb, Sr. and John Prim. Recorded 1 June 1821. (Pp. 208-209)

WILLIAM PETTEWAY Bill of Sale. 14 April 1821. Bill of sale to Jane Frazer. Recorded 2 June 1821. (P. 209)

JOURDAN WARD Bill of Sale. 12 February 1821. Bill of sale to Christopher Cooper. Witnesses: Abram Cooper, Nelson Bryan, and James Odum. Recorded 7 June 1821. (P. 211)

JAMES K. EASON Deed of Gift. 7 May 1821. Deed of gift to my nephews, Alfred Monroe and Montgomery Eason, and my nieces Eliza Frances and Anabella Eason, the children of Robert Eason. Recorded 18 June 1821. (P. 212)

JOHN B. YATES Deed of Gift. 10 September 1820. Deed of gift to my son, Lemuel Yates. Recorded 18 June 1821. (P. 213)

CYNTHIA HEGERTY Deed of Gift. 9 February 1821. Deed of gift to my nephew, John Evans, son of George Augustus Lynes Evans. Witnesses: Patrick Hegerty and Alexander Rutledge. Recorded 18 June 1821. (P. 214)

THOMAS D. BAKER Bill of Sale. 14 April 1821. Bill of sale to John McFarland, Jr. Recorded 25 August 1821. (P. 216)

JOHN MARSHALL Bill of Sale. 27 March 1820. Bill of sale to David Marshall. Witnesses: John L. Wynne and William Marshall. Recorded 25 August 1821. (P. 217)

PAULDIN and FRANCES ANDERSON Bill of Sale. 8 August 1821. Bill of sale to Jesse Cage of Sumner County. Recorded 25 August 1821. (P. 218)

MATTHEW DUKE Bill of Sale. 15 June 1821. Bill of sale to John M. Cherry and Robert C. Davis. Recorded 4 September 1821. (Pp. 219-220)

CHARLES COE Bill of Sale. 9 June 1821. Bill of sale to Wilson Webb. Recorded 5 September 1821. (P. 223)

JOHN B. BROWN and JOHN F. BROWN Bill of Sale. 10 August 1821. Bill of sale to Samuel Wray. Recorded 14 September 1821. (P. 224)

THOMAS K. RAMSEY Bill of Sale. 16 April 1821. Bill of sale to Mark Jackson. Recorded 16 September 1821. (P. 226)

NICHOLAS JONES Bill of Sale. Granville County, North Carolina. 25 September 1821. Bill of Sale to William Seawell. Recorded 17 September 1821. (P. 228)

LEWIS BALL Power of Attorney. Franklin County, Tennessee. 5 October 1821. Power of attorney granted to Samuel Dixon to represent me in Wilson County. Recorded 3 October 1821. (P. 229)

SHERIFF JAMES WILLIAMS Bill of Sale. Bill of sale to Obediah G. Finley. Recorded 30 November 1821. (P. 230)

MOTHERAL Bill of Sale. 16 February 1818. We, Robert and Jane Motheral have sold to Samuel Motheral our interest in the estate of John Kirkpatrick. Witnesses: Richard Anderson, Joseph Kirkpatrick, Halem Criswell, and John Motheral. Recorded 30 November 1821. (P. 231)

JOHN TELFORD Bill of Sale. 3 September 1821. Bill of sale to Hardin and J. T. Goodall. Recorded 3 December 1821. (P. 232)

JOSEPH COLE Bill of Sale. 22 August 1821. Bill of sale to Preston Henderson. Recorded 3 December 1821. (Pp. 232-233)

THOMAS HARRINGTON Bill of Sale. 3 August 1821. Bill of sale to Isaac Johnson. Recorded 3 December 1821. (P. 234)

WILLIAM EDINGS Bill of Sale. 24 February 1821. Bill of sale to James Johnson. Witness: James Adams. Recorded 1 March 1822. (P. 236)

WILLIAM H. BLACKBURN Bill of Sale. 27 December 1821. Bill of sale to Lewis Blackburn. Witnesses: Stephen Barton and Thomas Reed. Recorded 1 March 1822. (P. 237)

LUCY CLARK Bill of sale. 1 August 1821. Bill of sale to Edward Willis. Witnesses: William H. Blackburn and John G. Graves. Recorded 1 March 1822. (P. 238)

MARY and HENRY JACKSON Bill of Sale. 10 July 1821. Bill of sale to Anny D. Taylor. Witnesses: Mark Jackson and Edmund Jackson. Recorded 1 March 1822. (P. 239)

SOLOMON HARTSFIELD Bill of Sale. 22 December 1821. Bill of sale to John Guthrie. Recorded 1 March 1822 (Pp. 240-241)

JOHN PUGH Bill of sale. 22 September 1821. Bill of sale of Thomas R. Porterfield to John Pugh of Indiana. Recorded 4 March 1822. (Pp. 242-243)

JACKSON Articles of Marriage. 3 December 1810. Henry Jackson of Dinwiddie County and Mary Ramsey, widow of Zeral Ramsey, late of Dinwiddie County, and Robert King and Berriman Jackson both of the County of Dinwiddie. A marriage is shortly to be had between Henry Jackson and Mary Ramsey. Henry Jackson then is to have benefit of the slaves of Mary Ramsey. Robert King and Berriman Jackson, son (s) of William Jackson, to receive a deed of trust from Mary Ramsey. Witnesses: Julius King, Thomas B. King, and William King. Recorded 5 March 1822. (Pp. 243-248)

BERNARD P. BROWN Bill of Sale. 20 July 1821. Bill of sale to Dennis Kelly. Recorded 26 April 1822. (P. 248)

WILSON COUNTY COURT MINUTES 1814-1829

ASA TATOM Power of Attorney. 23 April 1822. Whereas Bernard Tatom late of the County of Wilson by deed bearing date the 5th day of May 1821 transferred to Asa Tatom his interest in the estate of Absolom Tatom, late of the State of North Carolina. Recorded 11 May 1822. (P. 249)

THOMAS and SAMUEL DONNELL Power of Attorney. 14 November 1821. Thomas and Samuel Donnell of Guilford County, North Carolina gave power of attorney to Samuel Donnell, Sr. of Wilson County to act as their agent in the transfer of a land warrant to William Edmiston of Lincoln County, Tennessee. Recorded 14 November 1822. (Pp. 250-251)

THOMAS SYPERT Bill of Sale. 22 February 1822. Bill of sale to Sally Sypert, my daughter. Recorded 18 May 1822. (P. 252)

MATTHEW and MARTHA H. FIGURES Bill of Sale. 29 November 1829. Bill of Sale to Pallis Neal. Witnesses: John L. Wynne and Mary L. Finley. Recorded 18 May 1822. (P. 253)

CHARLES BLALOCK Bill of Sale. 1 April 1822. Bill of sale to Joseph Kirkpatrick. Recorded 18 March 1822. (P. 254)

STEPHEN SYPERT Bill of Sale. 1 March 1822. Bill of sale to Lawrence Sypert. Witness: R. B. Sypert. Recorded 20 May 1822. (Pp. 254-255)

E. COFFIN Bill of Sale. 23 February 1822. Bill of Sale to John McGregor. Recorded 31 May 1822. (P. 255)

FRANKLIN FOSTER Bill of Sale. 28 December 1821. Bill of sale to John Telford. Recorded 1 June 1822. (P. 256)

STEPHEN SANDERS Bill of Sale. 1 May 1821. Bill of sale to Andrew Richmond. Witness: James Sanders. Recorded 3 June 1822. (P. 259)

DUDLEY CLIMER Bill of Sale. 29 August 1821. Bill of sale to Absolom Climer. Recorded 2 June 1822. (P. 260)

EVERETT MITCHELL Lease. 1 August 1821. Lease to Fed Malone. Recorded 7 June 1822. (P. 268)

MORRIS HALLUM Bill of Sale. 7 June 1822. Bill of sale to Ezekiel Coffin. Recorded 6 July 1822. (P. 270)

ABNER WASAN Bill of Sale. 9 August 1821. The administrators of Abner Wasan to Mary Quarles. Recorded 6 July 1822. (P. 270)

JESSE CAGE Bill of Sale. 18 September 1822. Bill of sale to John L. Tapp. Recorded 12 December 1822. (P. 274)

JEREMIAH McWHIRTER Deed of Gift. 9 October 1821. Deed of gift to Isaac McWhirter. Recorded 12 December 1822. (P. 274)

WILSON COUNTY COURT MINUTES 1814-1829

CHARLES LOCKE Bill of Sale. 1 October 1822. Bill of sale to James W. Locke. Recorded 12 December 1822. (P. 277)

CASPER HOUSHOLDER Power of Attorney. 26 September 1822. Casper Housholder of Rowan County, North Carolina gave power of attorney to William Steel to sell a tract of land. Recorded 13 December 1822. (P. 278)

SMITH Bill of Sale. 22 July 1820. Sherred Smith, Richard Smith, and Isaac Smith to Andrew Baird. Recorded 13 December 1822. (P. 280)

JAMES WILLIAMS Bill of Sale. 8 March 1821. Bill of sale to David Marshall, Sr. Recorded 13 December 1822. (P. 281)

JOHN G. GRAVES Deed of Gift. 22 June 1820. Deed of gift to Isaac, James, and Sally McWhirter that property that is now in the hands of Henry B. McWhirter. Witnesses: Thomas Guill and John Shepherd. Recorded 13 December 1822. (P. 283)

WILLIAM STEELE Guardian. 17 April 1822. Guardian of Thomas B. Taylor, the minor heir of Thomas B. Taylor. Recorded 1822. (P. 288)

THOMAS MITCHELL Deed of Gift. 21 March 1823. Deed of gift for the love and affection I have for my cousins, Levicy and George W. McWhirter. Recorded 14 May 1823. (P. 289)

NATHANIEL CARTMELL Deed of Gift. 24 March 1823. Deed of gift for the love and affection I have for my friend (s) to Jeremiah B. and Lucinda D. McWhirter. Recorded 23 May 1823. (P. 290)

JOHN TELFORD Bill of Sale. 22 March 182_. Bill of sale to William West. Recorded 23 May 1823. (P. 291)

JAMES WORD Bill of Sale. 13 November 1821. Bill of sale to Pauldin Anderson. Recorded 24 May 1823. (Pp. 291-293)

MILLER KORNEGAY Bill of Sale. 19 February 1823. Bill of sale to Henry Ward. Recorded 24 May 1823. (P. 293)

THOMAS KING Bill of Sale. 4 August 1819. Bill of sale to William Seawell. Recorded 24 May 1823. (P. 294)

JESSE WALDRAN and wife SALLY WALDRAN Power of Attorney. 19 March 1823. Power of attorney given to Wilson Sanders of Camden County, North Carolina to represent us in the settling of Anna Chamberlain and Ann Gamberling. Recorded 26 May 1823. (Pp. 295-296)

THEOPHILUS BASS Deed of Gift. 17 March 1823. Deed of gift to my son Etheldred Bass. Recorded 27 May 1823. (P. 297)

JOHN B. BROWN Bill of Sale. 1 February 1823. Bill

100

of sale to William Seawell. Recorded 27 May 1823. (P. 298)

WILSON SANDERLIN Power of Attorney. Camden County, North Carolina. 13 July 1820. Wilson Sanderlin given power of attorney by Joseph Gray and wife Milly, James Davis, Miles Jackson and wife Sarah, and Grandy Pritchard and wife Lydia, all of Pasquotank County, North Carolina and heirs at law of Benjamin Davis who was entitled to receive military land warrants as a private in the American Revolution. Witnesses: John C. Ehringham, Thomas Dozier, and William L. Ethridge. Recorded 1 June 1823. (Pp. 299-300)

JOHN RIEFF Bill of Sale. 19 June 1823. Bill of sale to Adline Criswell. Witnesses: Allen Ross and Ishmael Bradshaw. Recorded 25 April 1823. (P. 303)

ROBERT McLIN Bill of Sale. 10 June 1823. Bill of sale to James Elgin of Smith County. Witnesses: Robert Elgin and William B. Elgin. Recorded 25 August 1823. (P. 304)

ROBERT McLIN Bill of Sale. 11 January 1823. Bill of sale to William Bumpass of Rutherford County. Recorded 24 August 1823. (P. 305)

THOMAS DENTON Bill of Sale. 15 April 1822. Bill of sale to William Thomason. Recorded 24 August 1823. (P. 306)

WILLIAM C. GUTHRIE Bill of Sale. April, 1823. Bill of sale to Bennett Babb. Witness: Thomas Guthrie. Recorded 24 August 1823. (P. 307)

JOHN BONNER Deed of Gift. 21 November 1822. Deed of gift to my daughter, Mary Wright of Limestone County, Alabama. Recorded 24 August 1823. (P. 307)

COLEMAN STONE Bill of Sale. 11 August 1823. Bill of sale to James Frazer. Recorded 9 December 1823. (P. 308)

WILLIAM McHANEY Bill of Sale. 7 July 1823. Bill of sale to Hugh Marrs. Witnesses: Samson Smith, Martin Marrs, and Jacob Jennings. Recorded 9 December 1823. (P. 309)

JESSE WOODCOCK Bill of Sale. 18 April 1823. Bill of sale to Stephen McDonald. Witnesses: James S. Woodcock and John Bonner, Sr. Recorded 10 December 1823. (P. 311)

THOMAS BRADSHAW Bill of Sale. 16 September 1823. Bill of sale to Wilson Bradshaw. Recorded 2 December 1823. (P. 313)

EDWARD CLAY Bill of Sale. 12 October 1821. Bill of sale to John Gholston. Recorded 15 December 1823. (P. 314)

EDWARD TUCKER Bill of Sale. 25 February 1823. Bill·

of sale to David McMurray. Recorded 19 February 1824. (Pp. 315-316)

THOMAS RICHMOND Power of Attorney. 20 December 1823. Power of attorney granted to Humphrey Donalson, Sr. "to transact my business with Daniel Richmond of Wilson County. Recorded 19 February 1824. (P. 317)

JOSEPH WATSON Bill of Sale. 27 October 1823. Bill of sale to William H. White. Recorded 19 February 1824. (P. 317)

JOHN STONE Power of Attorney. Power of attorney to John Allcorn. Recorded 16 March 1824. (P. 318)

ELIJAH DAVIS Bill of Sale. 10 July 1822. Bill of sale to John M. D. Parks of Rutherford County. Witnesses: John Bell and Robert D. Bell. Recorded 16 March 1824. (P. 319)

HENRY D. NICKOLS Bill of Sale. 29 November 1823. Bill of Sale to Morgan W. and Robert N. Nickols. Recorded 15 March 1824. (P. 320)

JONATHAN WARD Bill of Sale. 24 March 1823. Jonathan Ward of Logan County, Kentucky to Michael Pitner of Wilson County. Recorded 15 March 1824. (P. 321)

EPHRAIM PAYTON Power of Attorney. 25 August 1807. Ephraim Payton of Washington County, Kentucky granted power of attorney to John Payton of Sumner County. Witness: William Payton. Recorded 4 May 1824. (Pp. 322-323)

TASWELL MITCHELL Executor. 24 February 1824. Executor of Thomas Mitchell. Recorded 17 June 1824. (Pp. 323-324)

JAMES SHAW Power of Attorney. 24 July 1823. John Shaw of Tuskalloosa County, Alabama gave power of attorney to Simon Hancock of Wilson County. Recorded 17 June 1824. (Pp. 324-325)

DAVID MARSHALL Articles of Agreement. 23 February 1823. Articles of agreement with William and Joseph Seawell. Recorded 18 June 1824. (Pp. 325-327)

CHARLES COE and WILLIAM COE Bill of Sale. 7 January 1824. Bill of sale to James Frazer. Witnesses: James W. Coe and Robert Ferguson. Recorded 22 June 1824. (P. 328)

HENRY BROWN Bill of Sale. 26 September 1823. Bill of sale to Benjamin Bonner. Recorded 22 June 1824. (P. 329)

RICHARD LYON Bill of Sale. 28 February 1824. Bill of sale to Ira E. Eason. Recorded 22 June 1824. (P. 330)

BARTON Bill of Sale. 1 August 1818. Stephen and Gabriel Barton to Benjamin T. Mottley sixty acres of land on Barton's Creek, formerly owned by Samuel Barton deceased. Recorded 10 August 1824. (Pp. 332-333)

CHARLES YOUNG Deed. 27 December 1823. Joseph Sharp of Wilson County, Edward Donoho of Rutherford County, and Samuel Dickins of Madison County to Charles Young of Wilson County. Recorded 10 August 1824. (Pp. 333-334)

ASAPH ALSUP Bill of Sale. 1 March 1824. Bill of sale to John Fakes. Recorded 19 November 1824. (P. 336)

ELIZABETH SNELL Bill of Sale. 29 April 1824. The heirs of Elizabeth Snell deceased to Robert Hallum. Recorded 17 November 1826. (P. 337)

WILLIS COLFIELD Deed of Conveyance. 29 September 1824. Deed of conveyance to Matthew Figures. Recorded 17 November 1824. (Pp. 338-339)

BENNY B. BEASLEY Bill of Sale. 25 May 1824. Bill of sale to Green B. Loe. Recorded 15 December 1824. (P. 344)

JOSEPH IRBY Bill of Sale. 20 July 1824. Bill of sale to Julius Walker. Recorded 22 February 1825. (P. 347)

MARRIOTT DAVIS Deed of Gift. 10 August 1824. Deeds of gift to my daughters, Sarah and Elizabeth Davis. Recorded 22 February 1825. (P. 348)

JAMES FREELAND Bill of Sale. James Freeland of Smith County to Green B. Lowe of Wilson County. Witnesses: Joseph T. Bell and R. C. Stubblefield. Recorded 22 February 1825. (P. 349)

JAMES GEORGE Power of Attorney. 19 March 1818. Power of attorney to Eli Leakley of Warren County, Tenn. James George is an heir of William Leakley. Recorded 29 March 1825. (P. 353)

HALLUM Power of Attorney. 19 November 1824. John and Susannah Hallum of Pike County, Mississippi, and heirs of Matthew Cartwright of Wilson County, gave their power of attorney to Matthew Cartwright of Pike County. Recorded 11 May 1825. (P. 354)

EDMUND HARDY Power of Attorney. 27 September 1824. Edmund Hardy, agent for Edmund Wier of Lunenburg County, Virginia, named Charles Blalock as attorney for his daughter, Frances Bacon. Recorded 26 May 1825. (P. 356)

THOMAS DENTON Bill of Sale. 25 January 1825. Bill of sale to Edward Denton. Witnesses: John Powell and William Walker. Recorded 26 May 1825. (Pp. 358-359)

WILLIAM NEW and FRANCES NEW Deed of Gift. 31 March 1825. Deed of gift for our son, Charles Turner New. Recorded 26 May 1825. (Pp. 359-360)

GEORGE McWHIRTER DEED OF GIFT. 7 February 1825. Deed of gift to my beloved grandchildren, to wit, Elizabeth, Martha, Benjamin, George, Sarah, and Samuel Briggs; also my confidential friend Samuel C. McWhirter. Witness: George F. McWhirter. Recorded 18 August 1825. (P. 362). ✓

BATT BAIRD MURCHESON Bill of Sale. 3 June 1825. Bill of sale to John Baird. Recorded 18 August 1825. (P. 364)

JOHN STEPHENSON Bill of Sale. 19 February 1825. Bill of sale to Isaac T. Stephenson. Recorded 20 August 1825. (P. 369)

HOBSON Bill of Sale. The heirs of Joseph Hobson, to wit, William and Benjamin Hobson, to George Scruggs. Recorded 22 August 1825. (P. 370)

HENRY CRISWELL Assignment. 2 May 1825. I assign the within to Rosannah Creswell. Recorded 23 August 1825. (P. 372)

WILLIAM WILLIAMS Deed of Gift. 26 April 1825. Deed of gift to my daughter Polly Tilman Mabry. Recorded in Register's Office in Deed Book DD, page 375. (P. 375)

SALLY HARRIS Deed of Gift. 26 March 1824. Deed of gift from Sally Harris, wife of John Harris deceased, to my two children, to wit, Eli A. and Patsy S. Harris. Fergus S. Harris is their guardian. Recorded 26 November 1825. (P. 376)

SAMUEL HOGG Bill of Sale. 26 February 1824. Bill of sale to John McLemore of Davidson County. Recorded 25 November 1825. (Pp. 377-378)

JOSEPH L. WILSON Guardian. 17 January 1826. Guardian of Mary Wilson, one of the minor heirs of Joseph Wilson. Recorded in the Register's Office in Deed Book DD, page 381. (P. 381)

WILLIAM WORD Bill of Sale. 9 March 1825. Bill of sale to John Lakes. Witnesses: Thomas Hodges and Harriet Word. Recorded 25 September 1826. (P. 385)

ELLENOR NICKONS Statement. 7 November 1826. Ellenor Nickons appeared before Josiah Walton, J. P. of Sumner County. She was a white woman and generally passed as such. It was generally assumed that Franky Nickons was the daughter of Ellenor Nickons. Recorded 3 January 1827. (P. 392)

WILLIAM L. SYPERT Statement. 5 February 1827. David Manley has always passed as a free person. (P. 392)

FRANKY SCOTT Statement. 5 February 1827. Franky Scott, whose maiden name was Franky Nickons, made oath that David, William, and Levi Manley were her children by her husband, Joseph Manley, a man of color but free. (P. 393)

ANDREW McHANEY Bill of Sale. 28 December 1826. Bill of sale to my children, to wit, William McHaney, Lucy Whitlow and husband Henry, Polly Pemberton and husband Thomas, and Nancy Smith and husband John A. Smith. Recorded 23 April 1827. (Pp. 399-401)

JAMES C. HARRISON Bill of Sale. 15 January 1827. Bill of sale to Alexander Penny. (P. 408)

ABRAM CANNON Title Bond. 23 July 182_. Abram Cannon of Rutherford County to John C. Smith and Thomas Smith of Wilson County. The land being part of the land belonging to James Cannon deceased. Recorded 18 January 1827. (P. 418)

DAVIDSON Bill of Sale. 2 February 1825. John Donnell, William B. Guill, W. P. Davidson, Francis P. Davidson, and Wilson Davidson, the heirs of Martha P. Davidson to Alford Bloodworth. Recorded 12 June 1828.

JAMES RUDD Power of Attorney. 22 November 182_. Power of attorney to Rutherford Rutland to act as my agent in the estate settlement of Jesse Clark.

WILSON BRADSHAW Deed of Gift. 11 May 1825. Deed of gift to Thomas Bradshaw. Recorded 18 June 1828.

J. WILLIAM WALLACE Power of Attorney. 5 July 1825. J. William Wallace of Dallas County, Alabama appointed Abram Shepherd of Wilson County his attorney. Recorded 6 April 1826.

GEORGE CUMMINGS Deed of Gift. 20 September 1828. Deed of gift to William R. D. Phepps. Recorded 3 November 1828.

J. W. WALKER Deeds of Gift. 30 October 1826. Deeds of gift to my beloved grandchildren, to wit, Susan Ann Martin, and Dosha Martin. Said grandchildren are the children of my daughter Nancy Martin. Witnesses: Josiah Ligon and Robert Shepherd. Recorded 3 November 1828.

JOHN TERRELL Bill of Sale. 28 February 1827. John Terrell of Weakley County to Benjamin Springs of Wilson County. Recorded 20 November 1828.

GEORGE B. BLASE Bill of Sale. 18 January 1827. Bill of sale to Absolom Gleaves of Davidson County. Recorded 20 November 1827.

JACKSON Power of Attorney. 30 December 1826. The heirs of Robert Jackson, to wit, Henry, Jesse, John M., Dolly, and Daniel Jackson, and Benny B. Beasley gave their power of attorney to Mark Jackson. Robert Jackson's widow is now the widow of James Lethe. There is land in Dinwiddie County, Virginia. Recorded 20 August 1827.

DEWS Bill of Sale. 2 October 1828. Richard Waller of Halifax County, Virginia, grandfather of my children, William W. and Sarah B. Dews. Said Richard Waller was the father of my first wife, Elizabeth, who died previous to her father. Her share of the estate to go to my children, both of said Elizabeth. Recorded 20 October 1828.

JOSHUA PIERCY Power of Attorney. 28 May 182_. Joshua Piercy of Pasquotank County, North Carolina gave power of attorney to Ewing Wilson of Wilson County to receive any land warrants that Christian Piercy was entitled.

Recorded 16 March 1829.

NATHANIEL DAVIS Bill of Sale. 15 March 1827. Thomas Drennan, guardian of Nathaniel Davis, to Henry H. Sugg. Witnesses: James and John Drennan. Recorded 22 January 1828.

WILLS & INVENTORIES   1853-1858

RICHARD W. HARRIS Will. 21 March 1848. Heirs:
wife Amelia Harris; my six children Mary J. Owen, Sarah
B. Allen, Evaline N. Debow, Joseph B., Harriet F., and
Susan E. Harris. Witnesses: Thomas J. Holman and Ila
Douglass. Executors: Amelia Harris, James H. Harris,
and Ila Douglass. Recorded 1 September 1853. (P. 1)

WILLIAM DAVIS Sale. 28 December 1852. J. W. Ewing,
administrator. Recorded 1 September 1853. (P. 2)

ALFRED McCLAIN Sale. 5 October 1852. George K.
Robertson, administrator. Recorded 1 September 1853.
(Pp. 3-4)

ISAAC HORTON Sale. 18 February 1853. John L. Britton, administrator. Recorded 3 September 1853. (P. 4)

BETHEL PHILIPS Sale. 22 August 1853. David Philips,
administrator. Recorded 17 January 1856. (P. 5)

MARY L. (POLLY) HARRIS Will. 24 June 1853. Heirs:
children Virginia and Erastus C. Harris. If they should
die, then to William W. Seay and my cousin, Sally Swain.
William W. Seay, executor. Witnesses: M. E. Johnson,
James Swain, and J. S. Davis. Recorded 15 September
1853. (P. 5)

JOHN SPICKARD Sale. 22 January 1853. William B.
Goldstone, administrator. Recorded 2 September 1853.
(P. 6)

JAMES LOYD Will. 6 October 1840. Heirs: wife
Matilda Loyd and children. The will was written by David
Bridges. Witnesses: David Bridges and Lovit Caraway.
Recorded 2 September 1853. (P. 6)

EBENEZER GILBERT Will. Heirs: wife Lucy Gilbert;
daughters; son John F. Gilbert; son James Gilbert's
son. Thomas C. Hott, executor. Recorded 3 September
1853. (P. 7)

EBENEZER GILBERT Codicil. 10 February 1850. My
three daughters are to use their share as they please.
Witnesses: James Arrington and D. H. Scruggs. Recorded
3 September 1853. (P. 7)

(ERRAND) HARRIS Sale. 15 October 1852. B. J. Tarver, administrator. Recorded 14 September 1853. (P. 8)

WILLIAM F. HEARN Sale. 25 October 1852. E. D.
Johnson, administrator. Recorded 15 September 1853. (Pp.
8-9)

MARGARET BARTHOLOMEW Sale. 24 December 1852. Isaac
N. Stewart. Recorded 15 September 1853. (P. 10)

STETH HIGHTOWER Sale. 7 March 1853. Sold after the
death of the widow. Elijah Williams, administrator. Recorded 15 September 1853. (Pp. 10-11)

A. G. HANKINS Sale. 28 October 1852. M. H. Hankins,
administrator. Recorded 15 September 1853. (Pp. 11-12)

WILLIAM CORLEY Will. 22 December 1852. Heirs: daughters Elizabeth Dillard and Clarissa Farley; sons Elisha, Robert, and William Corley; children by my last wife. Clarissa Farley and William Corley were children by first wife. Joel Allgood, executor. Witnesses: H. Snead and J. C. Terry. Recorded 19 September 1853. (Pp. 12-13)

B. HUTCHISON Sale. 28 February 1853. Administrators: Isaac Harvey and James M). Recorded 16 September 1853. (P. 13)

WILLIAM H. LAINE Widow's Allotment. 1 April 1853. The widow and child were given their allotment. (P. 15)

JAMES WOOD Will. 7 March 1853. Heirs: wife Elizabeth Wood; my seven heirs Martha Compton, Susan Kittrell, Moses A. Wood, Margaret Neal, William J. Wood, Yandell Wood, and J. S. Wood. Executors: Moses A. Wood and William J. Wood. Witnesses: Johnathan C. Doss and James P. Doss. Recorded 16 September 1853. (P. 15)

W. B. HARRIS Sale. 28 March 1853. J. T. Manson, administrator. Recorded 16 September 1853. (P. 16)

JAMES H. PEYTON Inventory. 4 April 1853. John Kelly, executor. Recorded 17 September 1853. (P. 17)

WILLIAM BAIRD Widow's Allotment. Lucinda Baird given her allotment. Recorded 17 September 1853. (P. 18)

MANSON B. LESTER Inventory. 30 March 1853. G. W. Jennings, administrator. Recorded 17 September 1853. (P. 18)

MARY JEWEL Will. 22 October 1851. Heirs: Nancy Jane Wilson and Thomas G. Wilson. Witnesses: H. H. Allison and J. B. Thomas. Recorded 17 September 1853. (P. 18)

ELI R. HARRIS Inventory. 25 January 1853. Said Harris lived in the 12th District. William S. Swan, administrator. Recorded 20 September 1853. (Pp. 19-20)

BERNARD CARTER Widow's Allotment. Recorded 19 September 1853. (P. 20)

THOMAS CONYERS Will. Stoddard County, Missouri. 25 August 1847. Heirs: wife Sarah Conyers; daughter Mary Jane Conyers; sons Clinton P., James H., Frederick A., and William F. Conyers. The estate includes a tract of land in Wilson County. Charles P. Conyers, executor. Witnesses: Thomas M. Adams, Hiram A. Shook, and William Gunnels. Recorded 21 September 1853. (Pp. 24-26)

JOHN RICE Will. 2 May 1853. Heirs: wife Nancy Rice; three children Polly, Nancy, and James Rice; son in law W. H. Johnson. Witnesses: B. M. Rogers and John W. Chandler. Recorded 23 September 1853. (Pp. 27-28)

ALEXANDER ASTON Will. 12 February 1853. Heirs: sons Joseph, James Aston; daughters Sally Aston, Polly

Scoby; grandchildren viz. Daniel Aston's children; and
Nancy Lyon's child J) A. Executors: William D. Smith
and Joseph Aston. Witnesses: Alexander Caruth and William B. Caruth. Recorded 23 September 1853. (P. 28)

THOMAS V. WIER Will. Heirs: wife Polly Wier; chil-
dren Lucus Paulden, Lurany Elizabeth, Mary Lucinda, Joseph
Thomas, Robert Wilson, Turner Shelby, and Littleberry
Williamson White. John Organ, executor. Witnesses: John
Cates and L. S. Whitehead. Recorded 24 September 1853.
(Pp. 29-30)

FRANCIS M. PEACE Will. 16 April 1853. Heirs: my
interest in my father's estate I give to Thomas J. Thomp-
son in trust for the use and benefit of my sister, Lucy
Ann Thompson, wife of said Thomas J. Thompson. Thomas J.
Thompson, executor. Witnesses: J. S. McClain and D.
Carr. Recorded 24 September 1853. (P. 30)

SARAH H. BAKER Sale. 26 March 1853. L. N. Robertson, administrator. Recorded 24 September 1853. (P. 31)

POLLY GEORGE Sale. 4 April 1853. R. W. George, administrator. Recorded 24 September 1853. (P. 32)

GEORGE HARPOLE Sale. 24 February 1853. Recorded 26
September 1853. (Pp. 33-34)

W. NEELY Widow's Allotment. 9 May 1853. Jane Neely
given her allotment. Recorded 26 September 1853. (P. 34)

WILLIAM L. DUNCAN Sale. 16 July 1853. (P. 37)

ELIZABETH HEARN Will. 18 March 1853. Lived in the
12th District of Wilson County, but formerly of Smith
County. Heirs: daughter Polly Harris; my two grandchildren Lilia Virginia and Arastus C. Harris. If they
should die before their mother, then to my niece Sallie
Swann. If Sallie Swann should die, then to her husband,
William Swann, and children. Other heirs brothers John,
William, Daniel, and Charles Seay; sister Johnson;
nephew Joseph Marks. Recorded 27 September 1853. (P. 37)

ISAAC HORTON Widow's Allotment. 17 February 1853.
Jane Horton given her allotment. Recorded 27 September
1853. (P. 38)

EMILINE KIRKPATRICK Orphan's Allotment. 16 June
1853. Recorded 27 September 1853. (Pp. 38-39)

HENRY SHANNON Inventory. 4 July 1853. John F. Posey,
administrator. Recorded 28 September 1853. (P. 41)

CHARLES BLALOCK Will. 8 June 1853. Heirs: wife
Rebecca Blalock; son Whitson Blalock. Witnesses: John
Epperson, Ezekiel Gwin, and A. Kirkpatrick. Recorded 29
September 1853. (P. 45)

JAMES MURRY Sale. 28 May 1853. Recorded 30 September 1853. (P. 45)

LYDIA LAWRENCE Will. 11 January 1844. Heirs: Vina

Beard, the wife of David Beard; David Malone; my two daughters Fatha Boyd, the wife of William Boyd, Polly Waters, the wife of Wilson F. Waters. James Young, executor. Witnesses: Ashley Neal, J. B. Bryan, and Doke Young. Recorded 1 October 1853. (P. 46)

M. E. CHANDLER Inventory. 10 August 1853. James Chambers, executor. Recorded 3 October 1853. (P. 47)

ASBAL SHERREL Widow's Allotment. 27 July 1853. Recorded 3 October 1853. (P. 47)

JAMES YANDELL Sale. 13 November 1852. (Pp. 48-49)

WASHINGTON TURNER Will. Lived in District #12 of Wilson County. Heirs: wife; my five children who are servants. Executor: good friend Philip Fisher. Witnesses: Johnathan Bailey and James Murphy. Recorded 4 October 1853. (P. 50)

FRANCIS E. MABRY Widow's Allotment. Recorded 4 October 1853. (P. 50)

WILLIAM W. SULLIVAN Will. 7 September 1853. Heirs: wife Elizabeth P. Sullivan. William P. Sullivan, executor. Recorded 4 October 1853. (P. 51)

ANN BARBEE Will. Heirs: sisters Parthena Barbee and Polly Edge; brothers Owen T., Levi D., Joseph L., and Joshua W. Barbee. Owen T. Barbee, executor. Witnesses: William J. Cragwall and Jacob Thomason. Recorded 4 October 1853. (P. 51)

JOHN HAWKS Will. 18 August 1855. Dinwiddie County, Virginia. Heirs: wife Sarah Hawks; my living children. Sarah Hawks, executrix. Witnesses: Robert W. Hawks and Thomas Chappell. Recorded 5 October 1853. (P. 52)

SAMUEL FUSTON Noncupative Will. 3 October 1853. Heirs: brother Leroy Fuston; my other brothers and sisters. He died at Leroy Fuston's house on the last day of August 1853. His wife was not expected to live long. She died two days later. Witnesses: David W. Wright, Martha J. Williamson, and Matilda Wright. Recorded 5 October 1853. (P. 53)

D. C. BUCKLEY Sale. (P. 53)

JAMES W. FERRELL Will. 25 October 1853. Heirs: wife Amanda Ferrell. Thomas C. McSpedin should help raise my children. Witnesses: J. F. Organ and James P. McSpedin. Recorded 5 November 1853.

WILLIAM F. JONES Will. 18 July 1853. Heirs: brothers Calvin and Alfred Jones. Executors: Calvin and Alfred Jones. Witnesses: Tom Waters and Doke Young. Recorded 30 November 1853. (P. 59)

GEORGE H. SHUTT Will. 6 October 1853. Heirs: wife Hannah H. Shutt; my children; the two children of my wife by a former husband. My wife's two children have received from their grandfather, Archelaus Carlos. Execu-

trix: Hannah H. Shutt. Witnesses: A. G. Muirhead and
L. W. White. Recorded 30 November 1853. (Pp. 60-61)

SAMUEL P. PATTERSON Widow's Allotment. 21 October
1853. Recorded 30 November 1853. (P. 61)

WILLIAM H. H. LEA Sale. 15 October 1853. Recorded
30 November 1853. (P. 62)

JAMES ROBINSON Gifts. 14 February 1853. Recipients:
wife Elizabeth Robinson; children Elizabeth Truett, Sarah
Jennings, Catherine Turner, Peggy Anderson's heirs, Mary
Jennings, Matilda Pritchett, Martha A. Martin, Edward
Robinson, Stephen Robinson, Moses Robinson, John Robinson,
and William F. Robinson. Witnesses: L. D. Fite and Isaac
Mullinax. Recorded 20 December 1853. (P. 63)

JOHN W. WHITE Will. 10 November 1852. Heirs: wife
Susannah White; children Lizzy Borum, Elizabeth Bradley,
Martha Tucker, Susannah White, and James White. Susannah
White, executrix. Witnesses: John F. Waters, George W.
Waters, and L. A. Swindell. Recorded 20 December 1853.
(P. 64)

I. J. DODSON Widow's Allotment. 8 November 1853.
Lavina Dodson given her allotment. Recorded 20 December
1853. (Pp. 65-67)

JAMES RAKES Widow's Allotment. 25 October 1853. Recorded 21 December 1853. (P. 67)

PATRICK FLORIDAY Sale. 5 December 1853. Thomas B.
Floriday, administrator. Recorded 21 December 1853. (P.
68)

R. C. LOCKE Sale. 18 November 1853. Recorded 21
December 1853. (Pp. 69-70)

PEGGY SMITH Will. 13 October 1853. Heirs: sons,
James and John S. Smith, to receive the tracts of land I
inherited from my father, James Canon, and husband, Thomas S. Smith. Witnesses: John H. Lillard and Moses H.
Thompson. Recorded 23 January 1854. (P. 72)

ELIZABETH COLEMAN Sale. 26 December 1853. Recorded
23 January 1853. (P. 74)

WRIGHT HUNTER Will. 3 December 1853. Heirs: sons
William P., James T., and Howel A. B. Hunter; daughters
Ann C., Nancy W., and Mary J. Hunter. Also, daughter
Mascey C. Hunter. Witnesses: Thomas H. ( ) and Lewis
Chambers. Recorded 21 March 1854. (Pp. 74-77)

WILLIAM CRAPPER Will. 16 December 1853. Heirs: all
my children. Son James Crapper, executor. Witnesses:
S. E. Belcher and Jarrett Tucker. Recorded 1854. (P. 77)

SAMUEL P. PATTON Sale. 6 February 1854. Recorded
22 March 1854. (Pp. 77-78)

SAMUEL STEWART Sale. 20 January 1854. (Pp. 78-81)

JOHN WOLLARD Sale. 3 January 1854. Recorded 24 March

1854. (P. 85)

ANDREW THOMPSON, JR. Inventory. 2 March 1854. Martha E. Thompson, executrix. Recorded 25 March 1854. (P. 86)

WILLIE ALFORD Will. 19 September 1853. Heirs: wife Sophia Alford; sons Britton D., James P., Benjamin M., Willie N. B., and Edmon S. Alford; daughters Louiza J. Walker, Ruth A. Cawthon, Mary P. Hays, Sophia Jannon, and Clarky M. Lumpkins children, to wit, Tirza, James B., and Mary A. Lumpkins. Witnesses: H. Carver and Barnet Guill. Recorded 26 March 1854. (Pp. 86-87)

MARTHA JOHNSON Sale. 27 December 1853. Recorded 16 August 1854. (P. 93)

JESSE S. DAVIS Inventory. 1 June 1854. Benjamin H. Davis, administrator. Recorded 16 August 1854. (Pp. 94-95)

JAMES GUILL Sale. 27 June 1854. Recorded 16 August 1856. (P. 96)

RICHARD LOCKE Widow's Allotment. 10 November 1853. Mary Locke given her allotment. Recorded 17 August 1854. (P. 97)

MARGARET THOMPSON Will. 2 July 1850. Heirs: nephew Andrew W. Thompson; dear friend Dr. John T. Gleaves; dear cousins John W. Tate and Alexander M. Cloyd, Mary Earheart, daughter of John Earheart. Executors: John T. Gleaves and Andrew W. Thompson. Witnesses: J. T. Gleaves and J. P. Cawthon. Recorded 17 August 1854. (P. 98)

AARON MURPHY Widow's Allotment. 28 February 1854. Nancy Murphy given her allotment. Recorded 24 August 1854. (Pp. 99-100)

ANDREW THOMPSON Will. 29 November 1853. Heirs: wife Martha E. Thompson; sons John P. and Henry C. Thompson; daughter Margaret Jane Thompson. Martha E. Thompson, executrix. Witnesses: Joseph Patton and Larance E. Tally. Recorded 24 August 1854. (P. 100)

WILLIAM SULLIVAN Sale. Recorded 24 August 1854. (P. 101)

JAMES THOMPSON Will. 20 May 1854. Heirs: children Mitchell H., Andrew J., Nancy Elizabeth, and Martha Jane Thompson. I direct that my body be interred in the graveyard at Mount Vernon Church. Executor: brother in law, George D. Young. Witnesses: William Thompson, James Ayres, and George Thompson. Recorded 26 August 1854. (P. 102)

LUCY LOYD Will. 29 May 1854. Heirs: children Martha James, Sarah Fine, Anderson Paulding, and Joseph William Loyd. Anderson Paulding Loyd has an afflicted arm. James Ingram to take Joseph William Loyd. My daughter and son, James and Catherine Ingram, to take charge of my younger daughters, Martha James and Sarah Fine Loyd, but they are to have the privilege of visiting their sisters, Margaret Mahoffer and Mary Parilla Mahoffer. John C. Organ, executor. Witnesses: F. Wilkinson and A. Cox. Recorded 26 August 1854. (Pp. 102-103)

JOHN WINTERS Sale. 4 June 1854. Recorded 26 August 1854. (P. 103)

(ALANON) KENEDY Sale. 24 September 1853. Thomas Vivrett, administrator. Recorded 26 August 1854. (P. 104)

THOMAS WRAY Sale. 13 January 1854. Sale took place at the residence of William Wray. William S. Clemons, administrator. Recorded 25 August 1854. (P. 106)

ELISHA CHASTAIN Inventory. 3 April 1854. Recorded 29 August 1854. (P. 106)

WILLIAMSON WILLIAMS Will. 4 August 1835. Heirs: wife Sidney Williams; children William, Elisha, Greenberry, (Ivisey), George Washington, Lavicy, E. C., and Drucilla Lancaster Williams. Also, daughter Lavina S. Jacobs. Executors: Sidney Williams and Joshua Lester. Witnesses: Henry B. Williams and John Bond. Recorded 29 August 1854. (P. 107)

JOHN BENNETT Widow's Allotment. 23 May 1854. Nancy Bennett given her allotment. (P. 109)

ELEANOR JOHNSON Will. 1 July 1841. Heirs: children John, Robertson, Daniel Johnson, and Mary Calhoun; children of my daughter Jane Barton, to wit, Joseph, Eliner, Alexander R., Martha, Elizabeth D., William J., and James C. Barton; grandson Edward D. Johnson. Executor: Daniel Johnson. Witnesses: James D. White and Stephen McDonald. Recorded 31 August 1854. (P. 110)

JAMES B. SELLARS Sale. 5 June 1854. Recorded 31 August 1854. (P. 111)

JOHN D. NORRIS Sale. 28 April 1854. Recorded 31 August 1854. (Pp. 111-112)

CATHERINE HARDY Sale. 10 March 1854. Recorded 1 September 1854. (Pp. 112-114)

EDWARD SWEATT Will. Ellis County, Texas. 11 January 1854. Heirs: wife Nancy Sweatt; children Quincy A., A. C., Richard V. B., George B., W. C., Cynthia, Mary P., and Sarah A. Sweatt, and Elizabeth Ligon; grandson James E. Scoby; the heirs of Eli C. Sweatt. Witnesses: Samuel T. Bledsoe and Robert P. Sweatt. Recorded 2 September 1854. (P. 117)

SARAH COLE Sale. Recorded 2 September 1854. (P. 118)

F. UNDERWOOD Sale. Recorded 2 September 1854. (P. 118)

ANDREW ESKEW Sale. 15 June 1854. Recorded 8 Septem-

113

ber 1854. (Pp. 121-127)

SPENCER W. TALLY Sale. 3 January 1852. Recorded 9 September 1854. (Pp. 128-139)

SAMUEL NORRIS Will. 7 July 1854. Heirs: wife Drucilla Norris; children Manerva Arnold, Harriet Norris, Elizabeth Chambers, Mildred Buckley, and Cassandra Norris; Manerva Arnold's children, to wit, John B. and William Arnold. Edward Willis, executor. Witnesses: Alexander Brett and S. W. Stevenson. Recorded 21 September 1854. (P. 141)

BURRELL PATTERSON Will. Heirs: Elizabeth Gibson, Kinchen Patterson, Tilman Patterson, Edny Orston, Martha Lee, Marinda Putman, and Green Patterson; grandson Joseph G. Bond. Executors: Kinchen Patterson and John H. Johnson. Witnesses: M. W. Henderson, John W. Buckner, and William M. Lasater. Recorded 21 September 1854. (P. 142)

GRAY ANDREWS Will. 13 September 1850. Heirs: wife Rebecca Andrews; son John A. Andrews; grandsons John W. and Elijah S. Andrews. Executors: John A. McClain and Price Curd. Recorded 21 September 1854. (Pp. 142-143)

HARRISON LESTER Will. 2 June 1854. Heirs: wife Nancy Adaline Lester; children; Bradley's Creek Baptist Church. Executors: Nancy Adaline Lester, R. H. Jarman, and A. Williams. Witnesses: R. H. Jarman and A. Williams. Recorded 13 October 1854. (P. 143)

SARAH EDDINGS Sale. 20 September 1854. John R. Davis, administrator. Recorded 13 October 1854. (P. 144)

JOHN BRASHER Sale. 25 September 1854. Alfred Brasher, administrator. Recorded 14 October 1854. (P. 147)

JAMES T. MARTIN Sale. Recorded 14 October 1854. (Pp. 148-149)

NANCY M. CALLIS Sale. 28 September 1854. Recorded 16 October 1854. (Pp. 149-150)

JONAS SWINGLEY Will. 8 July 1854. Heirs: wife Martha Swingley; children Mary Ann W. Carver, Catherine Stroud, Susannah Jackson, and John G. Swingley. Executors: John G. Swingley and Archibald Carver. Witnesses: W. R. Winters and A. W. Vick. Recorded 19 October 1854. (Pp. 153-154)

AUGUSTINE SNOW Will. 7 August 1854. Heirs: children Sintha, Elvirinda, J. B., and H. R. Snow, Mary Ramsey, Virinda Chapman, Frances Speares. Daughter Mary Ramsey is to inherit only if "she will never again live with Samhill Ramsey." J. B. Snow, executor. Witnesses: Thomas B. Chapman and Jeremiah Turner. Recorded 19 October 1854. (P. 155)

A. C. JOHNSON Widow's Allotment. 20 September 1854. Mary Johnson given her allotment. Recorded 20 October 1854. (P. 156)

JOHN MURRY Will.   11 October 1854.   Heirs: wife Any
A. Murry;   all my children except William W. Murry.   James
Hamilton, executor.   Witnesses: Barrett Guill and Burrell
T. Castleman.   Recorded 18 November 1854.   (Pp. 159-160)

CHARLES WRIGHT Widow's Allotment.   19 September 1854.
Mary Wright given her allotment.   Recorded 23 November
1854.   (P. 165)

WILLIAM STEWART Widow's Allotment.   6 November 1854.
Nancy Stewart given her allotment.   Recorded 23 November
1854.   (Pp. 165-166)

JOSIAH S. McCLAIN Inventory.   6 November 1854.   Recorded 23 November 1854.   (P. 166)

JAMES CARUTH Will.   18 September 1854.   Heirs: wife
Mary Caruth; American Bible and American Tract Societies.
Executor: Shiloh Presbytery.   Witnesses: Thomas C.
Smith, Edmond Oliver, and James C. Smith.   Recorded
1855.   (P. 171)

JAMES P. WILLIAMS Will.   28 October 1854.   Heirs:
wife Isabella Williams;   my heirs as the law may direct.
Recorded 12 February 1855.   (P. 172)

THOMAS MARKS Will.   2 October 1854.   Heirs: wife
Louiza J. Marks;   my children.   Witnesses: William J.
Cragwall and John Marks.   Recorded 12 February 1855.
(P. 173)

SHADRACK SMITH Will.   20 January 1851.   Heirs:
wife Nancy Smith;   children Elizabeth, Shadrack C., and
David B. Smith, Drucilla C. Jennings, Nancy Ann Ramsey,
Mary Grissom, and Rebecca Puckett;   grandchildren Eliza
Ann, Marshall, and James W. McAdow; grandchildren Oscar
A. S. Ewing and John L. Ewing deceased's daughter Nancy
Malinda and her brothers and sisters, to wit, Sarah M.
Allison, Lucinda C. Kennedy, Alexander B. Ewing, James
W. Ewing, Nancy E. Davis, Martha J. Kennedy, Benjamin D.
Ewing, and Shadrack N. Ewing;   great grand daughter Ann
Eliza Newbern (Latimer).   Executors: Nancy Smith, David
B. Smith, and Rial C. Jennings.   Witnesses: E. C. Witty
and Rial Penuel.   Recorded 19 February 1855.   (Pp. 182-
183)

JASPER R. ASHWORTH, SR. Will.   16 April 1853.   Heirs:
wife Cassander B. Ashworth; son Jasper R. Ashworth, Jr.;
daughter in law Adalaid Ashworth.   Recorded 1955.   (P.
183)

J. G. B. GRAVES Widow's Allotment.   18 December 1854.
Nancy Graves given her allotment for one year.   Recorded
20 February 1855.   (P. 187)

BURRELL JACKSON Will.   Heirs: brother Warren Jackson;   sister Mary Warren;   niece and nephew, Mary Jane
and William R. Jackson, the children of Robert Jackson;
and nephew William B. (Drenon).   Brother Coleman Jackson to
make no charges.   Joel Allgood, executor.   Recorded 11 July

1855. (Pp. 192-193)

WILLIAM ADAMS, SR. Will. 21 February 1855. Heirs:
all my children except William W. Adams who is to receive
my personal property. William W. Adams, Jr., executor.
Recorded 13 July 1855. (P. 194)

JOHN BARBEE Widow's Allotment. Recorded 26 July
1855. (P. 206)

WILLIAM JENKINS Will. February 1855. Heirs: wife
Jemima Jenkins; children G. W., (Lewis), W. H., E. H., L.,
H. T., and C. T. Jenkins, Jane and Nancy Castleman. Re-
corded 30 July 1855. (P. 209)

ISRAEL MOORE Will. 26 October 1854. Heirs: wife
Susanna F. Moore; children Jane, Frances, Jasper, Eliza-
beth B., Maria, Deca, Samuel, Sarah, and Marion Moore.
Recorded 30 July 1855. (P. 210)

THOMAS CALHOUN Will. Heirs: children Alexander J.
land in Missouri, P. B., Thomas P. all my interest in the
estate of William Johnston in Obion County, Samuel J. the
land given me by my father Samuel Calhoun; Lydia E. Calhoun, the widow of my son Ewing F. Calhoun and her children,
to wit, Ewing F., William C. and Mary O. Calhoun; daughter Nancy E. Calhoun's son Alexander C. Foster.; the
Theological Department of Cumberland University. Witness: Richard Beard. Recorded 31 July 1855. (Pp. 210-
212)

ARCHEBALD Y. HUFFMAN Will. 3 March 1855. Heirs:
wife Elizabeth Huffman; my three children. Recorded 1
August 1855. (P. 213)

DAVID BEARD Widow's Allotment. 8 May 1855. Lavina
Beard given her allotment. Recorded 1 August 1855. (P.
215)

JOHN PROVINE Will. 10 May 1855. Heirs: wife
Catherine Provine; children Alexander, William M., James
N., and John C. Provine, Nancy A. Hunt; Samuel F. minor
heir (being equal) to one of my children). Recorded 22
November 1855. (Pp. 227-228)

JAMES F. GEORGE Widow's Allotment. Recorded 11
December 1855. (P. 233)

WILLIAM SWINNEY Will. 23 July 1852. Heirs: wife
Elizabeth Swinney; children John J. and Sally T.; the
children of my daughter Emerilda V. Belcher, to wit,
William L., John A., Susan, and Marion J. Belcher. Recorded 11 December 1855. (P. 234)

J. HOWARD Will. 19 August 1853. Heirs: wife Sarah
R. Howard; son John K. Howard; other children. Recorded
10 December 1855. (P. 235)

FRANCES M. SELLARS Will. 3 May 1853. Heirs: brother Wesley M. Sellars; sister Caroline Puckett; sister
Mary F. Sellars. Recorded 10 December 1855. (P. 235)

RICHARD BRYAN Will. 19 June 1855. Heirs: wife Polly Bryan; children Nelson, Elizabeth M., Samuel W., John W., James B., and William R. Bryan. Recorded 10 December 1855. (P. 236)

JAMES H. JOHNSON Will. 9 June 1854. Heirs: my seven children by my first wife, to wit, Henry F., John W., Mathias, and James M. Johnson, Elizabeth Maddox, Nancy Wilburn, and Lavina Lain. I give the remainder to my wife, Susannah, and my youngest son, Samuel Johnson. I reserve one quarter of acre of land around my graveyard never to be sold. Witnesses: Henry Truett and Amos Martin. Recorded 10 December 1855. (P. 237)

M. A. BARRY Will. 2 October 1855. Heirs: my mother, brothers William F. and John Nichol Barry; cousin Isabella French; Mrs. Mitchell, a poor woman with four children. Recorded 10 December 1855. (P. 237)

EDWARD TRICE Will. 27 August 1855. Heirs: wife Lilly Trice; all my sons and daughters. Witnesses: E. Holloway and Levi Holloway, Jr. Recorded 10 December 1855. (P. 238)

HENRY T. CARTMELL Will. 12 July 1855. Heir: wife Adaline E. Cartmell. My wife is now pregnant. Father in law Alfred M. Hunt, executor. Recorded 10 December 1855. (P. 238)

JAMES B. DEBOW Will. 23 October 1855. Heirs: wife Evaline N. Debow; children. Recorded 10 December 1855. (P. 239)

WILLIAM W. HUDDLESTON Will. 11 September 1855. Heirs: my children when they come of age. Executors: Thomas L. Huddleston and E. S. Smith. Witnesses: J. W. Williams and Edward Donoho. Recorded 10 December 1855. (P. 240)

ELIZABETH BULLARD Sale. Recorded 13 December 1855. (P. 244)

MARGARET BODIN Sale. Recorded 14 November 1855. (P. 245)

NANCY DONNELL Will. 6 January 1851. Heirs: children Betsy, Nancy, John, Adlai Caruth, Rebecca, and Mary Donnell. Witnesses: John D. Donnell and John Donnell. Recorded 13 December 1855. (Pp. 241-246)

ISAAC EATHERLY Will. 16 February 1855. Heirs: wife Mary Eatherly; children William Eatherly, Margaret Webber; Sarah Bernard and her children except Mary Jane Lanius and Elizabeth Finney; children of my son, Andrew R. Eatherly, viz. Mary Ann, Mariah, and Andrew Eatherly; grandchildren Elizabeth Watkins and Wesley B. Wright. Recorded 1855. (P. 246)

JAMES A. HAWKINS Widow's Allotment. 20 July 1855. Jane Hawkins given her allotment. Recorded 17 December 1855. (P. 251)

HIGDON ROBERTSON Will. 28 October 1852. Heirs: wife Elizabeth W. Robertson; children George K., Thomas L., Nathaniel H., Lewis W., and Higdon Robertson, Martha W. Blacknall, and Susannah P. Tarver. Witnesses: John Holland and William Barton. Recorded 17 December 1855. (P. 253)

REBECCA SUBLETT Will. 18 September 1854. Heirs: children Elizabeth P., Rebecca M., and J. H. Puckett; son John B. Puckett's heirs; grandchildren Thomas and Juley Puckett. James Hamilton, executor. Witnesses: J. W. Hewgley and James Drennan. Recorded 17 December 1855. (P. 257)

NANCY PHILIPS Will. 4 December 1855. Heirs: children James R. Allen and wife Anna, John W. Philips, James M. Philips, James L. Patton and wife Mary, Sarah Jane Washburn, Robert C. Bass and wife Malissa, David Young and wife Margaret, A. Bryan and wife Elizabeth C., Ezekiel Bass and wife Catharine. Recorded 17 January 1856. (P. 261)

JOHN S. CHAPMAN Will. 8 June 1855. Heirs: wife Sarah A. Chapman. Recorded 17 January 1856. (P. 262)

MOSES RILEY Will. 3 January 1856. Heirs: wife Margaret Riley; our child, Mary Frances Riley. Executor: friend Dr. Joseph M. Anderson. Recorded 17 January 1856. (P. 262)

JOSEPH MOORE Widow's Allotment. 16 November 1855. Susannah Moore given her allotment. Recorded 17 June 1856. (P. 264)

WILLIAM CARVER Will. 17 August 1855. Heirs: wife Annie Carver; children Eunice, Archebald, Samuel, and Elizabeth S. Carver. William L. Clemmons, executor. Witnesses: Jeptha Clemmons and Willain F. Lain. Recorded 17 April 1856. (P. 268)

WILLIAM W. CALHOUN Will. 10 December 1855. Heirs: wife Sarah W. Calhoun; children. Executor: friend Hezekiah Reaves. Recorded 17 April 1856. (P. 270)

WILLIAM N. STONE Will. 13 March 1856. Heirs: son John W. Stone; daughters Martha M. and Elizabeth P. Sullivan. Witnesses: John Holland and Eli Sullivan. Recorded 21 April 1856. (P. 280)

T. T. ELLIS Widow's Allotment. Nancy Ellis given her allotment. Recorded 22 April 1856. (P. 281)

DAVID BILLINGS Will. 17 September 1855. Heirs: wife Fannie Billings; ?children James Carson and Christina Billings; brothers and sisters. Witnesses: James F. Organ and Haynie Thompson. Recorded 22 April 1856. (P. 282)

JOHN DONALDSON Widow's Allotment. 24 March 1856. Elizabeth Donaldson given her allotment. Recorded 1856. (P. 285)

118

WILLS & INVENTORIES 1853-1858

JOHN McFARLAND Will. 15 April 1856. Heirs: wife Sally McFarland; children John and James H. McFarland, Dicy Wynne; daughter Matilda Eskew's children; daughter Nancy Brigg's children. Executors: A. G. Wynne and J. H. McFarland. Witnesses: James Hamilton and John Kelly. Recorded 16 June 1856. (Pp. 288-289)

THOMAS HARLIN Sale. Recorded 30 June 1856. (Pp. 295-301)

R. B. JENNINGS Sale. 30 September 1856. Uriah Jennings, administrator. Recorded 30 June 1856. (Pp. 301-302)

TABITHA HEARN Sale. Nathaniel Murry, administrator. Recorded 1 July 1856. (P. 302)

WILLIAM CARVER Sale. 21 February 1856. Recorded 23 September 1856. (Pp. 303-306)

JESSE A. LINK Sale. 27 May 1856. John J. Link, administrator. Recorded 23 September 1856. (Pp. 306-307)

JOSIAH WOOD Widow's Allotment. Recorded 23 September 1856. (P. 307)

F. M. DAVIS Will. 4 January 1856. Heirs: brothers J. F., W. C., William, John, and R. A. Davis; sister Susan Curd; sister Elizabeth Donalson's children to receive nothing; Philip C. Lanius and his wife, Docia. Philip C. Lanius, executor. Recorded 24 September 1856. (P. 308)

NANCY SPARKS Sale. Recorded 26 September 1856. (P. 311)

J. C. PARRISH Inventory. Recorded 29 September 1856. (P. 316)

ABRAHAM HUGUELY Will. 18 June 1849. Heirs: children Margaret Ann Haraldson, Elizabeth Lain, George W. Huguely, John W. Huguely, Lewis Huguely, Nancy Huguely, Sally Huguely, Almedia Huguely; grandchildren Augustus Huguely, Henretty Huguely, and Alemedia Bodily; the heirs of son Alfred S. Huguely. If Elizabeth Lain is not living, then to her daughter, Sarah J. Eatherly. Executors: John H. Huguely and William Young. Witnesses: John Crudup and Wilie Alford

ABRAHAM HUGUELY Codicil. 29 September 1851. Sally Huguely's part to go to J. W. Huguely.

ABRAHAM HUGUELY Second Codicil. 10 February 1854. Heirs: daughters Nancy Young, Sarah Hamilton, Almedia Bodily, Margaret Ann Harelson, and Elizabeth Lain. William L. Young to be trustee for Almedia Bodily in place of Samuel Hamilton. Recorded 1 October 1856. (Pp. 318-320)

JAMES TIPTON Will. Heirs: wife; children Franklin J., Newton J., Rebecca, Joshua H., William, and Margaret J. Tipton, Sarah Hall, Mary Bumpass, and Elizabeth Whitson.

Executors: Elias Hall and Franklin J. Tipton. Witnesses:
H. B. Vaughan and Joseph Gray. Recorded 2 October 1856.
(Pp. 321-322)

JAMES McFARLAND Will. Heirs: wife Dicy McFarland;
daughters Jane Hamilton, N. Peyton, D. A. Whitsett, S.
Swingley, Frances Williamson, and Martha S. McFarland;
James P. McFarland; grandson John P. McFarland. Executors: James Hamilton and L. E. Williamson. Witnesses:
Edmond Jackson and William B. Guthrie. Recorded 2 October
1856. (Pp. 322-323)

DANIEL RICHMOND Sale. Recorded 23 October 1856.
(Pp. 324-336)

JAMES A. TAYLOR Will. 9 April 1856. Heirs: wife
Sophia S. C. Taylor; children Moses L. H., Thomas, Mar-
tha L., William B., and James A. Taylor. Executor: Sophia
S. C. Taylor. Witnesses: Sterling B. Peyton and James S.
Cartmell. Recorded 23 October 1856. (Pp. 336-338)

W. N. STONE Sale. 14 June 1856. W. P. Sullivan,
executor. Recorded 28 October 1856. (P. 340)

ANDERSON COX Widow's Allotment. 10 June 1856. Sally
C. Cox given her allotment. Recorded 28 October 1856.
(P. 341)

WILLIAM JEWELL Will. 24 May 1856. At home. Heirs:
wife Eleanor Jewell; my wife's two children; my child-
ren by my first wife; son J. T. Jewell; daughter Nancy
J. Jewell; grandson Smith S. Jewell. Executors: Eleanor
Jewell and John Putman. Witnesses: B. W. Smith and W. H.
McConikin. Recorded 28 October 1856. (P. 342)

ANDREW THOMPSON Will. 26 November 1853. Heirs:
wife Amelia A. Thompson; mother Polly Thompson; son
Dudley H. Thompson; brothers Samuel P. and Matthew N.
Thompson; sister Nancy E. Tribble. Executors: Samuel P.
Thompson and Matthew N. Thompson. Witnesses: Jordan
Stokes and Ro Hallum. Recorded 28 October 1856. (Pp. 342-
344)

DABNEY TATUM Sale. Recorded 29 October 1856. (Pp.
346-347)

CHARLES RICH Will. 31 March 1851. Heirs: children William Rich, Elizabeth Wilson and her husband Robert
Wilson. Witnesses: Anthony Owen and (Drura) McKee. Recorded 30 October 1856. (P. 348)

JOSEPH H. GATTON Will. 28 May 1856. Heirs: wife
Elizabeth Gatton; sons William A., Hiram, and Joseph W.
Gatton; daughters Elviry Chapman and Elizabeth Ann
McKee; daughter Synthia Moore's children. Joseph W. Gat-
ton, executor. Witnesses: Isaac Mullinax and Jacob A.
Jennings. Recorded 31 October 1856. (Pp. 348-349)

THOMAS S. SMITH Will. 24 April 1856. Heirs: I
hereby ratify the will of my wife, Peggy Smith, by giving
our sons, James C. and John S. Smith, the land that was

left by her father, James Cannon;   other daughters M. W.
C. Powell and Martha Garrison. Witnesses: J. H. Lillard
and Edmond Olliver. Recorded 31 October 1856. (Pp. 349-
350)

JACKSON VANHOOZER Will. 30 June 1856. Heirs: wife
Nancy Vanhoozer;   three children Mary Elizabeth Eliza,
John, and Frederick Vanhoozer. Isham F. Davis, executor.
Witnesses: J. B. Vivrett and J. F. Vanhoozer. Recorded
12 November 1856. (P. 356)

JAMES A. LINK Widow's Allotment. Elizabeth Link
given her allotment. Recorded 12 November 1856. (P.
356)

JOHN A. ROBINSON Will. 25 July 1853. Heirs: wife
Lucinda Robinson;   three children Polly Ann, James Pitts,
and Benjamin Wit Robinson. Executors: Benjamin Prichard
and brother Stephen Robinson. Witnesses: Edmund Gilliam
and William Arbuckle. Recorded 12 November 1856. (P.
357)

WILLIAM H. VANTREASE Will. 28 August 1856. Heirs:
wife Isabella Vantrease;   children. Executors: Isabella
Vantrease and brother A. J. Vantrease. Recorded 12 November 1856. (P. 358)

JAMES CHAMBERS Will. 3 August 1856. Heirs: wife
Susannah Chambers;   children. Executors: James D. White
and brother John Chambers. Witnesses: Samuel Calhoun
and S. B. Barr. Recorded 12 November 1856. (P. 359)

EVERETT BRADLEY Widow's Allotment. 30 September
1856. Ann Bradley given her allotment. Recorded 18 November 1856. (P. 366)

JAMES CARSON Sale. Recorded 15 November 1856. (P.
367)

ROBERT H. COLLIER Will. 25 September 1855. Heirs:
wife Sarah Ann Collier;   children Robert V. Collier, Aley
Patterson, Adaline W. Woodral, Charlotte C. Cotther,
Matilda Tipton, and Frances C. McDaniel;   other children,
Albert H. Collier, Tilman L. Collier, and Elizabeth
Parker, had been given their share earlier. Executors:
Vines L. Collier and Daniel Glenn. Witnesses: Daniel
Glenn, James F. Tipton, and Josiah J. Wood. Recorded 19
November 1856. (P. 368)

JOHN R. WILSON Will. 8 August 1856. Heirs: wife
Elizabeth Wilson to receive the lands I received by her
at the time of our marriage;   my two daughters Margaret J.
Eatherly and Nancy J. Wilson;   four sons;   daughter Elizabeth E. (Baijn) deceased children. The graveyard is not
to be sold. Executors: son Andrew R. Wilson and John
Crudup. Witnesses: John W. Tate and Zachariah Tate. Recorded 20 November 1856. (P. 369)

WRIGHT HICKMAN Will. 22 August 1856. Heirs: wife
Sally Hickman;   children George, Martha Ann, Rebecca,
Polly T., and S. B. Hickman. Henry Truett, executor.

Witnesses: R. S. Wilbourn and J. W. Rowlett. Recorded 20 November 1856. (P. 370)

WILLIAM C. DAVIS Will. 21 August 1856. Heirs: brothers and sisters Anderson L. Davis, Caroline A. Tally, America A. Smith, John W. Davis, and James H. Davis; Mary L. Davis. A. L. Davis, executor. Witnesses: William L. Alsup and S. C. Hamilton. Recorded 20 November 1856. (P. 371)

ABRAHAM A. MASSEY Will. 28 September 1856. Heirs: wife Elizabeth Jane Massey; children. H. Ragland, executor. Witnesses: Peter Thompson and Nathaniel Murray. Recorded 20 November 1856. (P. 372)

DAWSON HANCOCK Will. 4 November 1852. Heirs: wife; children Lesley, Nelson D., Dawson A., and William Hancock, Nancy Crutchfield; deceased daughter Priscilla's children; deceased son James Hancock's children. Executors: sons Nelson D. and William Hancock. Recorded 21 November 1856. (P. 374)

ROBERT McCAFFREY Will. 22 March 1844. Heirs: children Alsey Johnson, Levi McCaffrey, George Hays and Franky his wife, Elizabeth Johnson and William her husband, and Sarah McCaffrey; granddaughter Susan, a daughter of Leanna. I will to Polly Wallace one half share to be equally divided among my three grandchildren and her children by her first husband, to wit, John, William, and Nancy Moore. Levi McCaffrey, executor. Witnesses: Uriah Jennings, James Garther, and William Jones. Recorded 21 November 1856. (Pp. 375-376)

RUTHERFORD RUTLAND Sale. Recorded 18 December 1856. (Pp. 380-382)

JESSE JOHNSON Will. 23 August 1856. Heirs: Lovick Dies; Matilda Dies; Jesse Dies; niece Martha Smithwick; sister in law Elizabeth Johnson; sisters Sarah Gibson, Pheba Gray, Mary A. Shelton, Frances (Walker), Susannah Parkhurst, and Elizabeth Rutherford; brothers James, John A., and Samuel Johnson. Lovick Dies, executor. Witnesses: S. B. Barr and H. B. Mooningham. Recorded 20 December 1856. (P. 386)

MARGARET ANN MASSEY Will. 22 November 1856. Heirs: my interest in grandfather Hearn's estate to go to my brothers and sisters, to wit, George W., Benjamin L., Eli M., Elizabeth J., Mary E., Martha M., and Nancy M. Massey. Edwin Berry, executor. Witnesses: Martha Thompson, H. Ragland, and Edwin Berry. Recorded 20 December 1856. (P. 387)

ELIZABETH McCLAIN Will. 30 June 1856. Heirs: children Martha D. Swift and Polly D. Vivrett; daughter Parthena E. McClain's daughter; daughter of son Alexander F. McClain; sons of son W. P. McClain, to wit, Fitz-James and James H. McClain. Executor: son Josiah McClain. Witnesses: N. Green, Jr. and E. A. Foster. Recorded 21 March 1857. (P. 388)

ISAAC GREEN Widow's Allotment. 5 November 1856. Elizabeth Green given her allotment. Recorded 27 March 1857. (P. 394)

ISAIAH ALLISON Will. 1 December 1856. Heir: wife Anna Allison. Edmund Gilliam, executor. Witnesses: John A. Cason and Fountain W. Cheek. Recorded 27 March 1857. (P. 395)

THOMAS TELFORD Will. 24 February 1857. Heirs: children Jane, Margaret A., Hugh, and Robert A. Telford, Easter H. Cauthon, and Nancy Markham; granddaughter Nancy C. Williams; nephew T. C. Telford. I am guardian of John Markham. T. C. Telford, executor. Witnesses: James M. Brown, William C. Rutland, and G. W. Telford. Recorded 16 April 1857. (P. 411)

HARTWELL MABRY Widow's Allotment. 25 November 1856. Mary Mabry given her allotment. Recorded 21 April 1857. (P. 419)

JOSEPH M. PEYTON Will. 3 February 1857. Heir: wife Elizabeth Peyton. Lived in Lebanon, but owned land in the 22nd District. John Kelly, executor. Witnesses: Samuel Golladay and Thomas J. Stratton. Recorded 22 April 1857. (Pp. 423-424)

SAMUEL ALSUP Will. 8 April 1848. Heir: William L. Alsup. Executors: William L. Alsup and J. J. Alsup. Witnesses: L. R. Jennings, Daniel James, and E. C. Jennings. Recorded 4 December 1857. (Pp. 428-429)

GEORGE BROWN Noncupative Will. 26 December 1857. Heirs: wife; sons Richard and Daniel Brown; all his children. Richard Brown, executor. Witnesses: E. B. Martin and Martin Underwood. Recorded 10 December 1857. (P. 429)

THOMPSON MACE Inventory. Recorded 11 December 1857. (Pp. 431-433)

ROBERT M. DONNELL Will. 17 March 1857. Heirs: wife Jane F. Donnell; children. Jane F. Donnell, executrix. Witnesses: Peter Thompson and John Thomas Bass. Recorded 11 December 1857. (Pp. 433-434)

STEPHEN GOODMAN Widow's Allotment. 8 December 1855. Malinda Goodman given her allotment. Recorded 11 December 1857. (P. 440)

WILLIAM PALMER Will. 26 July 1849. Heirs: wife Sarah Palmer; children Margaret Palmer and Susan Reese; older children. Their grandmother is still living. Executor: son John Palmer and Sarah Palmer. Witnesses: H. A. Goodall and G. W. Edwards. Recorded 15 December 1857. (P. 441)

WILLIAM H. HARDWICK Sale. 27 June 1857. Recorded 16 December 1857. (P. 441)

SAMUEL JOHNSON Will. Heirs: wife Elizabeth Johnson; children; heirs of J. M. Johnson deceased to receive one ·

123

dollar; heirs of Lewis Glenn and Mary his wife, both deceased to receive one dollar; Mildred Ann Walker former wife of William Johnson deceased to receive one dollar; Samuel Johnson, son of William Johnson to receive an equal share. Lovick Dies, executor. Recorded 8 June 1856. (P. 444)

JOHN HESSEY Will. 9 June 1855. Heirs: children Anny A. Murry, Mary A. Wright, Rena Murry, John H. Hessey, James Hessey, and the heirs of Margaret Haralson. James Hamilton, executor. Recorded 17 December 1857. (P. 445)

JOHN MARKS Will. 2 June 1857. Heirs: wife Elizabeth Marks; infant child Martha Jane Marks. John S. Haley, executor. Recorded 17 December 1857. (P. 446)

SAMUEL E. MARRS Will. 16 July 1857. 19th District. Heirs: Robert A. Marrs, William D. Marrs, Martha Ann Edwards, and Rachel F. Climer who are my brothers and sisters; niece Martha Jane Henry. Robert A. Marrs to receive the land that belonged to my father, Alexander Marrs. He is to see to my mother. Robert A. Marrs, executor. Witnesses: Samuel C. Anderson, James H. Shannon, and Thomas Dellis. Recorded 15 February 1858. (P. 457)

ELIZABETH FERRELL Will. 17 December 1856. Heirs: children Isabella Adaline, Harriet Jane, Martha M., Benjamin B., and John B. Ferrell. Also, my married children J. W. Ferrell, Nancy Hatcher, Elizabeth Stephens, and William L. Ferrell. Witnesses: Jordan Johnson and E. C. Tally. Recorded 16 February 1858. (P. 458)

ELIZABETH McHENRY Will. 11 July 1857. Heirs: children James and Fannie McHenry, Pollie Goodin; granddaughters Elizabeth Fouch and Diretha McHenry. James McHenry, executor. Recorded 17 February 1858. (Pp. 458-459)

JEMIMA CARR Will. 10 September 1857. Heirs: grandchildren Mary Elizabeth, Nancy, and Philip S. Johnson; daughter Martha J. Carr. Dabney Carr, executor. Recorded 17 February 1858. (P. 459)

BENJAMIN GRAVES Will. 13 March 1856. Heirs: wife Mildred Graves; children; Ann Jones; grandchildren Fountain Hester and Savannah Richard Hester. Recorded 18 February 1858. (P. 460)

PRESTON HENDERSON Will. 13 September 1854. Heirs: wife Dorothy Henderson; children Harmon L. Henderson, Mary A. M. Blankenship, Henrietta Phillips, John B. Henderson, Jeremiah T. Henderson, Robert H. Henderson, Marsalite S. E. Henderson. Executors: Harmon L. Henderson and James A. Blankenship. Recorded 20 February 1858. (P. 463)

JOHN TELFORD Will. 16 September 1857. Heirs: children Susan E. Hallum, Samuel, and James H. Telford. The sons to receive my share of the estate of Joseph Telford. Recorded 20 February 1858. (P. 464)

JOHN E. DANCE Will. 14 December 1853. Heirs:
pephew John Russell Dance and niece Mary Elizabeth Dance
who are the son and daughter of my brother, Drury Dance.
I expect to live with my friend, William H. Doak. Recorded
20 February 1858. (P. 465)

WILLIAM C. ROBBINS Widow's Allotment. 14 September
1857. Susan Robbins given her allotment. Recorded 20
February 1858. (P. 465)

FRANCES PALMER Will. 29 November 1857. Heirs:
Bethlehem Church to receive $1000 to be handed over to
William K. Palmer; sisters Victoria Philips and Margaret
Palmer; sister Susan Reese's children, to wit, Thomas,
Nancy Margaret, Sarah, William, and Harriet Reese; sis-
ter Sarah Murphy's son, Francis Murphy; sister Martha
Bennett's children, to wit, William and Charles Oliver
Bennett; brother John Palmer to receive for the benefit
of James Tate. John Palmer, executor. Witnesses: S. E.
Belcher and J. Harris. Recorded 22 February 1858. (P.
467)

JOSHUA LESTER Inventory. Recorded 26 February 1858.
(P. 471)

ELIJAH TRUETT Will. 20 March 1852. Heirs: wife Sarah Truett; children Henry Truett, Rispah Bagwell, Nancy Fields, Elizabeth Bond, Ann Jones, Margaret Clemmons, Rachiel Clemmons, and Sarah Martin. Executors: son Henry Truett and son in law Jeptha Clemmons. Witnesses: R. B. Castleman, E. Holloway, and Samuel C. Anderson. Recorded 24 August 1858. (Pp. 1-3)

ELI M. HARRIS Will. 28 December 1857. Heirs: children: Mary P., John G., William W., Robert E., and Finis A. Harris, and Jane Hamlet. B. W. Harris, executor. Witnesses: D. B. Winchester and J. P. Harris. Recorded 24 August 1858. (P. 4)

EDWIN CLEMMONS Will. 21 December 1857. Heirs: wife Nancy Clemmons; sons Joseph A., Robert E., Rufus P., and William E. Clemmons; granddaughter Lemons. Executor: brother William L. Clemmons. Witnesses: Wiley Eskew and B. J. Eskew. Recorded 24 August 1858. (P. 5)

STERLING and LUCRETIA TARPLEY Sale. Recorded 16 November 1857. (Pp. 15-16)

JOHN ADAMS Sale. 27 November 1857. Nancy Adams, administratrix. Recorded 20 October 1858. (Pp. 16-17)

THOMPSON MACE Will. 16 February 1854. Heirs: wife Susannah Mace; children Thompson, Brice, Susan Emma, Martha T., and Mary Thompson Mace; Mary Buckley. Also, older children Elizabeth Russell and Phinias Mace. Rev. John Kelly, executor. Witnesses: John K. Howard, Joseph Mottley, and J. S. McClain. Recorded 24 October 1858. (Pp. 17-20)

JOHN W. ANDERSON Will. 3 April 1856. Heirs: wife Jane Anderson; children. H. L. Bass, executor. Witnesses: L. N. M. Cook and M. P. Anderson. Recorded 9 November 1858. (P. 24)

HENRY MOSER Will. 28 September 1857. Heirs: wife Elizabeth Moser; Albert, Pleasant, Henry, and Berry Moser; Elizabeth Patterson. Berry Moser, executor. Witnesses: Edmund Gilliam and Archibald A. Owen. Recorded 17 November 1858. (P. 30)

✔ CHARLES T. JENKINS Will. 27 May 1857. Fairfax County, Virginia. Heirs: children Charles T., Lelen, and Mason Jenkins, and Nancy Bridges. Witnesses: John Epperson, C. C. H. Reston, Richard Hunt, James Donaldson, and Thomas H. Nelson. Recorded 3 December 1858. (Pp. 37-38)

G. B. JOHNSON Widow's Allotment. 19 February 1858. Lockey Johnson given her allotment. Recorded 23 November 1858. (P. 38)

WILLIAM SEARCY Will. 8 February 1858. Heir: wife Nancy Searcy. She may sell three acres of the land that I purchased of Louis Manor, lying next to Mrs. Manor, the wife of Louis Manor as a homestead and at her death to go to Louis Manor, the son of Louis Manor now deceased.

WILLS & INVENTORIES   1858-1863

James Holmes, executor. Witnesses: D. A. McEacham, James Birchett, and John D. Allen. Recorded 26 November 1858. (P. 41)

NANCY PARRISH Will. 26 February 1858. Heirs: children Samuel E. Parrish and wife Mary Jane E., Howell G., William K., Eliza F., Elizabeth S., Joseph J. Parrish, and Margaret Byram; the heirs of Mary Jane Criswell. Executors: William K. Parrish and Samuel E. Parrish. Recorded 30 November 1858. (P. 42)

FRANCES HOBBS Will. 6 December 1857. Heirs: children Thomas L., Benjamin B., Mary J., Winny T., Lavina S., and Emily J. Hobbs, and Roxalana C. Riggin. Green Hobbs, executor. Witnesses: T. A. Swindell and James M. Johnson. Recorded 30 November 1858. (P. 45)

RICHARD J. CRUTCHFIELD Inventory. Recorded 2 December 1858. (P. 46)

JOHN F. KITTRELL Will. 5 December 1857. Heirs: wife Adaline D. Kittrell; four children. Executor: brother M. B. Kittrell. Witnesses: S. E. Belcher, Sr. and T. M. Edwards. Recorded 16 December 1858. (P. 49)

BUCHANAN JAMES Widow's Allotment. 22 March 1858. Recorded 16 December 1858. (P. 50)

JOHN LESTER Widow's Allotment. Mary Lester given her allotment. Recorded 17 December 1858. (P. 50)

JUDIDAH H. STEEL Will. 28 August 1857. Heirs: children Hiram G., Amanda, James, and Thomas J. Steel, and Isabell Binkley; deceased son Andrew Steel's son, John Andrew Steel. Witnesses: James R. Gleaves and F. Castleman. Recorded 4 February 1859. (P. 58)

J. W. WYNNE Widow's Allotment. 18 May 1858. Recorded 14 March 1859. (P. 62)

ROBERT GOODMAN Will. 19 January 1859. Heirs: wife Rhoda Goodman; heirs of Robert Goodman, Jr. and Albert Goodman's heirs. I do not remember the names of these heirs. James Thompkins, executor. Recorded 14 March 1858. (Pp. 62-63)

JOHN A. MAJOR Will. 28 May 1858. Heirs: wife; children; youngest daughter Nancy E. Eugenia Major; William Page. Samuel D. Major, executor. Recorded 16 March 1858. (P. 66)

JOHN CLEMMONS Will. 4 June 1858. Heirs: wife Polly Clemmons; children. William Clemmons, executor. Recorded 21 March 1859. (P. 75)

JAMES SPEARS Widow's Allotment. Recorded 21 March 1859. (P. 76)

REBECCA GWYNN Will. 3 November 1856. Heirs: children. Executors: Anderson Gwynn and S. F. Hooker. Witnesses: V. C. Haralson and J. H. Smith. Recorded 24 March 1858. (P. 84)

127

ISAAC CARVER Will. 31 May 1858. Heirs: wife; children Isaac N. Carver and wife Mary Ann, William H., George W., Henry, Rachael, and Mary Carver, Frances Clements. Recorded 24 March 1859. (Pp. 86-87)

HENRY ARRINGTON Will. 2 June 1857. Heirs: children Emma Carter, McHeny Bradley, Joel Arrington, Albert Arrington, Priscilla Biles, Thomas, Calvin, and William Arrington. Recorded 26 March 1856. (P. 88)

NICHOLAS VANTREASE Will. 23 August 1858. Heirs: wife Elizabeth Ann Vantrease; children Mary Ann Moore, Nicholas Dillard, Jacob, Andrew Price, Elizabeth, Lucinda, and Tennessee Vantrease, and Catharine Jones. James P. Doss, executor. Recorded 31 March 1859. (Pp. 90-91)

CATO BASS Widow's Allotment. 19 August 1858. Martha Bass given her allotment. Recorded 1 April 1859. (P. 91)

ED R. BENNER Sale. Recorded 1 April 1859. (Pp. 91-92)

WEBB BLOODWORTH Will. 25 October 1856. Heirs: wife; children Manerva Cocks, Lucinda, Elisabeth, Mary, Webb, Smith, and William Bloodworth; grandchildren Caroline, Malinda, and Elizabeth Tipton. Recorded 29 April 1859. (Pp. 104-105)

WILLIAM H. WHITE Will. Heirs: children Nancy Castleman, Sally Davis, Jesse and John White. Executors: Berryman White and Samuel Smith. Recorded 12 May 1859. (Pp. 110-112)

NATHAN GLENN Will. 19 October 1850. Heirs: wife Catharine Glenn; children; daughter Elizabeth and her husband C. W. Hazard. Recorded 13 May 1858. (Pp. 112-113)

CADER BASS Will. 7 April 1858. Heirs: wife; son H. L. Bass; deceased daughter Martha's children. Witnesses: L. M. N. Cook and Asa Jackson, Jr. Recorded 12 May 1859. (P. 114)

ROBERT and FRANCES BOND Division. 13 November 1858. Heirs: M. M., M. J., M. E., and M. A. Bond. Recorded 21 May 1859. (P. 128)

✓ DAVID BRIDGES Will. 30 November 1857. Heirs: wife Nancy Bridges; children Julia A., Mary J., John Bridges; John Bridges' three children Berrygrove, David, and Jonathan Bridges. Recorded 23 May 1859. (P. 131)

JOHN H. DRAKE Will. 6 June 1854. Formerly of Sumner County. Heirs: wife Caladonia Drake; children Martha H. and Benjamin M. Drake. Witnesses: William L. Martin, John F. Doak, and William W. Blythe. Recorded 25 May 1859. (Pp. 136-138)

WILLIAM WILLIS Inventory. 16 October 1858. Recorded 25 May 1859. (P. 138)

BENJAMIN L. TUCKER Sale. Recorded 25 May 1859. (Pp.

138-139)

THOMAS VAUGHN Sale. 14 January 1859. Recorded 27 May 1859. (P. 142)

B. A. RUCKER Widow's Allotment. Recorded 16 April 1859. (P. 150)

S. N. ROSS Widow's Allotment. S. H. Ross given her allotment. Recorded 16 June 1859. (P. 150)

ELIZABETH LINK Sale. 10 May 1859. Recorded 15 July 1859. (P. 153)

GEORGE LASH Widow's Allotment. 11 April 1859. Ellen Lash given her allotment. Recorded 15 July 1859. (P. 158)

FERGUS S. HARRIS Will. 2 June 1857. Heirs: wife Nancy Harris; children B. W., James S., William, and John P. Harris, Elizabeth Johnson. B. W. Harris, executor. Recorded 15 July 1859. (Pp. 161-162)

WILLIAM B. SAUNDERS Will. 14 November 1858. Heirs: wife Betty Saunders; children William Hallum, John Bowers, James Yancey, and Samuel A. Saunders; father in law William Hallum. Witnesses: L. C. Holt, W. B. Campbell, and W. R. Baylek. Recorded 16 July 1859. (P. 162)

ELIZABETH SCRUGGS Will. 31 May 1859. Heirs: children Elizabeth P. Brown, Martha Killingsworth, and Harriet Hamlett; grandchildren Flemming and (Hopard) Scruggs; heirs of Ann Hail; heirs of C. C. Scruggs; and heirs of D. H. Scruggs. Recorded 16 July 1859. (P. 163)

BENJAMIN WARREN Will. 21 June 1859. Heirs: wife Prudence Warren; children Benjamin Warren, Jane Cason, the wife of Samuel S. Cason, Mary F. Taylor, Nancy Afflack, the wife of James Afflack, and Katharine Kitrell, the wife of Samuel J. Kitrell. Executors: sons William G. Warren and John A. Warren. Witnesses: W. D. Smith and H. B. Mooningham. Recorded 16 July 1859. (Pp. 164-165)

WILLIAM H. HARDWICK Widow's Allotment. Recorded 20 July 1859. (P. 172)

WILLIAM L. WIER Will. 22 November 1858. Heir: mother Mary B. Wier. J. L. Bell, executor. Witnesses: William B. Pursley and Johnathan Whited. Recorded 5 August 1859. (Pp. 176-177)

JOHN H. NEAL Will. 14 June 1859. Heirs: wife Phanarita Neal; children Edward M., James A., Nancy M., Elizabeth C., and Samuel S. Neal. My wife to have use of the land that came to her from her father, Benjamin Johnson. Mrs. Susan D. Johnson to live with my wife. Executor: brother in law Joseph T. Manson. Recorded 14 June 1859. (Pp. 177-178)

JAMES H. MOXLEY Will. 23 June 1859. Heirs: wife Nancy L. Moxley; children Martha Ann, Richard N., Mary L., Joseph P., and John W. Moxley. Richard Moxley, executor. Witnesses: John F. Doak and T. H. Shannon. Recorded

7 August 1859. (P. 179)

JOHN HANKINS Will. 16 March 1857. Heirs: mother Sarah G. Hankins; brothers and sisters. M. C. Hankins, executor. Recorded 15 August 1859. (P. 180)

WILLIAM F. M. ALSUP Widow's Allotment. Recorded 15 August 1859. (P. 180)

ANN JEMIMA BAIRD Will. 22 June 1859. Heirs: mother Lucinda Baird; brothers Robert A., Andrew J., and Jerome R. Baird. William J. Baird, executor. Recorded 15 August 1859. (P. 181)

MARY TRACY Sale. 26 April 1859. Recorded 22 September 1859. (Pp. 183-184)

NANCY JACKSON Will. 12 October 1853. Heirs: children Manerva Underwood, John B., D. F., Thomas B., Julia, Lucy D., (Theareda) James, Charles M., Sarah A., and Mary C. Jackson. Recorded 18 October 1859. (P. 185)

C. F. NEAL Widow's Allotment. 12 May 1859. Emily Neal given her allotment. Recorded 20 October 1859. (P. 189)

J. C. GOODMAN Widow's Allotment. 13 September 1859. Mary J. Goodman given her allotment. Recorded 1859. (P. 196)

JAMES ADAMS Sale. 14 April 1859. Recorded 26 November 1859. (Pp. 202-203)

JOSHUA PARTLOW Inventory. 16 November 1859. One eighth interest in 160 acres. W. E. Denton, administrator. Recorded 16 December 1859. (P. 205)

MOSES WOOLEN Widow's Allotment. 27 September 1859. Elizabeth L. Woolen given her allotment. Recorded 20 December 1859. (Pp. 218-219)

JOSEPH PATTON Widow's Allotment. 20 December 1859. Margaret Patton given her allotment. Recorded 23 January 1860. (P. 219)

BARNEY B. TIPTON Will. 28 July 1856. Heirs: wife Harriet C. Tipton; niece Prunella Bridges, the daughter of Allen H. Bridges. Harriet C. Tipton, executrix. Recorded 24 January 1860. (P. 222)

LITTLEBERRY W. WHITE Will. 23 November 1859. Heirs: wife Martha J. White; children. Executors: son John C. White and son in law Joseph T. Manson. Recorded 24 January 1860. (P. 223)

JOHN EATHERLY, SR. Will. 30 June 1856. Heirs: children Turner Bynum and John C. Eatherly, and Dollie Caroline Young, the wife of P. B. Young. Turner Bynum Eatherly, executor. Recorded 14 February 1860. (P. 228)

ROBERT B. SHANKS Will. 14 January 1860. Heirs: Elizabeth West for waiting on me; Wiley and Delia A. West, the children of William P. and Elizabeth A. West; Albert J.

130

West; John West; and Mary West. William P. West, executor. Recorded 14 February 1860. (P. 229)

ELIZABETH SMITH Will. 28 June 1858. Heirs: brothers
Shadreck C. and D. B. Smith; sisters Mary D. Grissom,
Martha A. Ramsey, Drucilla E. Jennings, and Rebecca Jane
Puckett; children of deceased sister McAdow, to wit, J. W.
McAdow and Ann Marshall; children of deceased sister
Nancy Ewing, to wit, Sarah Allison, Lucinda Kennedy, Mar-
tha J. Kennedy, Nancy E. Davis, A. S., A. B., J. W., B. D.,
and Shadrack N. Ewing. Executors: James F. Puckett and
E. S. Smith. Recorded 16 February 1860. (P. 230)

MARY COUCH Will. 5 February 1858. Heirs: children
W. G. and Martha Couch; grandson Elvis Perry Couch. Mar-
tha Couch to receive from the estate of my brother, George
Clark. W. G. Couch, executor. Recorded 6 July 1860.
(Pp. 236-237)

JOHN W. KING Widow's Allotment. Recorded 24 February
1860. (P. 238)

JAMES SHORTER Widow's Allotment. Recorded 28 February 1860. (P. 244)

JAMES CLEMMONS, JR. Will. Heirs: wife; children.
William D. Hancock, executor. Recorded 22 June 1860.
(P. 252)

WILLIAM DUDLEY Widow's Allotment. 24 March 1860.
Nancy Dudley given her allotment. Recorded 26 June 1860.
(Pp. 252-253)

NANCY IRBY Will. 18 September 1858. Heirs: grandson Francis Marion Irby. M. T. Bennett, executor. Recorded 9 July 1860. (P. 255)

WILLIAM B. GILL Will. 17 July 1858. Heirs: children who are still with me and those who have left; daughters Susan and Larana Jane Gill. William Swann, executor.
Recorded 9 July 1860. (P. 256)

JACOB S. HORN Will. 27 February 1860. Heirs: children Mary K. and Viola P. Horn. If they are dead, then to
sister Rebecca P. Payne and her daughters, to wit, Rebecca
E. and Mary K. Payne. Recorded 9 July 1860. (P. 260)

ELI B. EASON Will. 27 March 1860. Heirs: son
Lunis W. Eason; daughter Nancy D. Bowen; children of
Joseph C. and Nancy Bowen, to wit, Phebe E. and George R.
Bowen; grandchildren Richard F., William, Casander, Vici
F., and James F. Eason, Nancy J., Sarah C., Thomas J.,
Elizabeth S., Martha, and Mary A. Rye. The grandchildren
are to receive the $200 owned me by John W. Rye. Executors:
W. T. Robertson and John W. Rye. Recorded 9 July 1860.
(P. 261)

JOSHUA WOOLEN Inventory. 23 May 1860. Recorded 10
July 1860. (P. 264)

GEORGE HAMILTON Widow's Allotment. 18 March 1858.
Rebecca Hamilton given her allotment. Recorded 10 June

1860. (P. 266)

WILLIAM R. PARRISH Will. 10 April 1860. Heirs: wife Tursa Emeline Parrish; children; children Francis, William Lowrey, John David, Nancy Caroline, and Sallie Ann Parrish. Joseph N. Anderson, executor. Recorded 12 July 1860. (Pp. 273-274)

ANDREW JOHNSON Will. 31 October 1856. Heirs: wife Calvary Johnson; nephew James Johnson. My wife had only a life estate in her former husband's property. Joseph Mottley, executor. Recorded 13 July 1860. (Pp. 275-276)

NANCY WHITE Will. 18 May 1860. Heir:: daughter Elizabeth White, formerly Elizabeth Castleman (both of our names having been changed from Castleman to White after divorcement from James H. Castleman, my former husband). If Elizabeth White should die, then to my brothers and sisters. James B. White to be guardian of Elizabeth White. Recorded 18 October 1860. (P. 277)

WILLIAM J. LAIN Widow's Allotment. 19 July 1860. Anna Lain given her allotment. Recorded 27 October 1860. (P. 280)

JOHN MUIRHEAD Will. 3 June 1858. Heirs: son William B. Muirhead; brothers William, Adam G., and Ludovie Muirhead; sister Agnes Anderson. Henry D. Lester, executor. Recorded 29 October 1860. (P. 283)

ELIZABETH C. WYNNE Will. 20 August 1860. Heirs: sisters Elizabeth S. Blythe and Dicy Wynne; brother Thomas K. Wynne for the use of his daughter, Lucy Ann Wynne; brother Alanson Wynne for his daughter Bettie Blythe Wynne; nephew Thomas K. Wynne to be paid by his father, Alanson G. Wynne; nephew John A. Wynne to be paid by J. Y. Blythe. Grave markers are to be placed at my grave and that of Isaac Bledsoe. Recorded 29 October 1860. (P. 284)

CHARLES STEWART Will. 1 June 1860. Heirs: wife Frances Stewart; grandsons Charles Wesley Stewart and King Darriel McDowell. Witnesses: F. W. Golladay and R. S. Haley. Recorded 29 October 1860. (P. 285)

JOEL JENNINGS Widow's Allotment. Cintha Jennings given her allotment. Recorded 29 October 1860. (P. 285)

ISAIAH TRIBBLE Sale. 27 August 1860. W. H. Tribble, administrator. Recorded 29 October 1860. (Pp. 287-288)

ISAIAH TRIBBLE, SR. Widow's Allotment. Recorded 30 October 1860. (P. 291)

MARY MOUNT Sale. Recorded 31 October 1860. (P. 291)

JAMES WILLIAMS Will. 20 March 1860. Heirs: wife Jane Williams; living children by my present wife, to wit, James R., Ailsa C., Martha H., Solomon S., Quentophenus, Sarah W., Lucinda F., Ruth T., and William F. Williams. Martha H. Williams is now intermarried to

Joseph Ragland. The two eldest sets of children to be
prorated according to what they have already received.
John D. Carson, executor. Recorded 2 November 1860.
(Pp. 292-293)

JAMES BAIRD Will. 10 September 1860. Heirs: wife
Emily C. Baird; children. Executors: sons John H. and
James R. Baird. Recorded 2 November 1860. (Pp. 294-295)

WILLIAM D. SMITH Will. 23 August 1860. Heirs:
wife Sarah Caroline Smith; children; youngest son Richard
Smith; son William D. Figures Smith; daughter; two
other children. Recorded 16 November 1860. (Pp. 296-
297)

J. A. JENNINGS Widow's Allotment. Nancy Jennings
given her allotment. Recorded 21 November 1860. (P.
302)

ELIZABETH DONALDSON Will. 22 March 1860. Heirs:
daughters Susan Donaldson, Catharine Lane, and Mary Ann
Donaldson; Patrick and Peloney Donaldson who are the
children of Robert Donaldson deceased. Joab P. Cawthon,
executor. Witnesses: J. B. Vivrett and William D. Hamblin. Recorded 23 November 1860. (P. 305)

AMELIA HARRIS Will. 11 October 1860. Heirs: daugh-
ter Susan E. Harris; my lawful heirs. Executors: James
H. Taylor and I. J. Wilkerson. Recorded 14 February 1861.
(P. 307)

JOSHUA WOOLEN Widow's Allotment. 18 October 1860.
Mary Woolen given her allotment. Recorded 11 February
1861. (P. 308)

CHARLES HUGUELEY Will. 8 September 1851. Heirs: ✓
sons Henry A. and Charles W. Hugueley; daughter J. H.
Hamilton. Executors: Charles W. Hugueley and William H.
Hamilton. Recorded 15 November 1861. (P. 323)

RICHARD CHUMLEY Will. 26 September 1860. Heirs:
wife Jane Chumley; all my children; George Chumley.
A. S. Young, executor. Recorded 18 November 1861. (P.
330)

JOHN F. W. JARRATT Widow's Allotment. Martha Jarratt given her allotment. Recorded 18 November 1861.
(P. 331)

GRANVILLE MANSFIELD Will. 15 January 1861. Heirs:
wife; children. Recorded 19 November 1861. (P. 339)

E. S. CARUTH Will. 27 February 1861. Heirs: wife
Elizabeth Caruth; children Angeline Barr and Charlotte
Caruth. My land in Kentucky is to be sold. Executors:
Elizabeth Caruth and Isaac Caruth. Recorded 19 November
1861. (P. 340)

FRANCIS M. GRAVES Widow's Allotment. 6 February
1861. Angeline Graves given her allotment. Recorded
19 November 1861. (P. 341)

ELIZABETH VIVRETT Will. 20 April 1861. Heirs: children Mary F., Rebecca, and Margaret L. Vivrett. Jonathan Eatherly, executor. Recorded 19 November 1861. (P. 342)

ARMSTEAD A. PUCKETT Will. 4 April 1861. Heirs: wife (Edura) Ann Puckett; father Charles Puckett. Recorded 19 November 1861. (Pp. 342-343)

CRISSA McFARLIN Will. 25 January 1861. Heirs: sisters Sibba McFarlin and Catharine Bradshaw; brother Alfred A. Canady. Recorded 19 November 1861. (P. 343)

BARTHOLOMEW BRETT Will. 8 January 1861. Heirs: children Martha E. Pitts, Elizabeth Vaughan, Sarah Welles, Hardy, Alexander, and Benjamin B. Brett; granddaughter Eliza N. Clayton; children of deceased daughter Mary C. Parker, to wit, Laura A. Wallace, Cherry, George, and Hanley Parker. Executors: Hardy Brett and Edward Welles. Recorded 19 November 1861. (P. 344)

W. B. WRIGHT Will. 10 December 1860. Heirs: wife Mary S. Wright; children. Recorded 19 November 1861. (P. 346)

J. W. SULLIVAN Will. 16 March 1861. Heirs: wife Susan Sullivan; sister Mary T. Sullivan. Recorded 19 November 1861. (P. 347)

LEROY B. SETTLE Will. 28 June 1861. Heirs: wife Margery W. Settle; children. Recorded 19 November 1861. (P. 348)

ROBERT JENNINGS Will. 27 March 1861. Heirs: wife Hannah Jennings; children Martha Ann Patterson, Betress E. Mount, Ann Eliza Witty, Nancy E. Grandstaff, Lucinda A. Sullivan, Jacob R., John W., and Susan F. Jennings. Recorded 19 November 1861. (P. 350)

ALLEN TOMLINSON Will. 9 March 1858. Heirs: wife Mary Ann Tomlinson; children Simeon, Zarena, James, Hudson, Reuben, Martha Ann, Nancy, Gilly A., and Elizabeth Tomlinson. Zarena is now Zarena Johnson. Martha Ann is now Martha Ann Gold. Nancy is now Nancy Ramsey. William M. Provine, executor. Recorded 19 November 1861. (P. 351)

JOHN B. THOMPSON Will. 20 December 1860. Heirs: wife Elizabeth S. Thompson; children. Recorded 20 November 1861. (P. 360)

HENRY H. CLUCK Will. 8 July 1861. Heirs: wife Polly Cluck; children Fountain, Smith, Meredith R., and Martin Green Cluck. Executors: John A. Cason and G. M. Alsup. Recorded 21 November 1861. (P. 361)

JAMES SCOBY Will. 1860. Heirs: wife Polly Scoby; children John Berry Scoby, Jane K. Sweatt, and Margaret L. Hunter. John Berry Scoby, executor. Recorded 21 November 1861. (P. 362)

BENJAMIN PRITCHETT Will.. 17 August 1861. Heirs:

wife Jane F. Pritchett; children Jasper, Nancy, Lavina, and Julia Ann Pritchett; four sons by my first wife John, David, James, and George W. Pritchett. William P. Berry, executor. Recorded 21 November 1861. (P. 363)

ROBERT JOHNS Widow's Allotment. Recorded 9 January 1862. (P. 378)

JOHN G. GREEN Widow's Allotment. 25 September 1861. Tracy Green given her allotment. Recorded 9 January 1862. (P. 379)

SELDON BAIRD Widow's Allotment. Recorded 11 February 1862. (P. 379)

THOMAS WOMMACK Sale. 21 January 1862. Recorded 11 February 1862. (P. 383)

W. B. H. WALKER Letter. Letter to brother. Heirs: brother; mother. Mentions Uncle Jackson Brown. (Pp. 387-388)

JOHN O. POYNER Will. 23 March 1860. Heirs: wife Elizabeth Poyner; my lawful heirs. Executors: James Poyner and son in law John Holland. Recorded 1862. (P. 389)

TURNER B. LAWRENCE Will. 22 May 1862. Heirs: wife Sarah Lawrence to receive the land from my father William Lawrence; brother Edward Lawrence of Smith County; Turner M. Lawrence, the son of my nephew, William B. Lawrence and his wife Sarah; Turner Lawrence Johnson, son of Duncan and Elizabeth Johnson; Susan F. Lawrence, daughter of my nephew, Pallas N. Lawrence and his wife Nancy; Churchwell Anderson; Horatio Betty; Joseph L. Lawrence, son of my brother Edward Lawrence; niece Susan Roy, the wife of James Roy; Rachel Jane Roy, the wife of Beverly Roy; and Delilah Wood, the wife of Moses A. Wood; Joseph D. Lawrence. Recorded 1862. (Pp. 390-392)

CHARLES L. CARTER Will. 2 January 1859. Heirs: wife; children William H. and Charles T. Carter. Daughter Martha Caplenor is dead. Recorded 7 November 1862. (P. 392)

JOHN REEVES Will. 25 May 1861. Heirs: wife Sarah Reeves; children Nancy Jane Wier, Rhoda Ann Sanders, Taletha Puryear, and John Reeves. Executors: J. G. Wier, R. C. Sanders, and Thomas Puryear. Recorded 3 November 1862. (P. 393)

WILLIAM WRAY Will. 18 November 1861. Heirs: wife Martha P. Wray; children Richard E. W., William W., and Martha Elizabeth Wray, Mary J. Jenkins, Susan Taylor, and Margaret A. Hewgley. Margaret A. Hewgley's husband, Lewis H. Hewgley is to have no control over her part. Witnesses: Jesse A. Grigg and J. E. Gibson. Recorded 7 November 1862. (P. 394)

LEVI HOLLOWAY Will. 11 January 1859. Heirs: wife;.

children Levi, Richard, John, and Sally Holloway; daughter Martha's children, to wit, Sally F., John Patra, and James Green Harrison; Jane's two children, Martha and James Lain, to have their mother's part. Witnesses: R. B. Castleman, Collier A. Steed, and J. L. Castleman. Recorded 7 November 1862. (P. 395)

HENRY F. SMITH Will. 7 November 1860. Heirs: wife Mary D. Smith; children William W., Edward M., Henry C. Smith, Martha Louisa Pennebaker, and Lucy A. C. Smith; grandchildren Martha Ella Johnson and Molly Ann Pennebaker. Executors: William W. Smith and son in law Edwin R. Pennebaker. Recorded 7 November 1862. (Pp. 396-397)

W. M. JUSTICE Will. 18 May 1861. Having enlisted in the service. . . to my brother Joseph C. Justice. Recorded 8 November 1862. (P. 397)

FOUNTAIN JARRELL Will. 9 January 1862. Heirs: wife; children. Recorded 8 November 1862. (P. 397)

SILAS TARVER Will. 20 June 1862. Heirs: wife Lucinda Tarver; children John B., Benjamin J. Tarver; Hannah Claiborn; all my children. Executors: Benjamin J. Tarver, John B. Tarver, and Nathan B. Burdine. Recorded 8 November 1862. (P. 398)

REUBEN SEARCY Will. 7 October 1857. Heirs: wife Harty Searcy; children Ann Alloway, Nancy Benson, Daniel Searcy, and Reuben Monroe Searcy; William P. Searcy's heirs: niece Sarah Hays; William P. Hays shall live with and take care of me. Executor: Joab P. Cawthon. Recorded 8 November 1862. (P. 399)

ARCHEBALD HUNT Will. Heirs: wife Eliza Hunt; Church Ellen Hunt, the only daughter I have by my wife Eliza Hunt; sons Thomas and Hardy Hunt; Polly Vanatta, the girl who now lives with me; heirs of daughter Delia Allen; heirs of daughter Sallie Floyd. The heirs of my first wife have already received their share. Recorded 8 November 1862. (Pp. 400-401)

AB CARUTHERS Will. Heirs: children. Executors: brother Robert L. Caruthers and son William A. Caruthers. Recorded 8 November 1862. (P. 402)

ROBERT HATTON Will. 18 May 1860. Heirs: wife Sophia Hatton; children. Recorded 8 November 1862. (P. 403)

MATTHEW HILL Will. Heirs: wife L. A. Hill; sister Elizabeth Etchison. W. H. Grimmett, executor. Recorded 10 November 1862. (P. 404)

WILLIAM E. CURD Will. 21 May 1861. Heirs: If I should not return from military service, then to my brother, John N. Curd. Recorded 10 November 1862. (P. 404)

BAILEY MARKS Will. 6 August 1862. Heirs: If I do not return from military service to Lucy Gannon if she.

is still living. The remainder to my mother, Elizabeth
Marks. Recorded 12 November 1862. (P. 405)

JOHN W. TUCKER Will. 7 May 1861. Heirs: brothers
Foster and Green H. Tucker; mother Priscilla Tucker.
Executrix: Priscilla Tucker. Recorded 12 November 1862.
(Pp. 405-406)

AMZI BASS Widow's Allotment. 14 October 1862.
Lucinda A. Bass given her allotment. Recorded 12 November
1862. (P. 406)

WILLIAM FOSTER Widow's Allotment. Recorded 17 November 1862. (P. 417)

JAMES W. HEARN Will. 5 October 1860. Heirs: wife
Mary C. Hearn; children Thomas N., William, Purnell,
Milbrey P., Henry L., Hardy, James, and Thomas Hearn;
daughter Catherine's children, to wit, Mary Catherine,
Elizabeth Jane, Martha C., and William B. Davis. Execu-
tors: Milbrey P. Hearn and Thomas N. Hearn. Recorded 9
December 1862. (P. 419)

JAMES MEASLES Sale. 1 October 1861. Recorded 6
January 1863. (Pp. 419-421)

SUSAN MEASLES Sale. Recorded 6 January 1863. (Pp.
421-423)

RICHARD WOMMACK Sale. 13 February 1862. Recorded
12 January 1863. (Pp. 423-424)

LANSFORD BAGWELL Will. 19 November 1861. Heirs: wife Raspah Bagwell; children; son William Bagwell. Sam C. Anderson, executor. Witnesses: J. W. McCartney and William Clemmons. Recorded 22 October 1863. (No page number)

JAMES DUKE Widow's Allotment. 26 December 1862. Mary Ann Duke given her allotment. Recorded 7 April 1864. (No page number)

WILLIAM C. BAIRD Will. 21 May 1861. Having joined the Army. . . Heirs: half brothers and sister, Benjamin, Jesse, and Mica A. Gleaves; cousin Z. A. Baird's daughter, about six months old. John Crudup, executor. Witnesses: J. F. Davis and John H. Guill. Recorded 7 April 1864. (No page number)

ALANSON G. WYNNE Will. 4 December 1862. Alanson G. Wynne died at his residence in Wilson County where he was raised and always lived except eight or ten years he lived in Texas. On Monday or Tuesday before his death on Friday, he made a noncupative will. Heirs: wife; five little children. Recorded 10 April 1864. (No page number)

ROBERT YORK Will. 12 May 1863. Heir: sister Martha York. Recorded 11 April 1864. (No page number)

MOSES ELLIS Will. 9 February 1863. Heirs: wife Elizabeth Ellis; children Eliza Ellis, Rebecca E. Allen, Lucy Ann Hatcher, Polly P. Hatcher, and Nancy J. Harris. Col. J. H. Allen is to be guardian of Eliza Ellis. Recorded 11 April 1864. (P. 1)

LITTLETON MOSELEY Will. 20 February 1862. Heirs: Rebecca Caplinor, Lucinda Bettes and husband, Albert Bettes, Sarah, Martha W., Parthena C., Nancy C., and Eliza J. Moseley. James Hewgley, executor. Witnesses: William S. Holman and John W. Thomas. Recorded 10 April 1864. (P. 3)

EPERSON BANDY Will. 5 June 1863. Heirs: children Mary C. Crutcher, Harriet Davis, Jonathan and Alexander Bandy; the rest of my children. Recorded 18 April 1864. (P. 4)

WILLIAM DUNCAN Will. 19 June 1863. Heirs: wife Nancy Duncan; children Sarah J. Powell, Harriet A. Hagan, Isabella Hagan, and George M. B. Duncan; heirs of son William S. Duncan; heirs of daughter Martha Ann Page, to wit, Merica, Lavisa, and Ann Page. Executor: son in law William Powell. Recorded 20 April 1864. (P. 5)

ELIZABETH HUDSON Sale. Recorded 21 April 1864. (Pp. 7-8)

JAMES M. CARTER Will. 21 July 1863. Heirs: wife Ellen Carter; children Nathaniel Henry, Charles G., W. B., Annie J., Louiza W., and James Carter. Answorth Harrison, executor. Recorded 25 April 1864. (P. 13)

JAMES PORTERFIELD Will. 7 June 1861. Heirs: child-

ren S. C., John M., Julianna P., and Jarvis M. Porterfield, and Mary H. Blankenship; Matilda Barton's children; Charles A. Porterfield's children. Executors:
L. D. Leeman and Jarvis M. Porterfield. Recorded 26
April 1864. (Pp. 13-14)

JOHN BASS Widow's Allotment. 9 May 1863. Mary Bass
given her allotment. Recorded 26 April 1864. (P. 14)

FRANCES YOUNG Will. 22 September 1856. Heirs: wife
Katharine Young; children Stacy Young, Ginsey Gibson,
Patsy Clemmons and husband, Alfred Clemmons; Allen Clem-
mons' children; son Gilbert Young's children. Stacy
Young, executor.

FRANCES YOUNG Codicil. 7 February 1857. Lamiza Hancock, Gilbert Young's youngest daughter, is dead. Her
mother, Rebecca Young, is to have the distributive share.
Recorded 27 April 1864. (Pp. 21-22)

NATHANIEL CARTMELL Widow's Allotment. Recorded 29
April 1864. (P. 35)

WILLIAM DUKE Will. 2 June 1854. Heirs: children
Malisa Caroline Peak and Daniel J. Duke; daughter Sally
H. Payne's two children, to wit, Henrietta and Daniel
Hubard Payne. Executors: Isaac Peak and Milton Taylor.
Witnesses: Milton Taylor and Paris Taylor. Recorded 4
May 1864. (P. 50)

SAMUEL JUSTISS Will. 4 October 1862. Heirs: children Joseph C. Justiss, Mary Shannon, Louisa Harrison,
John Justiss, Sarah R. Sparks, and Lucinda Wilburn. Executor: Lewis W. Robertson. Witnesses: Lewis N. Parham
and J. W. McCartney. Recorded 31 August 1863. (P. 51)

FRANCEWAY R. COSSETT Will. 24 April 1862. Heirs:
wife Matilda Cossett; daughter Lucinda L. Golladay;
granddaughter Alice A. Fisher; son in law Dr. John S.
Pearson; nephew Patrick H. Jewett; and Dr. Richard Beard.
Monuments are to be erected at the graves of Col. James
H. Fisher and his wife Ann C. Fisher, and Mary Ellen Pearson and her child. Executors: Nathan Green, Jr. and son
in law Ed J. Golladay. Recorded 5 May 1864. (Pp. 53-55)

SAMUEL RAMSEY Will. 8 September 1862. Heirs: wife
Mary Jane Ramsey; child Nelly Ramsey. Recorded 6 May
1864. (P. 56)

MARY J. RAMSEY Will. 27 July 1863. Heirs: child
Nelly Ramsey; sister Synthia Snow. Executor: brother
John Snow. Witnesses: T. E. Morris and Henry R. Snow.
Recorded 6 May 1864. (P. 56)

H. J. CLOAR Widow's Allotment. 4 February 1864.
Ann B. Cloar given her allotment. Recorded 7 May 1864.
(Pp. 59-60)

W. T. WILLIAMS Will. 27 August 1863. Heirs: wife
Nancy Williams; sisters Harriet Coker and Martha L. Williams. A. S. Williams, executor. Recorded 8 May 1864.

(P. 63)

SARAH R. HOWARD Will. 6 October 1863. Heirs: children George, Sallie, Crisp, and Sallie K. Howard. Executors: Sam Milligan and James M. Safford. Recorded 8 May 1864. (P. 64)

EDMUND H. TOMPKINS Will. 26 June 1863. Heirs: wife Linie Tompkins; children. Recorded 9 May 1864. (P. 67)

WILLIAMSON BIRTHRIGHT Will. 22 December 1862. Heirs: children Betty and Clabon Birthright, Fanny Hays; children of deceased daughter Mary Brett. William B. Jennings, executor. Recorded 10 May 1864. (P. 68)

MARTIN ORION Widow's Allotment. 1 April 1864. Recorded 10 May 1864. (P. 68)

JAMES H. WALKER Widow's Allotment. Frances C. Walker given her allotment. Recorded 10 May 1864. (P. 70)

JOHN T. NEW Widow's Allotment. Recorded 10 June 1864. (P. 77)

JACKSON N. BROWN Will. 16 July 1862. Heirs: children James F., Emily, and Elizabeth Jane Brown; afflicted daughter Eliza Ann Brown. Executors: A. M. Turner and M. S. Vaughan. Recorded 11 June 1864. (P. 77)

JOHN KELLY Will. 17 July 1862. Heirs: wife Margaret L. Kelly; children of son David C. Kelly. Margaret L. Kelly, executrix. Recorded 8 July 1864. (P. 78)

JOHN ROBB Will. 30 May 1861. Heirs: wife Jane Robb; children John S., William, Margaret Elizabeth, Jane M., Harvey W., and Mary Robb. Jane Robb, executrix. Recorded 8 July 1864. (P. 78)

JOHN CARR Will. 20 March 1863. Heirs: wife Mary B. Carr; wife's daughter Samantha A. Jolly; my children Dabney, Thomas H., Tolbert, and John O. Carr, Martha Gentry, Sarah Johnston, Nancy Travillian, and Mary Breedlove. Executor: son Tolbert Carr. Recorded 10 July 1864. (P. 79)

MARK WHITAKER Widow's Allotment. Elizabeth Whitaker given her allotment. Recorded 10 July 1864. (P. 80)

WILLIAM L. HOLMAN Widow's Allotment. 17 May 1864. Recorded 10 July 1864. (P. 82)

CARNES LOGUE Will. 24 October 1853. Heirs: present wife; children John Logue, Tapley G. Logue, Cordelia Luck, and Mary A. Telford; friends Sterling B. Hardy and James Hamilton; granddaughter Eleanor Peach. Executors: sons John Logue and Tapley G. Logue. Recorded 14 August 1864. (Pp. 85-86)

GEORGE W. CARROLL Will. 24 April 1855. Heirs: wife Susan Carroll; wife's little children. Recorded 1864. (P. 89)

140

WILLS & INVENTORIES 1863-1866

LUCINDA H. MOORE Will. 24 June 1864. Heirs: mother; father; brothers and sisters; Mary Shannon; Mount Zion Church. Executor: uncle Finis E. Shannon. Witnesses: Nancy Ragsdale, Martha E. Tatum, and F. E. Shannon. Recorded 15 September 1864. (Pp. 94-95)

PASCHAL P. HUDSON Will. 186?. Heirs: wife Allaphair Hudson; Mary P. Chapman, the daughter of Thomas B. Chapman; Methodist Episcopal Church South; Masonic Fraternity Lodge #98. My mother is to be looked after. Allaphair Hudson, executrix. Witnesses: Sarah A. Rutherford and Molly P. Chapman. Recorded 16 November 1864. (Pp. 102-103)

LUCY GANNON Will. 20 September 1856. Heirs: my Elizabeth Marks; grandson Bailey Marks. Bailey Marks, executor. Recorded 19 November 1864. (P. 103)

A. B. ROBERTSON Widow's Allotment. 14 November 1861. Martha Robertson and her seven children given their allotment. Recorded 15 January 1865. (Pp. 107-108)

JOHN PHILIPS and REBECCA PHILIPS Sale. Recorded 13 November 1864. (Pp. 108-109)

G. W. B. SHANNON Widow's Allotment. Mary C. Shannon given her allotment. Recorded 19 January 1865. (P. 124)

ROBERT HARLIN Children's Allotment. Recorded 3 February 1865. (P. 125)

SAMUEL MAJOR Will. 18 January 1865. Heirs: wife Frances Major; children. J. F. Hooker, executor. Witnesses: John Logue and J. A. Major. Recorded 15 February 1865. (Pp. 127-128)

BENJAMIN D. POWELL Will. May 1861. Heir: wife Mary G. Powell. Alfred R. Davis, executor. Recorded 20 May 1865. (P. 133)

ISAAC HARVEY Will. 20 March 1853. Heirs: wife Nancy Harvey; children Sarah Tarpley, Elizabeth Hutcheson's heirs, Nancy Hutcheson, and Isaac Harvey. Isaac Harvey, executor. Witnesses: Zadoc McMillen and Charley McMillen. Recorded 20 May 1865. (P. 133)

BENNETT WILLIAMS Will. 25 March 1858. Heirs: Ben Winford; William Bennett Winford. Benjamin Winford, executor. Recorded 25 June 1865. (P. 137)

POLLY PROCTOR Will. 2 January 1833. Heirs: brothers David and William Proctor; sister Sally Proctor to have the land given to us by our father Thomas Proctor; sister Patsey Proctor. David Proctor, executor. Witnesses: Etheldred P. Horn and Elizabeth W. Horn. Recorded 25 June 1865. (P. 138)

RICHARD BORUM Will. 6 July 1861. Heirs: John Borum; Hiram G. Borum's three sons, to wit, John, William, and Ransom Borum; Mary Bradley, daughter of Jonas Bradley. Recorded 25 June 1865. (P. 138)

JAMES T. HAYS Will. 9 October 1854. Heirs: wife Malinda Hays; children Leander, James T., (Frederickson), Mary, Tennessee, and John W. Hays; Louisa Cole's children. Witnesses: Samuel Hays, Nathaniel Hays, and Cornelius Keaton. Recorded 26 June 1865. (Pp. 140-141)

BENJAMIN F. LAIN Will. 25 November 1861. Heirs: father Tyra Lain; mother Nancy Lain; brother James Lain; nieces Martha Eubanks and Cordelia A. Lain. Executor: brother James H. Lain. Witnesses: Guy T. Gleaves and John Crudup. Recorded 26 May 1865. (P. 141)

THOMAS L. RAGLAND Widow's Allotment. 12 April 1865. (Pp. 145-146)

LUCRET1A NETTLES Inventory. 21 April 1864. (Pp. 148-152)

CHARLES JOHNSON Will. Heirs: wife Elizabeth Johnson; children Evaline M. Johnson, Elizabeth J. O'Neal, and Sarah Ann Green. D. K. Vaughter, executor. Recorded 10 July 1865. (P. 154)

WASHINGTON L. GRIGG Widow's Allotment. 18 March 1865. Susan E. Grigg given her allotment. Recorded 28 June 1865. (P. 155)

JOHN A. WARREN Will. 22 October 1861. Heir: brother William G. Warren. William G. Warren, executor. Recorded 28 June 1865. (P. 157)

JOHN REA Will. 19 April 1860. Heirs: daughter Mary J. Tailor; children of John Rea; children of deceased daughter Margaret Foster, to wit, James and Andrew J. Foster; children of James Rea, to wit, Mary A. Smith, Margaret Kirkpatrick, and James R. Rea; grandchildren John and Joseph C. Rea, and Margaret Ann Robbins. Recorded 29 June 1865. (P. 162)

PEYTON C. COWGILL Widow's Allotment. Recorded 30 June 1865. (Pp. 163-164)

JOHN Y. SMITH Widow's Allotment. (Lunny) Smith given her allotment. Recorded 30 June 1865. (P. 165)

C. L. MARTIN Widow's Allotment. S. A. Martin given her allotment. Recorded 10 July 1865. (P. 168)

JACOB B. LASATER Will. 14 June 1861. Heirs: wife Lavinia Lasater; children William M. Lasater, Elizabeth J. Allen, and Felice Ann Allen; grandchildren of deceased daughter Harriet Weatherly, Gideon, Deretha, Darthula, and Parallee to receive their mother's part. Recorded 15 July 1865. (Pp. 174-175)

√ NATHAN JENKINS Will. 8 May 1852. Heirs: wife Fanny Jenkins; children Dicey, Turner, and Benjamin Jenkins; deceased daughter Gincy Rouse's children, to wit, Polly, Nancy, and Betty Rouse; granddaughter Esther Eby Blackwell; grandchildren Betsy, Lucinda, Patsy, and Louiza Rouse, minor children of John Rouse. Recorded 15 July 1865. (P. 175)

DAVID C. JACKSON Will. 13 April 1865. Heirs: wife Bur   ) Jackson; Elizabeth Goldstone (child of my first wife); children Margaret Caroline, Philander, and Thomas Jackson. Timothy M. Shaw, executor. Recorded 15 July 1865. (Pp. 175-176)

JAMES T. PATTON Will. 23 June 1861. Heirs: mother father James H. Patton; brother John A. Patton; sister Rachel J. Patton. Witnesses: John Word and James M. Donnell. Recorded 15 July 1865. (Pp. 176-177)

ALEXANDER POSEY Will. 13 September 1850. Heirs: wife Martha Posey; children Benjamin, Frances, John, Susan, Alison, Robert, Thomas, and Alexander Posey, and Nancy Woodliff. Executors: Benjamin Posey and William Bilbro. Recorded 15 July 1865. (Pp. 177-178)

ELI MASSEY Will. 18 July 1865. Heirs: wife Mary Massey; son John T. Massey; all my children. Son Eli Polk Massey to have twice as much as the others because of his affliction. Recorded 14 August 1865. (P. 179)

JOHN CHAMBERS Widow's Allotment. Edna Chambers given her allotment. Recorded 14 August 1865. (P. 179)

JOHN SPINKS Will. 24 April 1861. Heirs: children Emily, James P., and John C. Spinks; other daughters. Recorded 16 August 1865. (P. 180)

BENJAMIN DOBSON Will. 17 May 1865. Heirs: wife Minerva Jane Dobson; children. Executors: Moses M. Currey and John N. Lannom. Witnesses: J. F. Hooker and M. W. Taylor. Recorded 13 September 1865. (P. 185)

RUSSELL ESKEW Will. 24 July 1865. Heirs: wife Martha D. Eskew; son E. P. Eskew; my three sons; sister Rachel Guill. J. F. Hooker, executor. Witnesses: Ransom R. Gwyn and James Bridges. Recorded 13 September 1865. (P. 186)

CASSANDRA ASHWORTH Will. 20 February 1864. Heirs: children David, Hardy S., and Lewis D. Barry; youngest son Jasper R. Ashworth. Older children already provided for. Jasper R. Ashworth, executor. Recorded 13 September 1865. (Pp. 186-187)

WILLIAM A. POWELL Will. 26 August 1865. Heirs: wife Mary A. Powell to receive my land in Coffee County; children Elizabeth, William D. N., and Thomas G. Powell. Executor: brother D. J. Powell. Recorded 13 September 1865. (P. 187)

MADISON NEAL Widow's Allotment. 18 August 1865. Nancy Neal given her allotment. Recorded 17 September 1865. (P. 192)

ALBERT G. BARKSDALE Will. 1 May 1861. Heirs: E. P. Lowe for my sister Elizabeth Brooks; brothers R. L., W. H., (Higgerson), and G. B. L. Barksdale. W. H. Barksdale has joined a volunteer company. E. P. Lowe, executor. Recorded 17 September 1865. (P. 193)

WILLS & INVENTORIES 1863-1866

ETHELDRED CLEMMONS Will. 31 August 1862. Heirs: wife (Jany) Clemmons; children. (Jany) Clemmons, executrix. Recorded 17 September 1865. (P. 194)

ALFRED C. CABLE Will. 3 June 1865. Heirs: wife Jane C. Cable; children. Martha E. Cable is to be sent to school like N. J. Mickel was. Recorded 3 June 1865. (P. 194)

NANCY FORRESTER Will. 15 May 1863. Heirs: granddaughter Mary Elizabeth Armstrong to receive land in Sumner County; grandson William Forrester; great grandson William Henry Forrester. Recorded 17 September 1865. (P. 195)

J. W. L. BETTES Will. May 1864. Sumner County. Heirs: wife; daughters. Witnesses: F. A. Myrick and R. F. Myrick. Recorded 28 September 1865. (P. 202)

ARCHIBALD CARVER Will. 9 August 1865. Heirs: wife Sarah K. Carver; Pleasant Jonas, John William, Areanah Turner, Elizabeth Lee, Cornelia Catherine, Samuel E., and Lucy Annis Carver. Pleasant Jonas Carver to receive my father's land. A monument to be erected at the grave of our little child, Susan A. Carver. Executors: William C. Clemmons and Pleasant Jonas Carver. Witnesses: Peyton F. Ligon and J. W. Chandler. Recorded 10 October 1865. (Pp. 204-205)

JOHN BOND Will. 18 April 1859. Heirs: deceased daughter Polly Richmond's children, to wit, John B. Richmond, Mary Sanders, and Sarah Powell; son James Houston Bond; grandchildren George L., Francis, Sarah E., Malissa, and John B. Lenoir. Executors: John B. Richmond, Jack D. Bond, and James H. Bond. The old Mount Pleasant School is on my land. Recorded 23 October 1865. (P. 206)

LAMBERT VANHOOZER Widow's Allotment. 14 September 1865. Mary Vanhoozer given her allotment. Recorded 23 October 1865. (P. 207)

WILLIAM VANTREASE Will. 3 June 1860. Heirs: wife Mary Vantrease to receive the land she will get from her father; children James K., Nicholas M., Levi D., Jacob, John L., Elizabeth, Delila, and Francis Vantrease, and Catherine Odum. Hardin Ragland, executor. Recorded 25 November 1865. (Pp. 214-215)

BRITTON ODUM Will. 2 January 1861. Heirs: wife Redley Odum; children Sally, Kinchen, John, Daniel, Nancy, Lucy, (Britton), and Dempsey Odum, Polly Wiley, and Redley Vantrease. Hardin Ragland, executor. Recorded 25 October 1865. (P. 215)

JOHN M. BLAN Will. 9 February 1862. Heirs: wife; children. Executrix: wife Elizabeth Blan. Witnesses: John Logue and James M. Brown. Recorded 26 October 1865. (P. 218)

ELIJAH WOMMACK Widow's Allotment. 27 September 1865. Esther Wommack given her allotment. Recorded 27 October ·

144

1865. (P. 222)

R. A. BARTON Family's Allotment. Recorded 27 October 1865. (P. 225)

JOHN ASKEW Will. 5 January 1865. Heirs: wife Ann Askew; oldest daughter Priscilla Barnes; children Mary C., John T., William M., Charles M., and Susan C. Askew, and Angelina J. Williams; Mathew W. Barnes, the heir of Elizabeth J. Barnes deceased. (P. 241)

JOHN ASKEW Codicil. 5 January 1865. In case of the death of my son John T. Askew who is now in prison, then his share to his children. Recorded 30 October 1865. (P. 241)

ALLEN DILLARD Will. 15 September 1865. Heirs: wife Selety A. Dillard; children. Selety A. Dillard, executrix. Witnesses: G. W. Lewis and W. H. Williamson. Recorded 12 November 1865. (P. 242)

SARAH HUGHES Will. Heirs: children Jessie Ann and Lee Hughes to receive the land on Barton's Creek conveyed to sister Margaret Ames and myself by Dr. Thomas Norman. The deed is found in the Register's Office in Deed Book #2, page 443. Dr. Thomas Norman, executor. Recorded 10 November 1865. (P. 242)

ED WILLIS Inventory. Recorded 12 November 1865. (P. 243)

WILLIAM NELSON Widow's Allotment. Elizabeth Nelson given her allotment. Recorded 12 November 1865. (P. 243)

HARDY M. HEARN Widow's Allotment. 7 October 1865. Recorded 12 November 1865. (P. 244)

R. P. DONNELL Widow's Allotment. 27 October 1865. Cleopatra Donnell given her allotment. Recorded 12 November 1865. (P. 244)

JOHN PHILIPS Widow's Allotment. 17 October 1865. Rebecca J. Philips given her allotment. Recorded 13 November 1865. (P. 250)

ARTHUR M. PATTON Widow's Allotment. 18 September 1865. Mary Patton given her allotment. Recorded 13 November 1865. (P. 250)

W. J. O'BRIANT Widow's Allotment. Recorded 14 November 1865. (P. 253)

JOHN HOUGHEN Will. 20 August 1864. Heirs: wife Hannah Houghen; children Alexander Haughen and wife Lucinda Houghen, and Ann Edwards, the wife of Robert Edwards. Stephen Woodrum, executor. Witnesses: George Sanders and Hugh R. Gwyn. Recorded 25 December 1865. (Pp. 259-260)

B. W. KIRKPATRICK Widow's Allotment. Recorded 25 December 1865. (P. 260)

145

WILLS & INVENTORIES 1863-1866

WILLIAM E. DONNELL Widow's Allotment. Recorded 25 December 1865. (P. 260)

W. M. JOHNS Widow's Allotment. 27 October 1865. Jane Johns given her allotment. Recorded 25 December 1865. (P. 261)

JAMES M. SWAIN Widow's Allotment. Sarah E. Swain given her allotment. Recorded 26 December 1865. (P. 263)

ELIZABETH LAWRENCE Inventory. Recorded 27 December 1865. (P. 266)

FANNY BILLINGS Will. 28 June 1859. Heirs: Christian and James Billings; Mary J., Laviny, and Emily Hobbs. Recorded December 1865. (P. 267)

PERRY P. BENSON Will. 10 November 1863. Heirs: wife Nancy Benson; blind son George W. Benson; other children. J. P. Cawthon, executor. Witnesses: William B. Jennings and John Cook. Recorded 29 December 1865. (P. 268)

HENRY R. SNOW Will. 7 October 1859. Heirs: brother John B. Snow; sister Sinthia Snow. John B. Snow, executor. Witnesses: Thomas B. Chapman and Silas J. Chapman. Recorded 29 December 1865. (P. 270)

JAMES HOLMES Widow's Allotment. Recorded 29 December 1865. (P. 270)

MITCHELL THOMPSON Widow's Allotment. 26 December 1865. Nancy Thompson given her allotment. Recorded 10 February 1866. (P. 273)

WILLIAM SWANN Widow's Allotment. 10 November 1865. Susan Swann given her allotment. Recorded 22 January 1866. (P. 277)

J. D. MAJOR Will. Heir: Bob Major. J. A. Major, executor. Recorded 22 January 1866. (P. 278)

LARKIN G. ALLEN Widow's Allotment. Recorded 16 February 1866. (P. 290)

NANCY W. WALKER Allotment. 20 October 1865. Nancy W. Walker, the infant child of Francis C. Walker, given her allotment. Recorded 16 February 1866. (P. 290)

JOHN MAHOLLAND Widow's Allotment. Elizabeth Maholland given her allotment. Recorded 17 February 1866. (P. 293)

JULIUS H. WILLIAMS Inventory. (Pp. 300-301)

ALEXANDER, ABNER. Died Wilson County, Tennessee 1837. Issue: Esther Alexander, Ezekiel Alexander, and probably others as well.

ALLEN, MOSES. Died Wilson County, Tennessee 1844.

AVERY, GEORGE. Born North Carolina 1750; died Wilson County, Tennessee 10 June 1853; married Pitt or Edgecomb County, North Carolina @1787 Elizabeth Allen, born North Carolina 1750; died Wilson County, Tennessee 27 November 1857. Private. North Carolina Continental Line. Issue: Allen Avery, Ann Avery, George S. Avery, John W. Avery, Sally Avery, and William Avery.

BARTON, DAVID. Served in Maryland during the American Revolution.

BARTON, SAMUEL. Born Virginia January 1749; died Wilson County, Tennessee May 1810; married Botetourt County, Virginia 10 March 1778 Martha Robertson. Dunmore's War. Seventh Virginia Regiment, Morgan's Rifles. Issue: Jane Barton, Margaret Barton, Elizabeth Barton, Samuel Barton, Jr., Joseph Barton, Gabriel Barton, and Stephen Barton.

BASHAW, PETER. Born Fauquier County, Virginia 31 March 1763; died Wilson County, Tennessee 20 May 1864; married 4 March 1785 Frances (?), born Virginia 14 February 1769; died Davidson County, Tennessee 16 June 1851. Virginia Militia. Last survivor in Tennessee of the Revolutionary War. Issue: James W. Bashaw, Hetty Bashaw, Byron Bashaw, John Bashaw, Fanny Bashaw, Hannah Bashaw, Betsy Bashaw, Nancy Bashaw, Benjamin Bashaw, Presley Bashaw, Lucy Bashaw, and Joseph E. Bashaw.

BEAUCHAMP, JOHN W. Died Wilson County, Tennessee 1846. Issue: Martha Jane Beauchamp, Annistasia Beauchamp, John Beauchamp.

BILLINGSLEY, JOHN. Died Wilson County, Tennessee 1849.

BLALOCK, CHARLES. Died Wilson County, Tennessee 1842. Issue: James Millington Blalock.

BONNER, JOHN. Born Sussex County, Virginia 20 August 1764; died Wilson County, Tennessee 14 September 1842; married 1796 Sarah Love, died 1843. Virginia Minuteman. Issue: Thomas L. Bonner, and probably others as well.

BUMPASS, WILLIAM, SR. Died Wilson County, Tennessee 1805; married Mary (?). Issue: William Bumpass, Jr.

BURTON, JAMES MINGLE. Born Mecklenburg County, Virginia 23 January 1761; died Wilson County, Tennessee 16 February 1844; married Elizabeth Riddle, born Granville County, North Carolina 27 August 1771; died Wilson County, Tennessee 4 January 1838. Issue: Robert Burton, Martha Ann Burton, Frances K. Burton, and Eliza R. Burton.

CAMPBELL, DAVID. Born Augusta County, Virginia 1752; died Wilson County, Tennessee 24 November 1832; married Jane (?), born @1770; died Wilson County, Tennessee 18 September 1840. Captain. Virginia Continental Army. Battle of Point Pleasant, 1774. Battle of Long Island Flats, 20 July 1776. Issue: David Campbell and Margaret Lavinia Campbell.

CHANDLER, JOSIAH. Born Henry County, Virginia 12 July 1762; died Wilson County, Tennessee 22 October 1827; married 24 August 1784 Sarah Eddins, born Culpeper County, Virginia 24 August 1762; died Wilson County, Tennessee 3 July 1848. North Carolina Continental Line. Battle of Ransom's Mill. Battle of King's Mountain. Issue: Josiah Chandler and probably others as well.

CLEMMONS, SAMUEL THOMPSON. Born Virginia 15 September 1751; died Wilson County, Tennessee 1837; married Martha Coggin, born North Carolina @1755. North Carolina Continental Line. Issue: Jeptha Clemmons, John Clemmons, William Clemmons, Mary Clemmons, Etheldred Clemmons, Sr., Lavina Clemmons, Priscilla Clemmons, Samuel Thompson Clemmons, Jr., James Clemmons, Nancy Clemmons, and Susannah Clemmons.

COLLY, AUSTIN.

COLLY, WILLIAM.

CONNER, THOMAS.

CRISWELL, HENRY.

CRISWELL, ROBERT.

CRUNK, JOHN.

CURREY, JOHN. Born Chester County, Pennsylvania 30 April 1762; died Wilson County, Tennessee 5 September 1840; married 29 July 1784 Sarah Currey, born 10 September 1766; died Wilson County, Tennessee 30 October 1843. North Carolina Continental Line. Issue: Isaiah Currey, Jane Currey, Elijah Currey, Susannah B. Currey, Abner B. Currey, Elizabeth Currey, Sarah Hix Currey, and Margaret C. Currey.

DABNEY, JOHN. Commissioned officer during the American Revolution.

DAVIS BENJAMIN. Private. North Carolina Continental Line. Issue: Lucinda F. Davis, Sion W. Davis, Phoney I. Davis, Octavia A. Davis, Matilda Tennessee Davis, and Lucretia E. Davis.

DEW, ARTHUR. Died Wilson County, Tennessee 1844. Issue: Elizabeth Dew.

DONNELL, WILLIAM. Born Greensboro, North Carolina 1749; died Wilson County, Tennessee 1822; married @1770 Nancy (Agnes) Denny, born 1757; died 18 March 1839. Captain. North Carolina Continental Line. Issue: William Donnell, John Donnell, James Donnell, Robert

Donnell, Adnah Donnell, Lyle Donnell, Josiah Donnell, Peggy Donnell Haley, and Jane Donnell Davis.

DRENNAN, JOHN. Born Pennsylvania 1740; died Wilson County, Tennessee 19 January 1816; married Delphan Drennan. Captain. South Carolina Militia. Issue: Thomas S. Drennan, Rachel Drennan Miller, James Drennan, Ann Drennan Partlow, David Drennan, (?) Drennan Arnold, William Drennan, and Joseph Drennan.

EDDINS, WILLIAM SR. Born 21 April 1758; died Wilson County, Tennessee 1841; married Rebecca Chandler. Virginia Militia. North Carolina Continental Line. Issue: Isaac Eddins, Nancy Eddins, Fanny Eddins, John Eddins, Joseph Eddins, Polly Eddins Bay, Tempsy Eddins Wright, Elizabeth Eddins Ozment, Catherine Eddins Drennan, Patsy Eddins Tatum, Lucinda Eddins Caple, Sally Eddins Caple, and William Eddins, Jr.

EDWARDS, ROBERT. Born Chatham County, North Carolina 13 February 1759; died Wilson County, Tennessee 17 November 1831; married Nancy F. Quesenbury, born 24 December 1767; died after 1839. Orderly Sergeant. North Carolina Continental Line. Issue: Nicholas Edwards, Elis Edwards, Mary Edwards Fakes, Edward Edwards, Elizabeth Edwards, Henry Edwards, Lucy Edwards, Hanah Edwards, Hugh Edwards, Polly Edwards, and Nancy Edwards.

FITE, LEONARD. Born Sussex County, New Jersey 1 February 1760; died DeKalb County, Tennessee 22 March 1842; married Sussex County, New Jersey 1781 Margaret Cross, born 1761; died Wilson County, Tennessee 1842. Private. New Jersey Troops. Issue: John Fite, Elizabeth Fite Robinson, Jacob Fite, Leonard Fite, Joseph Fite, Catherine Fite Moore, David Fite, Moses Fite, William Fite, Sarah Fite West, Margaret Fite West, and an infant child who died young.

FOSTER, JOHN SR. Born Pennsylvania; died Wilson County, Tennessee 1832. North Carolina Continental Line.

GARRISON, JOHN.

GREEN, JOHN.

GUNN, JOHN SR.

GWYNN, HUGH. Born North Carolina 1749; died Wilson County, Tennessee 11 January 1829; married North Carolina Sarah Rice. North Carolina Militia. Issue: Ransom Gwynn, Jordan Gwynn, Rebecca Gwynn, Frances J. Gwynn, Elisha Gwynn, Sarah Gwynn Telford, John Gwynn, Elizabeth Gwynn Smith, and Iverson Gwynn.

HANCOCK, MARTIN. Born North Carolina @1761; died Wilson County, Tennessee 1835; married Elizabeth (?). North Carolina Continental Line. Issue: Hope Hancock, Samuel Hancock, Dawson Hancock, Martin Hancock, Priscilla Hancock Skean, Nancy Hancock Sparks, Hannah Hancock, Edy Hancock Skean, Sally Hancock Sharp, and Milly Hancock Edwards.

REVOLUTIONARY WAR SOLDIERS IN WILSON COUNTY

HARPOLE, JOHN.

HARRISON, JOHN.

HORN, ETHELDRED.

KELLY, DENNIS. Born Sussex County, Delaware 25 August 1758; died Wilson County, Tennessee 11 December 1834; married 17 June 1784 Elizabeth Thompson, born 1759; died 9 May 1839. Private. Delaware Troops. Issue: Daniel Kelly, Cary Kelly, Dennis Kelly, Jr., Drucilla Kelly Johnson Stewart, Fanny Kelly Peyton, Anne Kelly Thompson, Elizabeth Kelly Hodges, Miranda Kelly Thompson, and John Kelly.

KIRKPATRICK, ALEXANDER. Born 1741; died Wilson County, Tennessee 1825.

McFARLAND, JOHN. Died Wilson County, Tennessee 1824; married Nancy (?). Revolutionary Soldier. Battle of Yorktown. Issue: Elizabeth McFarland Davis, Mary McFarland Castleman, Margaret McFarland Bilbro, Anne McFarland Somers, Jane R. McFarland, Arthur McFarland, and Benjamin M. McFarland.

McPEAK, JOHN. Born before 1760; died Rutherford County, Tennessee before 1820; married Esther Miller. South Carolina Militia. Issue: John McPeak, Jr.

McSPADDEN, THOMAS. Born ?Virginia 12 March 1748; died Wilson County, Tennessee 11 May 1833. Virginia Militia. Issue: William E. McSpadden, Thomas McSpadden, Jr., and probably other children as well.

McWHIRTER, JEREMIAH. Died Gibson County, Tennessee 1828; married Elizabeth (?). Issue: Hugh B. McWhirter, Elizabeth McWhirter, James B. McWhirter, George McWhirter, Eunice McWhirter Bridges, Cynthia McWhirter Sutton, Lovica McWhirter Bradshaw, Mary McWhirter Dickens, and Sally McWhirter Herron.

MITCHELL, EDWARD.

MORRISS, EDWARD. Born Virginia 1756; died Wilson County, Tennessee 10 February 1830; married Elizabeth Cary Whitaker. Virginia Militia. Issue: Nancy Morriss Tarver, Penny Morriss Sands, Elizabeth Morriss Elgin, Mary Morris Smith, Martha Morriss Massie, Louisa Morriss Tarver, Richard Morriss, Thomas Morriss, and John Morriss.

MOTHERAL, SAMUEL. Born 3 March 1757; died Wilson County, Tennessee 21 February 1840; married Sarah (?), born 21 June 1762; died Wilson County, Tennessee 23 March 1850. Issue: Robert Motheral, John Motheral, William Motheral, Ann Motheral Bass, Jane Motheral Stewart, Margaret Motheral Eagan, Mary Motheral Gray, Sarah Motheral Cartmell, and Aseneth Motheral.

OAKLEY, SUSAN.

PALMER, WILLIAM. Born King William County, Virginia 1752; died Wilson County, Tennessee 1824; married 1773 Caro-.

150

line Dulaney, born Maryland 1757; died Rutherford County, Tennessee 1826. Corporal. Virginia Militia. Issue: Mary Palmer Ready, William Palmer, Henry Palmer, Caroline Palmer Nelson, Francis Palmer, Phillip Palmer, and Susan Palmer.

POWELL, NATHANIEL. Born 1762; died 1827; married Elizabeth Cowper. Buried at Bellwood, Wilson County. His tombstone inscription reads, "A soldier of the American Revolution."

RUTLAND, ABEDNEGO. Born 1758; died Wilson County, Tennessee 1843. The NASHVILLE WHIG, 7 December 1843, states, "a soldier of the Revolution." Issue: Joseph Rutland.

SCOTT, JAMES. Died Wilson County, Tennessee 15 September 1815; married Elizabeth (?). Issue: John Scott.

SEAWELL, BENJAMIN. Born 1742; died Wilson County, Tennessee 16 July 1821; married Mary Booker. Captain. North Carolina Continental Line. Issue: William Seawell.

SEAY, JOHN. Died Wilson County, Tennessee 1830. Virginia Militia. Issue: John Seay, William W. Seay, Charles H. Seay, Daniel Seay, Mary Seay Spear, Sally Seay Johnson, and Elizabeth Seay Hearn.

SHACKLER, PHILIP. North Carolina Continental Line.

SHEPHERD, SAMUEL G. Died Wilson County, Tennessee 1846; married Jane (?). Revolutionary Soldier. Battle of Yorktown. Issue: James M. Shepherd, William Shepherd, Robert Shepherd, Samuel Shepherd, Martha Shepherd Ligon, Mary Shepherd Guill, and John Shepherd.

SMITH, CHARLES.

STONE, PICKETT.

SUMMERS, JAMES. North Carolina Continental Line.

SYPERT, WILLIAM L.

TARVER, BENJAMIN. Born 1765; died Wilson County, Tennessee 30 August 1821; married Hannah (?), died 28 November 1838. North Carolina Continental Line. Battle of Guilford Court House. Issue: Mary J. Tarver King, Edmund D. Tarver, Elizabeth A. Tarver Powell, Silas Tarver, Benjamin Tarver, Lucy Tarver Hobson, and Tabitha Tarver.

TEAG, WILLIAM.

TELFORD, HUGH.

TIPTON, JONATHAN. Virginia Militia.

VAUGHAN, ABRAM.

WILLIAMS, NANCY.

WILLIAMS, SAMUEL.

WILLIAMSON, JOHN. Born Montgomery County, Virginia 16 December 1764; died Wilson County, Tennessee 7 August 1829; married Montgomery County, Virginia 5 March 1781

Margaret Scott Cloyd, born 24 January 1766; died 3 October 1845. Private. North Carolina Continental Line. Battle of King's Mountain. Battle of Guilford Court House. Issue: Sarah Williamson Foster, Margaret Williamson, Robert Williamson, Rebecca Williamson Tate, George Williamson, Betsy Williamson Robertson, James Williamson, Rachel Williamson, William Williamson, and Ann Williamson.

WYNNE, JOHN K. Born 16 January 1765; died 7 January 1847; married Lucy (?), born 13 October 1777; died 29 June 1853. Colonel. Revolutionary War. Issue: Thomas K. Wynne, A. H. Wynne, Isaac Bledsoe Wynne, Eliza Caroline Wynne, Martha Wynne Bledsoe, and John L. Wynne.

YOUNG, BANNISTER.

WAR OF 1812   SOLDIER

PARTLOW, THOMAS. Born York County, South Carolina 1796;
died Wilson County, Tennessee 16 September 1849; married Wilson County, Tennessee 2 September 1819 Chloe
Hooker, born Bertie County, North Carolina 11 September
1799; died Wilson County, Tennessee 11 November 1876.
Tennessee Mounted Militia. Issue: William Albert Partlow, Benjamin Eddins Partlow, Thomas Allen Partlow,
James Wesley Partlow, Joshua Partlow, Ann Frizelle Partlow Thompson, Nancy Eddins Partlow Pride, Johnathan Newton Partlow, Mary Elizabeth Partlow Martin, Robert D.
Partlow, Rebecca Frances Partlow, and Sarah Jane Partlow
Dobson.

Sugg's Creek Church, founded in 1800,
became Cumberland Presbyterian in
1810. The first Constitution of the
Cumberland Presbyterian Church in
the United States of America con-
taining the Confession of faith,
Catechism, Government and Discipline,
and Directory for Worship was rati-
fied and adopted by the Synod of
Cumberland, held at Sugg's Creek
April 5-9, 1814.

Historical Marker

NAMES	BIRTHS	MARRIAGES	DEATHS
David Foster,Pastor	4 May 1780	1 July 1806	
Ann Foster	10 Feb 1780		
(children)			
Robert	4 Jul 1807		
John Carson	7 Nov 1809		
William Calhoon	22 Nov 1811		
Isabel	28 Jan 1814		
Nancy Allen	2 Jan 1817		
Elizabeth Ann	7 Mar 1820		
Hugh Telford,Elder	20 Aug 1764		5 Jun 1833
Jane Telford			
(children)			
Thomas	11 Nov 1786		
Robert			
John	12 Oct 1790		
Mary	20 Mar 1793		30 May 1845
Elizabeth			
Hugh A.	27 Oct 1798		
Ann	9 Jun 1805		
(second marriage)			
Jane Telford	12 May 1777	7 Jan 1808	
(children)			
Samuel	25 Apr 1809		
Jane	18 Nov 1810		
Tirzah	10 Feb 1815		
Washington	15 Jan 1823		
(third marriage)			
Sarah Telford			
Robert Telford		1813	
Nancy Telford	7 Apr 1791		
(children)			
Thomas E.	1 Feb 1815		
Elizabeth	6 Jun 1816		
Benjamin Dobson	19 Aug 1769	27 Jan 1800	
Elizabeth Dobson	20 Jun 1777		27 Sep 1828
(children)			
Elizabeth	27 Oct 1800		
William R.	20 Apr 1803		
Jane	24 Jul 1805		
Margaret	31 Dec 1807		
Benjamin	1 Dec 1812		
Ignatious Jones			7 Jul 1824
Wineford Jones			
John Roach, Jr.	15 Jun 1769	14 Jan 1790	May 1847
Rachael Roach	22 Jun 1770		
(children)			
William			
John			
Needham	23 May 1797		
Angelina	19 Dec 1799	10 Apr 1819	

SUGG'S CREEK CHURCH

NAMES	BIRTHS	MARRIAGES	DEATHS
ROACH			
Elizabeth	6 Nov 1802		
James P.	18 Oct 1804		
Celia	26 Oct 1806		
Joseph	9 Jan 1811		
Isaac J.	13 Oct 1813		
Isaac Johnston			
Wineford Johnston			19 Apr 1836
James Law, Elder	18 Jun 1766	17 Mar 1791	
Rosannah Law	29 Sep 1768		
(children)			
Margaret C.	15 Jan 1792		
Elizabeth	15 Oct 1793		
Rachael	7 Oct 1795		
Thomas T.	30 Nov 1797		
John	3 Apr 1800		
Jane C.	15 Oct 1802		
Mary	10 Nov 1806		
James Porter	23 Oct 1808		
Rosannah	14 Jul 1812		
John Kirkpatrick,E.	14 Feb 1770		
Jane Kirkpatrick	20 Jan 1774		
(children)			
John H.			
Mary			
Thomas			
Josiah	7 Aug 1798		
James	10 Jan 1800		
Jane M.	17 Nov 1801		
Alex A.	11 Dec 1803		
Margaret	16 Nov 1805		
Aseneth	15 Jul 1807		
William B.	5 Feb 1810		
Nancy E.	15 Aug 1813		
Ransom Gwyn			1848
Rebecca Gwyn			1848
(children)			
Mary	3 Oct 1793		
Sarah	2 Oct 1796		
Hugh	25 Sep 1798		1827
Robert	18 Nov 1803		
Margaret	24 Mar 1809		
Elenor	20 Jun 1811		
William	30 Jan 1815		
Rebecca	23 Dec 1819		
Robert Smith	Jul 1758	1791	1823
Margaret Smith	4 Mar 1762		
(children)			
John	25 May 1784		11 Oct 1822

NAMES	BIRTHS	MARRIAGES	DEATHS
SMITH			
Rosannah	6 Dec 1786		Sep 1846
William			
Rachael	21 Sep 1892		26 Sep 1818
Jane	20 Oct 1794		23 Apr 1823
Robert	17 Nov 1796		
Hugh	12 Oct 1798		
Samuel C.	17 Nov 1801		
Jesse	3 Jan 1803		Oct 1848
Thomas Telford, E.	11 Nov 1786	20 Oct 1808	2 Mar 1857
Elizabeth Telford	13 May 1783		16 Jan 1842
(children)			
Hugh	29 Sep 1809		
Nancy	15 Apr 1811		
Jane	14 Apr 1813		
Esther H. twins	7 Apr 1815		
Maryan F.	7 Apr 1815		1820
Elizabeth S. twins	17 Sep 1817		1822
Isabel C.	17 Sep 1817		1822
Margaret O.	29 Jan 1820		
Robert A.	1 Apr 1822		
Rachael	27 May 1824		
Thomas F. M.	6 Jan 1827		
Samuel Brown		26 Mar 1801	6 Sep 1840
Elizabeth Brown			7 Aug 1833
(children)			
James M.	14 Apr 1803		
Robert twins	26 May 1807		
Margaret	26 May 1807		
Elizabeth	3 Dec 1809		
Rosannah	7 Dec 1811		
John S.	27 Apr 1815		
William	14 Apr 1819		
(second marriage)			
Nancy Brown		30 Oct 1834	
Samuel Houston	9 Sep 1835		
John Currey	30 Apr 1762	29 Jul 1784	5 Sep 1840
Sarah Currey	10 Sep 1766		30 Oct 1843
(children)			
Isaiah	8 Jul 1788		
Jane	12 Apr 1790		
Elijah	10 Jul 1792		
Susannah B.	15 Oct 1795		
Abner B.	1 Dec 1797		
Elizabeth	15 Nov 1801		
Sarah H.	26 Dec 1804		
Margaret	5 Nov 1807		1847
John Hamilton	30 May 1769		
Mary Hamilton			
(children)			

SUGG'S CREEK CHURCH

NAMES	BIRTHS	MARRIAGES	DEATHS
HAMILTON			
Margaret	1 Dec 1801		
Hannah K.	2 Aug 1803		
Mary	6 Mar 1805		
George G.	23 Apr 1808		
James Bradford	29 Sep 1775	12 Jul 1803	1848
Elizabeth Bradford	13 Feb 1783		1876
(children)			
Eli M.	30 Aug 1804		26 Jul 1838
Malinda D.	31 Mar 1806		
William M.	13 Jul 1807		24 Jul 1831
John Rea		1804	
Anna Rea			1848
(children)			
James W.	6 Jan 1805	18 Sep 1830	
Margaret	23 Feb 1807		
William	20 Apr 1809		22 Oct 1836
John	5 May 1811		
Isabel	21 May 1814		3 Mar 1834
Elizabeth Ann	9 Jul 1817		7 Mar 1834
Josiah T.	2 Dec 1819		5 Mar 1834
Samuel	22 Nov 1822		11 Jun 1824
Mary Jane	27 Feb 1826		
Reuben Wood, Elder	10 Oct 1787	13 Nov 1810	9 Sep 1835
Jane Wood	12 Apr 1790		28 Sep 1846
(children)			
John C.	7 Jun 1812	21 Sep 1831	
Susannah M.	8 Dec 1813		
David F.	11 Mar 1816		29 May 1845
Reuben M.	3 Oct 1817		
Jane H.	28 Dec 1820		
Isaiah B.	10 Mar 1824		7 Jul 1840
John Roach, Elder	23 Jan 1794	24 Aug 1815	
Mary Roach	13 Jan 1792		
(children)			
John N.	15 May 1816		
Thomas K.	13 Oct 1817		
Alex A. F.	18 Sep 1819		
Angelina M.	1 May 1821		2 Jan 1822
James P.	17 Feb 1823		
Louiza Jane	7 Jan 1825		
Rachael E.	1 Jan 1828		
Emeline			
E. C.			
William Roach	23 Feb 1791	15 Sep 1814	
Anna Roach	1791		
(children)			
Rachael F.	15 Apr 1816		
Mary S.	27 Nov 1817		

NAMES	BIRTHS	MARRIAGES	DEATHS
ROACH			
Elizabeth Ann	7 Feb 1820		
Nancy A.	21 May 1822		
Angelina C.	10 Jul 1824		
Elenor P.	1 Mar 1827		
John F.	16 Aug 1829		
Celia B.	1 May 1832		
Elijah Currey, E.	10 Jul 1792	20 Jul 1813	
Margaret C. Currey	15 Jan 1792		
William Telford	8 Jun 1777	Apr 1802	
Elizabeth Telford	15 Oct 1778		
(children)			
Samuel K.	29 Jan 1803		
Mary	8 Oct 1804		
Elizabeth S.	22 Jan 1807		
Thomas E.	31 Oct 1808		
John	27 Jul 1810		
Ann	14 Aug 1812		
William W.	19 Feb 1815		
Louiza	5 Mar 1819		
John Telford	12 Oct 1790	20 Mar 1817	
Sarah Telford	3 Jul 1786		
(children)			
Hugh			
Mary			
Elizabeth Ann			
Andrew J.			
William G.			
Hugh A. Telford	2 Oct 1798		1842
Mary W. Telford			
(children)			
Elizabeth Ann			
David Bradford	1 Aug 1778	3 Nov 1803	
Mary Bradford	7 Oct 1787		
(children)			
Susannah	24 Oct 1804		
Samuel C. F.	24 Jul 1808		
Mary A.	30 Jun 1811		
Sarah W.	13 Feb 1814		
Josiah Kirkpatrick	7 Aug 1798	Apr 1819	
Nancy Kirkpatrick	7 Apr 1791		
(children)			
Robert			
Sarah	17 Jan 1820		
Aaron Sprouse	8 Mar 1771	31 Dec 1799	
Elizabeth Sprouse			
(children)			
John G.	21 Aug 1801		

NAMES	BIRTHS	MARRIAGES	DEATHS
SPROUSE			
Margaret C.	1 Sep 1803		
Nancy	8 Oct 1805		
Rachael	3 Nov 1807		
Mary	11 Dec 1810		
George D.	24 Apr 1815		
William	19 Jul 1817		
Joseph H. Roach	9 Jan 1811	1 Dec 1830	
Mary D. Roach			
(children)			
John Beard			
James Yandle			
Mary Yandle			
(children)			
John	16 Oct 1805		
Catharine	31 Aug 1807		
William	31 Aug 1809		
Thomas	6 Aug 1811		
Polley Ann	15 Sep 1813		
James H.	2 Jul 1815		
William Smith			5 Jul 1819
Elizabeth Smith			
(children)			
Iveson	24 Nov 1816		
Margaret			
Andrew Gwyn	13 Oct 1800	30 Aug 1821	
Esther Gwyn			
(children)			
Hugh R.	23 Feb 1823		
Ransom R.	27 Mar 1825 baptized		
James			
Elizabeth E.			
Esther R.			
Rebecca M.			
Jesse Smith	3 Jan 1803		1848
Latty Smith			22 Apr 1840
(children)			
John S.			
Margaret J.			
Robert Monroe			
Nancy Currey (widow)			
(children)			
John B.			
Robert B.			
James H.			
Ezekiel S.	1800		
Jane S.			18 Feb 1833
Lavina B.			
Elizabeth			1815

NAMES	BIRTHS	MARRIAGES	DEATHS
CURREY			
Isaac N.	8 Jun 1809		6 Aug 1840
Moses M.	23 Mar 1811		
Owen Quinley			
Mary Quinley			
(children)			
Mary Ann			
William C.			
David M.			
John C.			
Nancy E.			
Robert Brown	26 May 1807	10 Aug 1827	
Mary Brown	10 Aug 1808		3 Aug 1846
(children)			
Elizabeth J.	26 Jun 1828		
Nancy Ann	22 Sep 1829		
Ira E.	11 Mar 1832		
Margaret R.	27 Apr 1835		
Needham Roach	23 May 1797	10 Apr 1819	
Fanny Roach	25 Dec 1797		
(children)			
Sarah H.	30 Jan 1820		
Evaline L.	20 Apr 1822		
Rachael E.			
John H.			
Josiah E.			
James M. Brown	14 Apr 1803		
Celia Brown	26 Oct 1806		
James Drennan, E.	8 Sep 1787	22 Jun 1809	
Frances Drennan	13 Jun 1787		1836
(children)			
John	2 Mar 1810	Aug 1830	
Joseph A.	2 Dec 1811		
Sarah W.	4 Dec 1814	21 Sep 1831	
Catharine A.	10 Oct 1816		
Eliza J.	15 Sep 1818		
William B.	30 Oct 1820		19 Oct 1840
Rebecca A.	6 Dec 1822		
James A.	20 May 1825	1842	25 Dec 1857
Rachael A. F.	5 May 1827		
Thomas J.	27 Jun 1829		
Andrew J.	27 Jun 1829		
Hugh Smith	12 Oct 1798		
Elizabeth Smith	6 Nov 1802		
(children)			
Rachael R.	2 Apr 1822		
Celia L.	19 Jan 1824		
Margaret A.			

NAMES	BIRTHS	MARRIAGES	DEATHS
William Brown			
Jane Brown			
(children)			
Sarah L.			
Margaret			
Ann B.			
Rachael C.			
Ross			
Hugh			
Elizabeth L.			
Matt H. Hooker			
Nancy B. Hooker			
(children)			
Mary J.			
Martha C.			
Ezekiel S. Currey			
Rebecca Currey			
Jacob Woodrum			
Benjamin F. Woodrum			
William Woodrum	15 Aug 1807	30 Jul 1829	
Martha Woodrum	7 May 1809		
(children)			
Frances	17 Aug 18?6		
Colantha Jane	17 Dec 1836		
Reuben M. Wood	3 Oct 1817	30 Jul 1839	
Hester A. Wood	23 Aug 1821		
(children)			
Thomas Lunsford	14 Feb 1841		
Reuben Mariette	4 May 1843		
Elizabeth L. A.	9 Sep 1845		13 Dec 1848
Martha Jane Taylor	8 Jan 1848		
Thomas Glisson			
Sarah Glisson			1846
Plesent M. Markham			18 Oct 1844
Jane Markham			
Hugh Brown	4 Dec 1815	20 Aug 1835	
Lamiza Brown	16 Apr		
(children)			
James M.	2 Mar 1837		
Elizabeth A.	4 May 1839		
William C.	22 Aug 1841		
William C.			6 Nov 1913
Ross Brown		1 Sep 1835	
Rosannah Brown	7 Dec 1811		
David F. Wood	11 Mar 1816	7 May 1835	29 May 1845
Ann B. Wood	18 Jun 1814		
(children)			

NAMES	BIRTHS	MARRIAGES	DEATHS
WOOD			
Sarah J.	16 Mar 1836		
Susannah A.	4 Jan 1838		23 May 1865
John C. Wood	7 Jun 1812	21 Sep 1831	
Sarah W. Wood	4 Dec 1814		
(children)			
James D.			
F. J.			
J. B.			
C. A.			
Moses M. Currey	23 Mar 1811		
Margaret Currey	31 Dec 1807		
Thomas K. Roach	13 Oct 1817	16 Jul 1835	
Nancy W. Roach	4 Sep 1817		1840
(children)			
L. C. Roach			
Isaac Barr			
Caroline Barr			1844
Hugh Telford, Min.	29 Sep 1809	20 Apr 1842	
Julia A. B. Telford	1 Feb 1819		
(children)			
William Thomas A.	5 Sep 1843		
Samuel Brown	13 Jan 1845		
Richard Beard	9 Mar 1847		
Rebecca E. B.	27 Jun 1850		
Hugh B. Hill	31 Aug 1852		29 Aug 1895
Andrew J.	22 Sep 1855		
James Bradford, Jr.			
Rachel Bradford			
Robert Foster, E.	4 Jul 1807		
Margaret Foster	23 Feb 1809		
(children)			
William	9 Jul 1828		9 Jan 1844
Ann J.	10 Oct 1831		19 May 1851
Isabel R.	7 Jan 1834		
James D.	12 Jun 1836		
John	8 Jan 1839		1 Oct 1840
Andrew J.	24 Apr 1841		
(second marriage)			
Nancy Foster	29 Oct 1810		
(children)			
Robert E.	7 Jun 1847		
Henry Devault			
James Robbins			
Elmira A. Robbins			27 Aug 1844
Elizabeth Barr			
Malinda Carter			1844.

SUGG'S CREEK CHURCH

NAMES	BIRTHS	MARRIAGES	DEATHS
William McGinness			1844
Tennessee Randall			1848
John B. Kirkpatrick			
Flamen M. Robbins			1846
James (Parum)			
Hugh R. Gwynn			
Morris Gooden			
Rachael Drennan			
Rachael Telford			
Elizabeth Telford			
Elizabeth A. Telford			
Rhoda Ann Ford			
Delanta Ann Robbins			
Priscilla Finney			
Mrs. Patsy Dobson			
William S. Rice			
Mary Wright			
Elizabeth E. Osborn	21 Aug 1836	baptized	
Hester A. Osborn	21 Aug 1836	baptized	
Margaret Telford	21 Aug 1836	baptized	
Hubbard Cawthon	23 Aug 1836	baptized	
William Cawthon	23 Aug 1836	baptized	
Sally Ward			26 Sep 1839
Sally Davis			18 Jan 1843
Jane Davis			
Cintha Davis			
Stephen Woodrum			
Polly Ford			
R. C. Brown			
Lucinda Beard			
Rebecca McDaniels			
Susannah Hamilton			
Delilah Welch			
Tabitha Aheart			
Mitchel Welch			
Ezekiel S. Currey			
Mary E. Hamilton			
Mrs. Ann Chandler			
Nancy Smith			1840
Robert A. Finney			
Martha Woodrum			
Tabitha J. Woodrum			
Demaris Parum			
Mrs. Margaret Hooker			
J. Jacobs			
Nancy Brown			
Caroline Huddleston			1844
Burrel P. Smith	15 Aug 1841	baptized	
Robert Climer			
Hugh (Kelsey) Bell			
Samuel Hamilton			
Ira P. Davis			?4 Feb 1846

164

SUGG'S CREEK CHURCH

NAMES	BIRTHS	MARRIAGES	DEATHS
John H. Bush			
Rachael Roach			
Venetta Glisson			
Jane Cunningham	15 Aug 1841 baptized		
Lucinda H. Cawton			
Susannah F. Cawthon			
Isaac N. Cawthon	14 Aug 1842 baptized		
Maryan Huddleston			
James A. Drennan			
Alfred Vernum			
William Morgan			
Ida Rea			
Malinda Sullivan			
John B. Jackson			
Elizabeth Dobson			
Houston Cawthon			
Emeline Roach			
Thomas J. Drennan			
Elizabeth Jackson			
Manerva Jackson			1849
Malinda Barefoot			1845
Ann Foster			
Isabel Foster			
W. S. Woodrum			
James N. Yandell			
C. C. Roach			
M. C. Bonner			
P. B. Jackson			
A. D. Jackson			
Caroline Dobson			
Joseph W. Cawthon			
Susan M. Barr			
Sarah Carter			
Preston Sublett			
Thana Barr			
Will Kirkpatrick			1842
S. E. C. Kirkpatrick			
(Lissie) Jackson			
Nancy Jackson			
Mary R. Carter			
Elizabeth Harrison			
Sophona Gwyn			
William Brown			
Monroe Smith	1850 baptized		
Edward Eakes			
William (Sackrey)			
r. W. Miers			
Margaret Brown			
Tho B. Dobson			
Thankful Griffin			
Ely Griffin			
S. J. Griffin			

165

SUGG'S CREEK CHURCH

NAMES	BIRTHS	MARRIAGES	DEATHS
A. E. Dobson			
Elisa Dobson			
Amanda Cothern			
Julya Winters			
S. J. Yandell			
R. J. Kirkpatrick			
S. A. Kirkpatrick			
Margaret Smith			
Bedford Rice			
Ross Brown			
Randy Dobson			
Jane Bearfoot			
Robert W. Hooker			
(Isaiah) M. Cothern			
Rachel E. Cothern			
Olley Kirkpatrick			
Joseph Smith			
Thena Rice			
Mrs. (Sinna) (Hiers)			
Elizabeth Morrison			
Hiram Hugle			
Elizabeth Woodrum			
Elem Rice			
Martha Rice			
Ruth J. Rollins			
William Mires			
Sarah Ann Dobson			
Ester J. Dobson			
Eveline Mires		1852	
Lucy Jones			
Sarah Wiley			
Amanda Walker's Servant			
Mina Sherel			
Martha Jane Devault			
Cordelia Ann Mires			
Rachel Elizabeth Wood			
Sarah Elizabeth Telford			
William T. Telford		Oct 1858	
Reb. Ann Ceay			
John B. Fields			
J. E. Sanders	12 Jun 1839		
Will E. Sanders	3 Jul 1872		

RUTLAND BAPTIST CHURCH

(Located about four miles southeast of Mount Juliet, Tennessee)

WILSON COUNTY COURTHOUSE
Register's Office
I 216

     This indenture made the fourth day of September in the year of our Lord one thousand eight hundred and twenty between Blake Rutland, Benjamin F. Stevenson, and Elizabeth Stevenson of Wilson County and State of Tennessee of the one part and John Ligon in trust for the Baptist Church that may hereafter be constituted holding of the doctrines held by the United Baptists in America in the County of Wilson and State aforesaid of the other part. Witnesseth that the said Blake Rutland, Benjamin F. Stevenson, and Elizabeth Stevenson for and in consideration of the sum of twenty-five cents in hand paid by the said John H. Ligon in trust for the aforesaid Baptist Church and for other valuable considerations receipt whereof is hereby acknowledged hath given granted bargained sold aliened and confirmed unto the said John H. Ligon in trust as aforesaid forever a certain tract or parcel of land situated lying and being in the County of Wilson and State aforesaid as follows to wit. Beginning at the mouth of Harris' Spring running north six poles to Benjamin Graves' south boundary line, thence east with said line fifty-four poles to the road, thence south with said road to the old schoolhouse fourteen poles, thence to the beginning so as to include the privilege of getting water for the use of the school and congregation that may occasionally asemble for divine worship. To have and to hold the aforesaid lands with all and singular rights, profits, emoluments, and appurtenances of and to the same belonging or in any wise appertaining for the only proper use and behoof of him the said John H. Ligon in trust as aforesaid forever and the said Blake Rutland, Benjamin F. Stevenson, and Elizabeth Stevenson for themselves, their heirs, executors, and administrators do covenant and agree to and with the said John H. Ligon in trust as aforesaid Baptist Church their successors in order that the before recited land and bargained promises will warrant and forever defend against the rights, titles, interest, or claims of all and every person or persons whatsoever.

     In witness whereof the said Blake Rutland, Benjamin F. Stevenson, and Elizabeth Stevenson hereunto set their seals the day and year above written.

Witnesses:	JOHN G. GRAVES	BLAKE RUTLAND
	JOHN CURD	BENJAMIN F. STEVENSON
		ELIZABETH STEVENSON

Recorded 4 July 1822

RUTLAND BAPTIST CHURCH

NAMES	BIRTHS	MARRIAGES	DEATHS
Elizabeth Lumpkin			7 Mar 1865
Sally Clemmons			
Mary Rutland			
Elizabeth Puckett			
Sally Ames			30 Sep 1865
Martha Baird			10 Sep 1865
Elizabeth A. Lane			
Susan Curd			Jun 1871
Mary L. Rice			
Dorcas Martin (Stone)			
Jane Gwyn			
Roxey Tilford			
Elizabeth B. Lane			
Elizabeth Graves			
Rebecca Carver			
Betsy P. Sullivan			
Brunetty Carver			
Elizabeth Carver			3 Jun 1865
Frances Casell			
Polly Hamblin			
Martha Hamblin			14 May 1867
Rebecca Puckett			
Eleanor Barton			17 Feb 1867
Harriet Goldston			
Mary Carver			
Rachel Carver (Cook)			
Frances Clemmons			
Patsey Smith			Excluded
Parmelia Hamblin			
Sally Hamblin			24 Aug 1875
Elizabeth Curd			
Margaret Wright			14 Dec 186_
Mary Spickard			
Caroline Drennan			
Nancy Curd free			Expelled
Eliza Hamblin (Webber)			
Johanna Harpole (Jarrett)			2 Feb 18__
Anna Lane			
Louisa Lane			
Julia Gleaves			
Martha J. Lane			
Nancy A. Wright			
Sarah Hamblin			
Elizabeth Martin (Sullivan)			
Susan Donaldson (Neal)			
Mary Sullivan			
Martha R. Martin			12 Oct 18__
Blilza C. Lane			
Sarah Ann Sullivan			
Almeda Lane			
Zuritha Lane			
Lucinda Drennan			

RUTLAND BAPTIST CHURCH

NAMES	BIRTHS	MARRIAGES	DEATHS
Elizabeth Drennan			Excluded
M. A. Rutland			
Mary Sullivan			
Melissa Loyd			
(?) Loyd			
E. B. Lane (Jones)			
Alashaba Moss			5 Feb 1866
Louisa Wright			
Rebecca Graves			
Nancy A. Graves			
Moriah Earnest			
Jane Johnson			
Martha Drennan	10 Oct 1861	baptized	
Nancy Bradshaw	10 Oct 1861	baptized	
Amanda Osment	11 Oct 1861	baptized	
Susan Cawthon	11 Oct 1861	baptized	
Elizabeth Neal	11 Oct 1861	baptized	
Eliza Bradshaw Lane	11 Oct 1861	baptized	
M. H. Carver	11 Oct 1861	baptized	
Melinda Loyd	11 Oct 1861	baptized	
Ardenia E. Climer (Jones)	1861	baptized	
Susan E. Lennard	11 Oct 1861	baptized	
Mary F. Walker	11 Oct 1861	baptized	1871
Victoria Baird			
Izilla Lane	4 Nov 1861	baptized	
Eliza Ames			
Matilda Wright	4 Aug 1861	baptized	
Willie Jones	13 Oct 1862	baptized	
Martha Jane Carver	20 Oct 1862	baptized	
Mary Eldridge Brett	20 Oct 1862	baptized	
Martha McChesney			
Charity J. Wright	7 Aug 1864	baptized	
Surilda Carver	7 Aug 1864	baptized	
Mary Wright			
Anis Campbell	6 May 1865	baptized	
Margaret Crudup	Sep 1865	baptized	Excluded
Mary Clemmons	4 Jun 1865	baptized	
Cordelia Lane	15 Sep 1865	baptized	
Martha Lane	10 Sep 1865	baptized	
Hellen Loyd	15 Sep 1865	baptized	
Mary Chriswell	10 Sep 1865	baptized	
Martha Chriswell	10 Sep 1865	baptized	
L. E. Finney			
Louise Chriswell			Excluded
Nancy Young			
Martha Lohman			
Martha A. Hamblen	27 Jul 1867	baptized	
Nancy Chriswell	27 Jul 1867	baptized	
Sallie Chriswell	27 Jul 1867	baptized	
Sarah Lane	27 Jul 1867	baptized	
Sophia Lane	27 Jul 1867	baptized	
Claranda Lane	6 Oct 1867	baptized	

RUTLAND BAPTIST CHURCH

NAMES	BIRTHS	MARRIAGES	DEATHS
Almedia A. Carver			
Mary J. Chriswell	6 Sep 1868	baptized	
Nancy W. Lane			Excluded 1871
Mary J. Lane	6 Sep 1868	baptized	Excluded 1871
Kitty Rutherford	6 Sep 1868	baptized	
Nancy A. Lane	3 Oct 1868	baptized	
Mary E. Young	3 Oct 1868	baptized	
Rachel Clemons (Wright)			
Sallie Carver (Cawthon)			
Frances Chriswell	14 Sep 1868	restored	
Rebecca Brandon			
Cleopatra Cook			
Michal Gleaves			
Jane Brown			
Margaret Chriswell			
Caroline Miller			
Harriet J. Miller			
Hary J. Miller			
Elizabeth Bilbro			
Margaret Bilbro			
Eli Sullivan			
William D. Hamblin			
Henry Carver			18 Aug 1868
Andrew Baird			20 Oct 1863
James W. Barton			
John N. Curd			
S. G. Shepard			
Alvah Sperry			
Armsted Lain			10 Sep 1864
George Eaks			
Pierce W. Bashaw			Killed in Battle
David Lane			
Barnet Guill			
R. P. Lane			
Johnson Lane			
William Blackburn			
Harvey S. Lane			
Joab Sullivan, Jr.			
William C. Rutland			
Thomas P. Walker			
William H. Carver			
Jeptha Clemons			
Thomas L. Lane			Dec 1864
Richard Johnson			Excluded 65
James Loyd			
Rubern Searcy			Apr 1862
Richard Bradshaw			Excluded 69
Alexander J. Carver	deacon		
James Bashaw			
J. F. M. Martin			
J. M. Carver	11 Oct 1861	baptized	12 Mar 1862
John Osment	4 Nov 1861	baptized	

RUTLAND BAPTIST CHURCH

NAMES	BIRTHS	MARRIAGES	DEATHS
L. W. Wright	4 Nov 1861	baptized	
B. F. Lane	4 Nov 1861	baptized	
James W. Wright	4 Nov 1861	baptized	7 Feb 1865
Milton Lane	5 Jan 1862	baptized	Excluded 68
Pleasant S. Carver	4 Jun 1862	baptized	
P. M. Carver	10 Sep 1865	baptized	
Larkin Moor	10 Sep 1865	baptized	
John W. Bradshaw	10 Sep 1865	baptized	Excluded 67
George H. Sullivan	10 Sep 1865	baptized	
Peter Bashaw	5 Nov 1865	baptized	
C. W. Young	5 Nov 1865	baptized	
Robert P. Hamblin	5 Nov 1865	baptized	
John W. Chriswell			
Robert Young deacon			
Lewis Lohman			
Woodson Jones	27 Jul 1867	baptized	
George Young	27 Jul 1867	baptized	
David Bowie	27 Jul 1867	baptized	
Leander Chriswell	6 Sep 1868	baptized	
William Chriswell	6 Sep 1868	baptized	
George Chriswell	6 Sep 1868	baptized	Excluded 1875
John Bowie	6 Sep 1868	baptized	
James McFarland	6 Sep 1868	baptized	Excluded
Joseph W. Hamblin	6 Sep 1868	baptized	
Josiah Wright	6 Sep 1868	baptized	
Ellie Fuqua	16 Sep 1868	baptized	
George Martin	16 Sep 1868	baptized	
Fount Harlaine	16 Sep 1868	baptized	Excluded 1876
Jackson Chriswell	16 Sep 1868	baptized	Jul 1874
(?) Shreeve			
John W. Lane	8 Oct 1868	baptized	
Milton Lane			Restored 68
William Swingley	1 Nov 1868	baptized	Excluded
Peter Fuqua	1 Nov 1868	baptized	
Gardner Guill	1 Nov 1868	baptized	
John Bond	1 Nov 1868	baptized	Excluded 1872
Robert Chriswell	6 Nov 1864	baptized	
J. P. Miller	5 Dec 1868	baptized	
(?) Smith			1874
W. G. Sweeney	31 Apr 1869	baptized	
James Miller	5 Oct 1869	baptized	
Henderson Clemmons	6 Nov 1869	baptized	
Thomas Martin	12 Sep 1870	baptized	Excluded 1875
Cates Young	16 Sep 1871	baptized	
D. H. Carver	10 Sep 1871	baptized	
Harrison Osment	11 Sep 1871	baptized	
Charles H. Cook	11 Sep 1871	baptized	
Patrick Donnell	10 Sep 1871	baptized	
W. Lane			
J. Barton			
David Young	1 Oct 1871		

171

RUTLAND BAPTIST CHURCH

NAMES	BIRTHS	MARRIAGES	DEATHS
H. N. Sullivan			
A. ?. Leek	5 Nov 1871 baptized		
Lafayette Whitsett	3 Oct 1872 baptized		
Robert G. Lane			
James H. Carver			
William Cawthon			
Joab Sullivan			
R. L. Lane			
John Clemmons			
George Lane			
John Martin	Sep 1874 baptized		16 Nov 1879
Dayton Martin			
Jasper Fuqua			
Stephen Barton			

SUGG'S CREEK CEMETERY

1. Margaret Long, born 16 Sep 1873; died 20 Jul 1874.

2. Josephine A. M. Gwyn, born 1845; died 1873.

3. Martha Carter, born 21 Mar 1812; died 27 Jul 1827.

4. John Logue, born 25 Jun 1818; died 17 Oct 1889.

5. Catherine Harkreader, born 22 Jan 1820; died 30 Sep 1908. Wife of John Logue.

6. Nannie C., born 18 May 1862; died 8 Feb 1885. Wife of M. P. Omohundro. Daughter of J. and C. Logue.

7. George W. Northcott, born 31 Oct 1847; died 27 Oct 1889.

8. Cinthia Baggerly, born 1 Jul 1801; died 28 Jul 1879.

9. L. L. Jenkins, born 22 Apr 1883; died 7 May 1883. Son of W. F. Jenkins.

10. Solon Jenkins, born 11 Mar 1889; died 16 Dec 1890. Son of W. F. and D. J. Jenkins.

11. Caroline Drennan, born 1826; died 1904. Wife of William Williams.

12. William Williams, born 1820; died 1897.

13. Z. F. Williams, born 1817; died 1901.

14. Bettie Logue, born 1851; died 1925.

15. Emaline Eaks, born 19 Jan 1842; died 30 May 1883.

16. Lucy Ann Eakes, born 1859; died 1878.

17. Eliza J., born 18 Jan 1845; died 16 Apr 1881. Wife of R. F. Wood.

18. Infant, born 1 July 1874; died age 7 months. Daughter of R. F. and E. J. Wood.

19. R. M. Brown, born 1844; died 1911.

20. Alice K. Edwards, born 1 Nov 1848; died 16 Feb 1885. Wife of R. M. Brown. Erected by her daughter, Maud Ozment.

21. John Robert Boyd, born 19 Jul 1870; died 15 Nov 1935.

22. Willie Bradford Boyd, born 12 Dec 1868; died 26 Jan 18__.

23. Perry S. Boyd, born 26 Apr 1912; died 5 Dec 1938.

24. Willie Thomas, born 12 Nov 1858; died Dec 1859. Son of J. H. and E. Smith.

25. Mollie E., born 3 Sep 1858; died 4 Dec 1862. Daughter of F. E. and M. J. Kirkpatrick.

26. Martha J., born 15 May 1835; died 27 Mar 1842. Daughter of James W. and Mary M. Rea.

27. Margaret Ann Robbins, born 26 Nov 1811; died 9 Sep 1869.

28. Mary J. Taylor, born 27 Feb 1826; died 9 Dec 1912.
29. John Rea, born 22 Nov 1779; died 23 Jul 1862.
30. Mollie Baker, born 24 Nov 1855; died 28 Apr 1905.
31. Wallace Baker, born 5 Mar 1856; died 11 Jun 1903.
32. Ira E. Peach, born 11 Jun 1818; died 25 Oct 1896.
33. Mildred Burnette, 12 Jun 1908.
34. T. P. Burnette, born 3 Mar 1872; died 25 May 1916.
35. Annie B. Burnette, born 19 May 1878; died 8 Feb 1946.
36. Eugenia Burnette, born 20 Apr 1912; died 26 Oct 1928.
37. W. Hannah.
38. M. Hannah, died 22 Mar 1816 in the 29th year of life.
39. C. Crawford, died 31 Mar 1816. Age 62 years.
40. Nathaniel Davis, born 6 Mar 1765; died 1837.
41. W. F. Yandell, born 1809; died ?1870.
42. Sarah Davis, born 3 Feb 1760; died 18 Jan 1813.
Consort of Nathaniel Davis.
43. (?) Harrison, born 20 Sep 1862; died 1865.
44. R. G. Harrison, born 10 Apr 1865; died 20 May 1865.
45. Harrison. Infant, born and died 11 Aug 1860.
46. V. C. Dobson, born 7 Jan 1832; died 13 Apr 1865.
47. William R. Dobson, born 2 Apr 1802; died 11 Oct 1880.
48. (?) Bland, born April 1856; died 28 Sep 1858. Infant of J. M. and Elvira Bell Bland.
49. John M. Bland, born 8 Oct 1820; died 19 Feb 1862.
50. J. M. Bland, born 3 Apr 1862; died 16 Aug 1862.
51. Elizabeth Bland, born 23 Nov 1830; died 28 Feb 1863.
52. Martha Dobson, born 1784; died 22 Sep 1869.
53. Matilda Dobson, born 9 Mar 1813; died 1865.
54. John Dobson, born 19 Sep 1810.
55. Henry Dobson, died Mar 1824 in the 24th year of life.
56. Martha Dobson, died Apr 1838 in the 63rd year of life.
57. John Dobson, died Feb 1853 in the 81st year of life.
58. Elizabeth Dobson, born 23 Jun 1775; died 27 Sep 1828.
59. Benjamin Dobson, born 18 Aug 1769; died 23 Nov 1836.
60. Isaac N. Curry, died 6 Aug 1840. Age 31 years, 29 days.
61. Isaac N. Curry, age 23 years, 8 months. Co. 11, 45th Tennessee Infantry, C. S. A. Son of I. N. Curry and Jane Curry.

62. Benjamin Dobson, died 25 Oct 1838. Age 2 years, 2 months. Son of I. N. Curry.

63. S. Dobson, born 1812; died Oct 1839.

64. Elizabeth Dobson, died 1817 in the 13th year of life.

65. Temperance Wiley, born 4 Feb 1843; died 22 Jun 1852.

66. Jane Wiley, born 21 Jun 1807; died 21 Dec 1887.

67. Martha Wiley, born 20 Jun 1844; died 1 Jun 1903. Wife of J. S. Osment.

68. Josephus Osment, died 28 Aug 1906. Age 49 years.

69. Thomas A. Bagarly, born 10 Jun 1831; died 22 Jan 1921.

70. Sallie Ann Huggins Baggarly, born 12 Nov 1861; died 22 Mar 1942.

71. Henry Miller, born 8 Jan 1773; died 24 Nov 1857. Son in law of John Drennan, Sr.

72. Rachel Miller, born 13 Dec 1775; died 8 Jan 1860. Wife of Henry Miller.

73. Here lies the body of John Drennan who departed this life 19th day of January 1816 in 76th year off his age. August 24, 1819. (A very elaborate Masonic emblem is on his tombstone.)

74. Elanor Logue, born 2 May 1826; died 21 of 1847. Consort of G. Peach.

75. Cairnes Logue, born 14 Jul 17__; died 11 Apr 1864.

76. Margaret, born 1785; died 30 Mar 1843. Wife of Cairnes Logue. Member Methodist Episcopal Church.

77. Joshua, born 1 Jul 1822; died 30 Aug 1843. Son of Margaret Logue and Cairnes Logue.

78. Infant, born and died 9 Dec 1845. Daughter of T. G. Logue and Nancy Logue.

79. Flo Sillivin, died 26 Jan.

80. Anna, died 28 Feb 1852. Age 76 years, 11 months, and 17 days. Wife of John Rea.

81. Cinthy H., born 17 Jan 1803; died 18 Dec 1861. Wife of James Drennan.

82. James Drennan, born 17 Sep 1788; died 31 Jan 1867. Son of John Drennan, Sr.

83. Fanny W., born 13 Jun 1788; died 16 Jul 1831. Wife of James Drennan.

84. William B. Drennan, born 31 Oct 1820; died 19 Oct 1840.

85. Infant, born and died 1 Mar 1839. Daughter of John C. Hampton and Ann Hampton.

86. Infant, born 11 May 1811. Son of J. C. Hampton and Ann Hampton.

87. Infant, born 7 Feb 1878; died 1 Apr 1878. Son of F. Goodrick.

88. Burton Williams, born 15 Nov 1877; died 26 Feb 1880. Son of L. A. Williams.

89. Callie Williams, born 10 Nov 1879; died 12 Apr 1881. Daughter of L. A. W. Williams and J. O. Williams.

90. Willie Williams, born 16 Jul 1889; died 16 Jul 1889.

91. James G. Hamilton, born 16 Oct 1812; died 24 Aug 1895.

92. Margaret M. Hamilton, born 11 Apr 1817. Married 27 Aug 1835 James G. Hamilton.

93. Ellen Lane, born 4 Jan 1849; died 1 Dec 1880. Wife of C. B. Lane. Daughter of James Hamilton.

94. Eliza H. Eskridge, born 28 Jul 1851; died 17 Sep 1943.

95. Richard Woodroof, born Jul 1820; died 1894.

96. Maggie Harkreader, born 17 Mar 1852; died 17 Sep 1899.

97. Samuel S. Luckey, born 12 Jun 1821; died 5 Sep 1872. Erected by John Luckey.

98. A. D. Pugh, born 23 Mar 1865; died 14 Feb 1927.

99. W. T. Pugh, born Apr 1860; died Jul 1888.

100. M. A. Pugh, born 1880; died 1881.

101. Aney Pugh, born 15 Jun 1860; died 8 Jun 1882.

102. Al L. Marean, born 1872; died 1873. Son of G. T. Nikens and J. E. Nikens.

103. I. B. Castleman, 18 Oct 1849.

104. Maggie E. Castleman, born 25 Jun 1852; died 11 Dec 1923.

105. William Burnette Castleman, born 8 Jun 1880; died 1 Oct 1913. A Medical Doctor.

106. Sophia E., born 1884; died 1887. Daughter of L. B. Castleman and M. E. S. Castleman.

107. Infant, 1878. Son of L. B. Castleman.

108. Thomas Telford, born 1 Feb 1815; died 27 Nov 1881.

109. Wickliffe, born 13 Dec 1871; died 4 Aug 1873. Son of L. Burnette and E. B. Burnette.

110. Mary Ann, born 22 Nov 1816; died 3 Jan 1875. Wife of T. C. Telford. Married 17 Nov 1836.

111. Herman Rufus Castleman, born 26 Aug 1910;   died 9 Feb 1943.

112. L. W. B.

113. Fannie C. Birdwell, born 10 Jul 1855;   died 21 Apr 1875.

114. John Wick   ), born 9 Aug 1871;   died 30 Aug 1875. Erected by T. C. Telford.

115. Jo Ed, born 2 Nov 1901;   died 27 Dec 1903.   Son of J. K. Bradford and Lena Bradford.

116. Sarah Books Jones, born 11 Mar 1825;   died 26 Dec 1897.   Wife of Jasper Ozment.

117. Hannah Frances Hewgley, born 30 Sep 1827;   died 9 Feb 1905.

118. Birdie I. Vaughn, born 23 Jan 1874;   died 30 May 1904.

119. Ola May Vaughn, born 12 Dec 1903;   died 14 Aug 1904.

120. Inez Hale, born 1903;   died 1905.

121. U. T. Hewgley, born 6 Feb 1845;   died 3 Oct 1885.

122. Harriet E. Hewgley, born 18 Jul 1854;   died 17 Dec 1875.

123. Rubin N. Hewgley, born 19 Feb 1873;   died 7 Oct 1875.

124. J. T. Hewgley, born 10 May 18__;   died 21 May 18__.

125. Eugene Burnette, born 1878;   died 1910.

126. W. J. Burnette, born 1848;   died 1913.

127. Orville Burnette, born 1880;   died 1903.

128. Robert Ann Burnette, born 1851;   died 1917.

129. J. W. Ozment, born 1855;   died 1926.

130. Wade Baker, born 24 May 1873;   died 1 May 1899.

131. Roxie Boyd, born 28 Feb 1879.   Daughter of J. W. Boyd and M. A. Boyd.   Married Wade Baker 9 Jan 1899.

132. Robert C. Hale, born 16 Apr 1881;   died 28 Jan 1899.

133. Emily A., born 1 Sep 1841;   died 16 May 1903.   Wife of G. Hale.

134. Sarah E. Bland, born 27 Nov 1854;   died 27 Nov 1939.

135. William A. Bland, born 19 Dec 1851;   died 29 Jul 1895.

136. James Arthur, born 17 Feb 1885;   died 19 Jul 1890. Son of W. A. Bland and S. E. Bland.

137. Lizzie, born 1 Apr 1887;   died 7 May 1887.   Daughter of J. E. Humble and L. M. Humble.

138. George P. Bland, born 19 Jul 1898;   died 21 Oct 1918.

139. America V., born 25 Jul 1865;   died 13 Sep 1886. Wife of C. G. Smith.

140. A. B. Smith, born 28 May 1809; died 18 Jan 1888.

141. Hannah J. Hamilton, born 20 Aug 1828; died 25 Feb 1896. Wife of A. B. Smith.

142. Abbie R., born 19 Oct 1846; died 30 Mar 1898. Daughter of A. B. Smith.

143. Ida Underwood Smith, born 2 Sep 1879; died 1 May 1952.

144. Minnie, born 5 Jun 1881; died 9 Mar 1913. Wife of W. A. Smith.

145. Ona Smith, born 25 Dec 1916.

146. Mack Smith, born 16 May 1911; died 10 Jun 1944.

147. Linda Gaye Smith, born 29 Sep 1939; died 10 Jun 1944.

148. Mary Williams, born 10 Feb 1845; died 15 Nov 1887.

149. Sarah Williams, born 27 Jul 1863; died 18 Oct 1874.

150. Joseph L. Patterson, born 18 Jun 1873; died 8 Feb 1951.

151. J. L. Matthews, born 10 May 1842; died 6 Dec 1921.

152. Nancy Jane, born 23 Jan 1853; died 25 Nov 1906. Wife of J. L. Matthews.

153. Willie Doris Matthews, born 12 Dec 1911; died 12 Dec 1911.

154. Martin Vick, born 18 Jan 1862; died 22 Aug 1875.

155. W. H. Carter, born 27 Feb 1830; died 1 May 1911. Married Nov 1853 Adline Spain.

156. Adline, born 31 Jan 1837; died 12 Mar 1907. Wife of W. H. Carter.

157. Bettie Hamilton Burnette, born 6 Mar 1844; died 23 Oct 1906.

158. Darrah Hamilton, born 23 Nov 1870; died 23 Jun 1906.

159. Cora E. Carter, born 20 Oct 1881.

160. Harvey J. Carter, born 11 Jul 1886; died 26 May 1950.

161. Joe A. Carter, born 1856; died 1942.

162. Amanda L. Carter, born 1858; died 1943.

163. Vicie Smith, died 1885.

164. C. D. Bland, born 29 Jul 1850; died 22 Aug 1921.

165. E. N. Bland, born 30 Sep 1860; died 24 Oct 1909.

166. M. E. Bland, born 26 Sep 1861; died 14 Jun 1921.

167. Mildred Bland, born 9 Sep 1917; died 12 Sep 1917.

168. Nancy, born Jan 1789; died 31 Jul 1873. Wife of Samuel Brown.

169. S. H. Brown, born 9 Sep 1835; died 12 May 1909.

170. N. R. Jones, born 16 Nov 1875; died 25 Apr 1885.

171. William E. Underwood, born 17 Jul 1859; died 28 Apr 1911.

172. Mary Underwood, born 8 Dec 1860; died 11 Aug 1917.

173. H. R. Gwyn, born 25 Oct 1822; died 27 Feb 1871.

174. Hugh Gwyn, born 1749; died 11 Jan 1829.

175. Hugh Gwyn, born 25 Sep 1798; died 17 Dec 1826.

176. Two Infants, born and died 24 Jun 1851. Infants of James R. Gwyn and N. S. Gwyn.

177. Josephine Alice, born 23 Jun 1850; died 2 Jul 1850. Daughter of James R. Gwyn.

178. Ransom Gwyn, died 13 May 1848. Age 76 years.

179. D. M. Sullivan, born 25 May 1810; died 31 May 1856.

180. Eli M. Bradford, born 30 Aug 1801; died 26 Jul 1831.

181. William M. Bradford, born 13 Jul 1807; died 21 Jul 1831.

182. James Bradford, born 29 Sep 1775; died 29 Feb 1849.

183. Elizabeth Bradford, born 13 Feb 1784; died 11 Aug 1876. Born in Chester District of South Carolina.

184. W. H. Bradford, born 12 Dec 1836; died 25 Jan 1904.

185. Sallie E. Bradford, born 10 Nov 1838; died 27 Nov 1904.

186. Lydia Carter, born 1800; died 14 Apr 1857.

187. James R. Boyd, born 17 Feb 1907; died 16 Oct 1934.

188. Valentine Stull, died 20 Jul 1827.

189. Nancy Eveline, born 1 Aug 1831; died 1 Apr 1832. Daughter of John Drennan and Rebecca Drennan.

190. Infant.

191. John W. Brewer, born 21 Feb; died 15 Jul 1861.

192. A. O. Harrison, Jr., born 12 Jun 1879.

193. J. W. Brown, born 18__.

194. J. D. Shelton, born 1834; died 7 May 1871.

195. James Franklin, died 7 Mar 1865. Age 1 month, 12 days. Son of James R. Sullivan and S. E. Sullivan.

196. Esther C. Hamilton, born 6 Oct 1817; died Aug 1877.

197. George Hamilton, born 29 Oct 1858; died 18 Aug 1861. Son of E. Hamilton and Thomas Hamilton.

198. John Hamilton, born 1 Oct 1861; died 13 Nov 18__. Son of Thomas Hamilton.

179

199. Leon McCall, born 6 Apr 1907; died 20 Mar 1927.

200. Alice McCall, born 10 Sep 1885; died 4 Aug 1935.

201. Thomas Hamilton, born 6 Dec 1806; died 16 Aug 1885.

202. Rachel Williams, born 27 May 1821; died 16 Apr 1856.
Her 2 children, J. T., born 15 Sep 1850; died 1 Sep
1852. M. E. W., born 22 May 1853; died 15 Oct 1855.

203. John Roach, born June 1769; died 26 May 1847.

204. Elmira Jane, born 19 Nov 1821; died 27 Aug 1813.
Wife of John Roach.

205. M. Angelina, born 19 Dec 1797; died 17 Sep 1849.
Consort of Thomas Kirkpatrick.

206. Nancy W., born 11 Sep 1817; died 21 Sep 1840. Consort of Thomas K. Roach.

207. Sarah Glison, born 1790; died 13 Apr 1846.

208. Lee Baker, born 1861; died 1944.

209. John Elliott Baker, born 8 Jan 1781; died 23 Oct
1866.

210. Elizabeth Beasley, died 9 Sep 1829. Age 27 years,
7 months, and 5 days. Wife of John E. Baker.
Erected by Wade Baker in memory of his father and
mother.

211. Jane Wood, born 12 Apr 1790; died 28 Sep 1840.

212. Reuben Wood, born 10 Oct 1787; died 9 Sep 1835.

213. Isaiah B. Wood, born 10 May 1821; died 7 Jul 1840.

214. (?) Brown, born 10 Apr 1819; died 6 Sep 1893.

215. Hugh Brown, born 1815; died 21 May 1899.

216. William Brown, died 9 Jul 1855. Age 74 years.

217. Jane, died 28 Aug 1855. Age 72 years. Wife of William Brown.

218. Alfred Osborn, born 16 Oct 1788; died 26 Feb 1848.

219. Sarah Currey, born 10 Sep 1756; died 30 Oct 1813.

220. John Currey, born 30 Apr 1762; died Sep 1840.

221. Isaac N. Cauthon, died at Rock Island Prison 3 Jan
1861. This put here by James M. Brown.

222. Sarah Shelden, born 30 Oct 1811; died 4 Jan 1849.
Wife of J. M. Shelden.

223. James W. Telford, born 18 Jan 1838; died 15 Jan
1839.

224. H. M. Robbins, born 16 Nov 1820; died 9 Aug 1847.

225. Ruth Robbins, born 21 Sep 1816; died 3 May 1865.

226. Colonel A. D. Robbins, born 11 Oct 1822; died 15
May 1848.

227. Edmond Eakes, born 20 Jan 1800; died 7 Jun 1852.

228. Marette, born 4 May 1843; died 13 Dec 1848. Son of R. M. Wood and E. A. Wood.

229. Martha, born 5 Dec 1797; died 26 Apr 1866. Wife of Alfred Osborn.

230. Ruphus Eaks, born 1852; died 1854.

231. Lorena T. Mires, born 21 Dec 1870.

232. William Mires, born 14 Feb 1862; died 9 Mar 1926.

233. Morgan Mires, born 16 Feb 1831; died 29 Feb 1920.

234. T. F. Mires, born 15 Feb 1845; died 6 Jul 1929.

235. Charity Mires, born 23 Dec 1842.

236. Peter Myers, born 10 Dec 1793; died 15 Feb 1868.

237. Dinah Mires, born 20 Dec 1803; died 1 Feb 1885.

238. J. A. Hamilton, born 1 Feb 1819; died 2 Feb 1889.

239. Reverend Hugh Telford, born 29 Sep 1809; died 27 Sep 1869.

240. Thomas Griffin, born 3 Apr 1803; died 23 Sep 1885.

241. Thankful Griffin, born 3 Sep 1807; died 17 Feb 1863.

242. Erinvola, born 12 Feb 1878; died 6 Nov 1879. Daughter of Henry Strong and Bettie Strong.

243. Charlie, born 4 March 1867; died 10 Oct 1869. Son of Henry Strong.

244. Birdie, born 3 Apr; died 25 Sep 1869. Daughter of Henry Strong.

245. May, born 8 May 1861; died 22 Aug 1866. Daughter of J. Wright and E. Wright.

246. Margaret Logue, died 16 Mar 1867. Age 82 years. Wife of C. Logue.

247. Sallie Ann Sanders, born 16 Apr 1856; died 5 Feb 1902. Wife of Z. P. Blaine.

248. Zechariah P. Blaine, born 17 Feb 1854; died 21 May 1888.

249. George Sanders, born 14 Sep 1832; died 15 May 1902.

250. Z. P. Bland.

251. John William Bland, born 29 Nov 1877; died 5 Dec 1877. Son of Z. P. Bland and S. A. Bland.

252. Howard Eaks, born 7 Feb 1892; died 20 Mar 1910.

253. Infant children, born and died 20 Aug 1879. Children of H. Eaks.

254. Newton Eaks, born 10 Jun 1816; died 16 Oct 1873.

255. Luther Eaks, born 22 Aug 1873; died 6 Nov 1885.

256. Price Henry Garvin, born 31 Mar 1905; died 24 Jul 1950.

257. Lillie A. Bannister, born 23 Jul 1889; died 4 Dec 1923. Wife of John Boner.

258. Laura Jane Boner, born 10 May 1862; died 7 Apr 1927.

259. Albert G. Boner, born 17 Aug 1860; died 23 Jan 1925.

260. Gorge Stanley, born 1913; died 1935.

261. U. P. Jenkins, born 5 Mar 1855; died 25 May 1915.

262. F. M. Jenkins, born 11 Jun 1855; died 31 Dec 1934.

263. J. G. Jenkins, born 27 Aug 1892; died 27 Oct 1918.

264. Taylor Jenkins, born 3 May 1847.

265. Fannie E. Jenkins, born 30 Aug 1857; died 6 Dec 1914.

266. Alvie Jenkins, born 9 Nov 1890; died 30 May 1907.

267. Minnie Jenkins, born 9 Nov 1888; died 11 Nov 1904.

268. James L. Wright, born 21 Dec 1838; died 25 Feb 1910.

269. Ruey Jane Wright, born 6 Feb 1846; died 2 Feb 1916. Married 21 Dec 1865. Lived together 45 years.

270. J. Staley Wright, born 11 Mar 1874; died 10 Feb 1940.

271. W. A. Williams, born 5 Oct 1864; died 10 Jun 1927.

272. Emma Wright, born 18 May 1869.

273. Mattie, born 2 Dec 1897; died 9 Mar 1898. Daughter of W. H. Brown and F. Brown.

274. Newton, born and died 23 Jul 1894. Son of W. H. Brown and F. Brown.

275. Paizzetta, born and died 5 Oct 1895. Daughter of W. H. Brown.

276. Infant, born and died 25 Nov 1896. Infant of W. H. Brown.

277. Salura T. Eakes, born 8 Jan 1883; died 5 Jun 1963.

278. L. G. Eakes, Sr., born 10 Sep 1879; died 7 Mar 1944.

279. William C. Eakes, born 30 Jan 1906; died 21 Sep 1938.

280. Ida Jane Harrison, born 7 Mar 1870; died 9 Jan 1953.

281. W. P. Harrison, born 1868; died 1939.

282. Jim Carter, born 10 Nov 1880; died 6 Aug 1956.

283. Burnice Carter, born 25 Apr 1918; died 16 Nov 1968.

284. Baby Mai Lane, born 1917.

285. Son.

286. Mirtha H. Carter, born 2 Jun 1894;   died 13 Aug 1953.

287. B. A. Carter, born 14 Feb 1887.

288. John J. Hartman, born 11 Apr 1862;   died 15 Jan 1916.

289. Mary A. Hartman, born 14 Aug 1872.

290. Ethelene, born 12 Oct 1918;   died 20 Jan 1920. Daughter of H. E. Murphy.

291. Florence, born 26 Jan 1873;   died 23 Jun 1920. Wife of J. W. Powell.

292. James Udell, born 13 Aug 1917;   died 10 Apr 1918. Son of Alvis McPeak.

293. Beatrice, born 4 Nov 1897;   died 8 Jan 1926. Wife of A. T. McPeak.

294. H. T. Eakes, born 28 Apr 1868;   died 31 Aug 1914.

295. Johnnie Pearl, born 29 Oct 1915;   died 9 Oct 1918. Daughter of H. Bright and S. M. Bright.

296. Etta Eakes, born 5 Jan 1868;   died 19 Oct 1918.

297. George Eakes, born 19 Apr 1861.

298. James Marshall Robbins, born 31 Dec 1846;   died 20 Aug 1864.

299. Susan Matthew Robbins, born 8 Dec 1813;   died 27 Mar 1867.   Wife of William C. Robbins.

300. Daisy Sullivan, born 4 Jan 1884;   died 16 Feb 1910.

301. Charlie Robbins, born 23 Jan 1877;   died 14 Jun 1939.

302. Tempa A. Robbins, born 26 Apr 1844;   died 23 May 1924.

303. John P. Robbins, born 25 Apr 1848;   died 21 May 1917.

304. Ruth Ann Robbins, born 11 Oct 1870;   died 1 Nov 1870.

305. John Lunsford Robbins, born 4 Feb 1882;   died 9 Jul 1954.

306. Maggie Lane, born 20 Jun 1874;   died 3 Nov 1878. Daughter of David T. Robbins.

307. A. O. Harrison, born 8 Jul 1839;   died 21 Feb 1907.

MOUNT VERNON CEMETERY

(Located off the Statesville Highway between Watertown and Statesville)

1. William H. Talley, born 10 Mar 1842; died 25 Jan 1902.
2. Robert E. Talley, born 4 Jan 1883; died 27 Jun 1913.
3. Infant, born 8; died 21 Feb 1905. Daughter of F. Delay.
4. W. A. Whitlock, born 5 Feb 1840; died 9 Oct 1898.
5. Nancy E. Cornelius, born 9 Oct 1861; died 6 Feb 1911.
6. Mattie Whitlock, born 1868; died 1923.
7. Maggie J. Bass, born 14 Apr 1847; died 16 Apr 1865.
8. Louaney Cassit), born 17 Jul 1869; died 4 Sep 1899.
9. Julia A. Patton, born 7 Oct 1896; died 19 Feb 1903.
10. Thomas P. Cassity, born 4 May 1818; died 6 Nov 1902.
11. Margret E. D., born 16 Sep 1887; died 16 Aug 1888. Daughter of H. C. Jones and M. E. D. Jones.
12. Ora Z. Oakley, born 9 Oct 1878; died 29 Jul 1870.
13. Elmer Alvin Young, born 23 Nov 1876; died 30 Nov 1878.
14. M. E. D. Jones, born 15 Aug 1852; died 29 Sep 1887.
15. John G. Thompson, born 26 Feb 1844; died 1 Sep 1859.
16. James O. Thompson, born 5 Dec 1836; died 30 Sep 1845.
17. John Williams, born 10 Nov 1824; died 3 Jan 1886.
18. Elizabeth Cantrell, born 20 Aug 1830; died 17 Aug 1911.
19. J. P. Cunningham, born 25 Jan 1852; died Sep .
20. Samuel Thompson, born 12 Dec 1838; died 1 Dec 1840.
21. John N. Thompson, born 16 May 1811; died 10 Jun 1846.
22. J. Wilson Payne, born 1867; died 1937.
23. Stella T. Payne, born 1879; died 1955.
24. Betty Bell, born 1873; died 1938.
25. Clara Bell, born 1889; died 1968.
26. Fate Patton, born 1864; died 1949.
27. Dora M. Patton, born 1868; died 1943.
28. J. H. Griffin, born 25 Oct 1861; died 16 Feb 1938.
29. Mary Ellen Griffin, born 1 Jun 1869.
30. Newbern Jennings, born 1875; died 1942.
31. Lillie W. Jennings, born 1875; died 1951.
32. Dee R. Patton, born 25 Aug 1875; died 17 Jan 1949.
33. Mandie A. Patton, born 1 Aug 1875; died 6 Feb 1963.

34. Elzie Hue Tarpley, born 1915; died 1951.
35. Shelvie Eugene Tarpley, born 1876; died 1958.
36. Alice Bess, born 1871; died 1965.
37. W. G. Ricketts, born 12 May 1804; died 27 Jun 1877.
38. J. Wilson Patton, born 1860; died 1920.
39. Minnie M. Patton, born 1870; died 1950.
40. Homer Lofton Jennings, born 1897; died 1924.
41. Ettie Payne Jennings Word, born 1889; died 1963.
42. Infant, born 19 Jan 1917; died 21 Jun 1917. Daughter of H. L. Jennings.
43. J. C. Payne, born 1838; died 1920.
44. E. J. Payne, born 1848; died 1937.
45. Dovie E. Chastain, born 22 Sep 1881; died 2 Jul 1918.
46. S. S. Ayers, born 25 Feb 1827; died 10 Aug 1919.
47. Rebecca Patton Ayers, born 17 Aug 1845; died 19 Jun 1888.
48. James Edgar. Son of T. M. Johnson and A. G. Johnson.
49. James Ricketts, born 6 Oct 1797; died 23 Jan 1887.
50. Catherine Ricketts, born 17 Oct 1805; died 14 Jul 1881.
51. James Nelson, born 11 May 1872; died Dec 1873. Son of J. B. Patton and S. E. Patton.
52. S. S. Ricketts, born 16 Jan 1803; died 15 Jul 1871.
53. Esther Thompson, born 15 Mar 1814; died 21 May 1894.
54. T. E. Patton, born 1865; died 1877.
55. C. M. Patton, born 13 Feb 1876; died 22 Aug 187?.
56. J. H. Patton, born 16 Aug 1871; died 22 Aug 1872.
57. Nancy L. Patton, born 28 Aug 1844; died 10 Jan 1880.
58. M. M. Oakley, born 185?; died 1906.
59. John C. Oakley, born 18 Apr 1854; died 3 Jan 1923.
60. Ollie Mack Payne, born 18 Dec 189?; died 20 Jan 1968.
61. Samuel A. Ricketts, born 27 Jul 1839; died 7 Mar 1912.
62. Laurence E. Talley, born 20 Aug 1810; died 16 May 1880.
63. Jane E. Talley, born 20 Jan 1811; died 20 Sep 1887.
64. Vina M. Talley, born 1868; died 1936.
65. Annie Patton, born 7 Apr 1844; died 22 Oct 1869.
66. Agnes Patton, born 8 Mar 1861; died 26 May 1884. Wife of W. M. Sherrill.

67. Mary Phillips, born 6 Nov 1820; died 16 May 1865.
    Wife of James T. Patton.

68. James T. Patton, born 5 Nov 1818; died 7 Jan 1901.

69. Lucy Fay, born 1 Jan 1829; died 25 Dec 1906. Wife
    of James T. Patton.

70. John G. Talley, born 30 Oct 1871; died 10 Feb 1936.

71. A. A. Patton, born 22 Oct 1866; died 1 Dec 1878.
    Daughter of R. H. Patton.

72. John W. Herman, born 7 Oct 1818; died 29 Jan 1881.

73. Mollie T. Marler, born 1876; died 1959.

74. Donnell Patton, born 10 Jun 1832; died 26 Feb 1895.

75. Sallie Jane Patton, born 27 May 1827; died 27 Nov
    1898.

76. Josie, born 1878; died 1914. Wife of E. E. Keaton.

77. Porter Graves, born 1884; died 1949.

78. Phillip S. Patton, born 1933; died 1935.

79. Dessie Patton, born 1884; died 1964.

80. Turney Patton, born 1880; died 1939.

81. Thomas Lynn Gammons, 1949.

82. Wanda K. Gammons, 1950.

83. Maude Murphey Simpson, born 27 Dec 1886; died 27
    Jun 1933.

84. Charlie Hall Simpson, born 11 Jan 1888; died 20 Apr
    1932.

85. George D. Chastain, born 1903; died 1916.

86. W. T. Talley, born 1868; died 1940.

87. Eudora E. Talley, born 1863; died 1925.

88. Stasie T., born 1890; died 1891. Son of Levi Harden
    and Fannie Harden.

89. Freddie, born 21 Oct 1894; died 13 Aug 1902. Son of
    W. T. Talley.

90. Dan G. Talley, born 1856; died 1935.

91. Effie, born 26 Jan 1877; died 2 Jul 1886.

92. W. C. Talley, born 1847; died 1919.

93. M. J. Talley, born 18 Jan 1848; died 16 Jul 1921.

94. S. E. Thompson, born 19 Sep 1870; died 18 Jan 1879.

95. Mary Payne, born 1857; died 1947.

96. Nancy Ayers, born 28 Oct 1847; died 12 Feb 1851.

97. M. T. Ayers, born 11 Aug 1817; died 7 Sep 1861.

98. Susan B. Ayers, born 19 Apr 1827; died 4 Mar 1908.

99. Elizabeth Patton, born 28 Sep 1850; died 29 May 1872.

100. Elizabeth. Wife of L. T. Patton.

101. Laura A. Patton, born 16 Nov 1874; died 26 Aug 1880.

102. Rutha Patton, born 15 Jul 1796; died 16 Jan 1869.

103. Jonathan Patton, born 1803. Elder, Mount Vernon Presbyterian Church.

104. Sam Payne, born 1859; died 1938.

105. James Godfrey Patton, born 21 Sep 1828; died 13 Sep 1850. Elder, Mount Vernon Presbyterian Church.

106. Ann A. W. Patton, born 19 Oct 1800; died 10 May 1835.

107. Joseph Patton, born ?1 Sep 1792; died 6 Nov 1859.

108. Margret, born 8 Mar 1808; died 15 Jan 1885. Wife of Joseph Patton.

109. Nancy E., died 16 Nov 1858. Age 22 years. Wife of S. D. Patton.

110. Zella Bland, born 1886.

111. Mary E. Patton.

112. Cornelia A., born 7 May 1869; died 7 Aug 1878. Daughter of Ed Patton.

113. Effa, born 24 Feb 1874; died Aug 1878. Daughter of Ed Patton and M. J. Patton.

114. Jimmie W., born 1 May 1871; died 20 Aug 1878. Son of Ed Patton.

115. Edward Patton, born 25 Nov 1837; died 1 Apr 1880.

116. Malinda Patton, born 20 Feb 1834; died 22 Nov 1902.

117. Fannie E. Patton, born 18 Oct 1866; died 6 Jul 1884. Wife of L. R. Ayers.

118. Nancy Margaret Patton, born 1838.

119. John Patton, born 20 Jan 1836; died 22 Apr 1886.

120. Samuel Patton, born 21 Sep 1808; died 12 Jul 1890.

121. Elender Compton, born 20 Sep 1808; died 3 Aug 1890. Wife of Samuel Patton.

122. L. J. Patton, born 8 Apr 1833; died 29 Nov 1891. Wife of James T. Patton.

123. Samie Marler, born 1919; died 1920.

124. John L. Lewis Marler, born 1903; died 1909.

125. Etter B. Patton, born 8 Dec 1875; died 30 Aug 1878.

126. Nancy Patton, born 22 May 1871; died 17 Aug 1878.

127. Joseph S. Patton, born 15 Jul 1874; died 13 Aug 1878.

128. Mary Tribble, born 5 Dec 1823; died 20 May 1877.

129. Lowry Ayers, born 15 Mar 1831; died 13 Dec 1858.

130. Fannie Jennings Ayers Dean, born 30 Sep 1836; died 23 Apr 1896.

131. James L. Ayers, born 17 Dec 1853. Age 27 years, 28 days.

132. Arabella Ayers, born 11 Jul 1854; died 16 Oct 1863.

133. Margaret Ayers, born 16 Feb 1789; died 23 Feb 1868.

134. Thomas R. James, died 15 Apr 1869. Age 18 years, 1 month, 27 days.

135. Rachel Marler, born 1855; died 1929.

136. Harrison B. Marler, born 9 May 1890; died 5 Aug 1927.

137. Robert W. Marler, born 13 Apr 1915; died 24 Feb 1917.

138. Nina, born 5 Jun 1892; died 19 Jan 1893. Daughter of E. M. Thompson.

139. Ressie, born 14 Jan 1869; died 8 Jan 1893. Wife of S. Coffman.

140. J. M. Vaught, born 18 Oct 1821; died 5 Apr 1900.

141. Elizabeth Jane, born 24 Jan 1832; died 12 Jun 1888. Daughter of E. M. Thompson. Wife of John M. Vaught.

142. Josephine G. Womack, born 1 Jul 1853; died 5 Jul 1887. Wife of E. T. Vaught.

143. Martha T. Wife of Reverend J. G. Patton.

144. Abigil Godfrey, born 16 Oct 1801; died 4 Jul 1881. Wife of E. M. Thompson.

145. John F. Patton, born 17 Dec 1825; died 6 Mar 1900.

146. Andrew Thompson, born 15 Sep 1806; died 25 Aug 1866.

147. Milly Thompson, born 16 Mar 1802; died 19 Aug 1897.

148. Tom Bland, born 1878; died 1956.

149. J. G. Thompson, born 27 Mar 1823; died 2 Sep 1855. Son of E. M. Thompson. Joined Presbyterian Church 30 Apr 1845. Ordained Elder at Mount Vernon 11 May 1851.

150. T. W. Patton, born 1832; died 4 May 1898.

151. Martha, born 15 Apr 1833; died 10 Sep 186?. Wife of T. W. Patton.

152. James N. Patton.

153. Margaret Aldona Patton, born 10 May 1870; died 4 Dec 1873.

154. M. E. Patton, born 3 Jan 1845; died 23 May 1875.

155. Andrew Patton, born 1800.

156. Elizabeth, born 12 Aug 1800; died 5 May 1881.
Wife of Andrew Patton.

157. Billie Louis Ferrell, born 1932; died 1936.

158. C. M. Patton, born 14 Dec 1864; died 1 Aug 1891.

159. Samuel Hill Patton, born 22 Aug 1883; died 19 Aug
1896.

160. A. F. Moore, born 1888.

161. James A. Young, born 14 Mar 1854; died 19 Jun 1909.

162. V. V. Moore, born 18 Oct 18?4; died 26 Jul 1887.

163. M. E. Moore, born 22 Feb 1854; died 20 May 1886.

164. Elizabeth Walden, born 1822; died 1885.

165. W. H. Walden, born 14 Sep 1822; died 10 Oct 1892.

166. G. D. Young, born 23 Oct 1823; died 26 Apr 1905.

167. Maranda Thompson, born 2 May 1827; died 16 Apr
1896. Wife of G. D. Young.

168. Anna Thompson, born 1788; died 1863.

169. Andrew Thompson, born 1778; died 1858.

170. G. G. Thompson, born 10 Oct 1846; died 28 Jan 1898.

171. Infant, born 8 Dec 1904; died 20 Dec 1904. Infant
of J. W. Payne.

172. Tennie Harden, born 1868; died 1933.

173. Mary Jane Patton, 11 Dec 1924.

174. T. W. Harvey, born 26 Jun 1916; died 13 Dec 1966.

175. Mattie H. Harvey, born 15 Nov 1885; died 17 Apr
1918.

176. C. L. Harvey, born 17 Nov 1878; died 9 Apr 1939.

177. Tom D. Patton, born 10 Mar 1849; died 6 Apr 1913.

178. Martha J. Patton, born 30 Jun 1849; died 6 Sep 1908.

179. John Patton, born 12 May 1824; died 17 Apr 1904.

180. Octie Lee Sherrill, born 22 Jul 1880; died 30 Sep
1899.

181. Rhoda, born 12 Dec 1819; died 12 Feb 1878.

182. Sam A. Harden, born 1862; died 1945.

183. Sarah Fisher, died 27 Mar 1836. Age 57 years, 6
months, and 4 days. Consort of John Fisher.

184. Gallie Patton, born 1875; died 1918.

185. M. Patton, born 12 Dec 1847; died 19 Dec 1894.
Wife of W. Patton.

186. J. W. Marler, born 1860; died 1940.

187. Mary Marler, born 1865; died 1934.

188. Johnie Patton, born 1874; died 1947.

189. J. R. Bell, born 23 Jan 1874; died 26 Oct 1945.

190. Della Bess, born 18 Jun 1882; died 29 Mar 1935.

191. Infant of J. R. Bess and Della Bess.

192. Henry Clay Ricketts, born 23 Aug 1894; died 23 Nov 1921.

193. Lotie Grimes Ricketts, 24 Aug 1899.

194. Anna Rakes, born 19 Oct 1878; died 29 Nov 1920.

195. Johnnie Rakes, born 20 Nov 1906; died 29 Oct 1918.

196. Lassie Patton, born 1890; died 1935.

197. Z. F. Marler, born 1892; died 1896.

198. Minnie Marler, born 4 Aug 1872; died 24 Nov 1907.

199. Mattie M. Porterfield, born 10 Sep 1897; died 10 Dec 1915.

200. Nancy Payne, born 1867; died 1940.

201. Minnie Sorrells, born 1886; died 1920.

202. Mary E. Payne, born 1843; died 1913.

203. Henry Payne, born 1842; died 1912.

204. M. Z. Davis, born 9 Dec 1878; died 1879.

205. Al J. Rakes, born 1871.

206. William Newton Ricketts, born 19 Nov 1845; died 4 Oct 1896.

207. Annie E. Lane Ricketts, born 11 Jan 1851; died 13 Feb 1917.

208. Orro Virginia Ricketts, born 25 Oct 1869; died 6 Jun 1897.

209. William Lane Ricketts, born 3 Jan 1890; died 23 Mar 1902.

210. Kathy Ferguson, 1959.

211. J. W. Thorn, born 1848; died 1933.

212. Margaret Walden, born 1887; died 1935.

213. Joe M. Walden, born 1859; died 1898.

214. Emily G. Bess, born 11 Jun 1838; died 6 Feb 1921.

215. W. L. Bess, born 7 Jun 1837; died 14 Feb 1898.

216. Ernest Lofton, born 1895; died 1897. Son of John Tarpley.

217. Chris Ashworth, born 1860; died 1907.

218. William Toy Tarpley, born 1904; died 1926.

219. Sallie Ashworth Beadle, born 1868; died 1934.

220. J. Thompson, born 22 Jan 1858; died 5 Sep 1907.

221. Girtie Porterfield, born 1883; died 15 Aug 1907.

222. James I. Porterfield, born 29 Feb 1835; died 13 Feb 1917.

223. Indiana Thorn, born 1852; died 1921.

224. Charlie M. West, born 28 Jan 1883; died 10 Apr 1944.

225. Maud T. West, born 27 Sep 1889; died 31 Mar 1954.

226. Edith Mary West, born 1909; died 1913.

227. T. B. Thorn, born 1872; died 1918.

228. S. J. Thorn, born 17 Apr 1876; died 24 Mar 1917.

Ayres cont.
S. S. 185
Samuel T. 77
Susan B. 186
Ayres, Alfred M. 39
James 31,112
Miles L. 39
Miles T. 58
Rufus B. 39
Samuel 68
Samuel S. 66,74
Babb, Bennett 1,6,18,73,
101
Elizabeth 37
Hicksey 11
Mary J. 37
Pamelia 37
Sintha T. 45
Thomas 11,37
William 84
William P. 45
Bacon, Frances 103
Bagarly, Thomas A. 175
Baggarly, Sallie A. 175
Baggerly, Cinthia 173
Bagwell, Allen 91
Lansford 138
Raspah 138
Rispah 126
William 138
Baijn, Elizabeth 121
Bailey, Johnathan 49,110
Jonathan 34
Baird, Andrew 55,100,170
Andrew J. 130
Ann 55,61
Ann J. 130
Charles L. 62
Elizabeth 4
Emily C. 133
James 133
James H. 45
James R. 133
Jerome R. 57,130
John 3,51,57,104
John H. 133
Lucinda 108,130
Martha 168
Mary 62
Matilda 34
Miles 4
Nancy M. 66
R. A. 66
Robert 55,61
Robert A. 130
Sally 4
Seldon 135
Victoria 169
William 3,4,55,57,61,
108
William C. 45,138
William J. 55,130
Wilson 4,51
Z. A. 138
Z. H. 80
Zebulum 45
Baker, John E. 180
Lee 180
Martha 18
Mary 25
Mollie 174
Sarah H. 109
Thomas D. 97
Wade 177,180
Wallace 174
Ball, Green L. 17
Lewis 97
Bandy, Alexander 51,138
Eperson 87,138
Epperson 51
Harriet 51
Jameson 87
Joseph 87

Bandy cont.
Mary 51
Peron 87
Richard 87
Solomon 87
Wilcher 87
William 26
William P. 65
Bangle, Griffin 85
Bannister, Lillie A. 182
Barbee, Ann 110
Daniel 69
Elias 67
Eliza 8
Elizabeth J. 8
John S. 58
John W. 59
Joseph L. 110
Joshua W. 110
Levi D. 110
Margaret A. 59
Mary 13
Owen T. 110
Parthena 110
Sally J. 59
Sarah H. 58
Tabitha 59
Barclay, Benjamin G. 24,32
Barefoot, Malinda 165
Barkley, George 76
James 76
Jane 75
Joseph H. 44
Lucinda 44
Lydia A. 44
Martha 44,76
Nicey 76
Thomas 74
Barksdale, Albert G. 143
G. B. 143
Higgerson 143
W. H. 143
Barnes, Charles 95
Elizabeth J. 145
Mathew W. 145
Priscilla 145
Turner 19
Barnet, Nancy 93
Barr, Angeline 133
Caroline 163
Chana 165
Elizabeth 163
Isaac 163
John 80
John L. 80
Laura 80
S. B. 71,121,122
Susan M. 165
Thomas 80
William 23
Barrett, William 85
Barry, David 143
Hardy S. 143
John N. 117
Lewid D. 143
M. A. 117
Mark 3
Mary P. 25
William F. 117
Bartholomew, Margaret 107
Barton, Alexander R. 113
David 147
Eleanor 168
Eliner 113
Elizabeth 147
Elizabeth D. 113
Gabriel 89,102,147
J. 171
James C. 113
James W. 170
Jane 113,147
Joseph 113,147
Margaret 147

Barton cont.
Martha 113
Matilda 139
R. A. 145
Rutherford R. 19
Samuel 102,147
Samuel Jr. 147
Samuel Sr. 93
Stephen 89,98,102,147,
172
William 118
William J. 113
Bashaw, Benjamin 147
Betsy 147
Byron 147
Fanny 147
Frances 147
Hannah 147
Hetty 147
James 170
James W. 147
John 147
Joseph E. 147
Lucy 147
Nancy 147
Peter 147,171
Pierce W. 170
Presley 147
Bass, A. 6
Alexander 1
Amzi 72,137
Andrew N. 80
Ann M. 150
Archemack 16
Cader 68,128
Catharine 118
Cato 128
Crawford E. 62
Elias 62
Etheldred 100
Ezekiel 69,89,118
H. L. 126,128
Job 90
John 2,81,139
John B. 81
John T. 72,123
Lucinda A. 137
Lycurgus 72
Malissa 118
Martha 128
Martha J. 61
Mary 139
Mattie J. 184
Robert C. 118
Sion 15
Susan 81
Tabitha B. 69
Tennessee 69
Theophilus 100
Thompson 55
William G. 15,80
Wilson T. 69
Bates, Candia 15
Eliza 15
James 83
John 15
Susan 15
William 15
Baxter, H. A. 47
Rebecca A. 47
Bay, Polly E. 149
Baylek, W. R. 129
Beadle, A. A. 76
Abram L. 76
Eli 76
Hardin R. 76
Martha F. 76
Sallie A. 190
Thomas 84
William 76
Wilson H. 76
Beard, Alexander 85
David 110,116

193

194

Brown cont.
Nancy 75,157,164,178
Nancy A. 161
Newton 182
Paizzetta 182
R. 78
R. C. 164
R. M. 173
Rachael C. 162
Richard 93,123
Robert 157,161
Rosannah 157,162
Ross 162,166
S. H. 179
Samuel 157,178
Samuel H. 157
Sarah L. 162
W. H. 182
William 38,45,50,67,
157,162,165,180
William C. 162
Eliza A. 140
Bruce, John 76
Bryan, A. 118
Aljournal 6,40
Aljurnal 16
Caroline A. 68
Christeny 6
Elizabeth C. 118
Elizabeth M. 117
J. B. 110
James B. 117
John 40
John B. 6,16,40
John W. 117
Nelson 6,7,10,68,94,97,
117
Nelson J. 7
Polly 117
Richard 117
Samuel W. 117
Sarah 7
Tennessee 40
William M. 7
William R. 117
William Sr. 83
Willis 83
Bryant, Caswell 54,69
James 48,54,69
John 48
Julia 9
Masible 12
Milford 16
Miseble 9
Richard 54,69
Richardson 48
Samuel 9
Bryson, D. 15
John Jr. 2
Joseph 2
Robert 15
Buck, Cornelius 93
Buckley, D. C. 110
Mary 126
Mildred 114
Buckner, Jacob 14
John W. 114
Richard 14
Suton 14
Usley 14
Bugle, Joseph 61
Bullard, Elizabeth 117
George H. 3,60,83
Bumpass, Garrett 13,29,31
Henrietta 33,51,56
Mary 119
Robert 13
William 101
William Jr. 147
William Sr. 147
Burchett, William 43
Burdine, Jefferson 69
Margaret 69

Burdine cont.
Nathan B. 136
Sophia 69
Burk, Fielding 67
Burke, Caladonia 58
Edward 93
Fielding 58
James L. 58
John G. 65
Sarah A. 58
Burnette, Annie B. 174
Bettie H. 178
E. B. 176
Eugene 177
Eugenia 174
L. 176
Mildred 174
Orville 177
Robert A. 177
T. P. 174
W. J. 177
Wickliffe 176
Burres, David 50
Burton, Albert 27
C. C. 74
Edmund 54
Eliza R. 147
Frances K. 147
James M. 147
Martha A. 147
Martha H. 28
Pleasant C. 54
Robert 147
Robert M. 32
Susan F. 27
Bush, John H. 165
Byne, William B. 17
Byram, Margaret 127
Byrd, Willie 93
Byrn, William 13
William B. 23,29,47
Cabell, Elizabeth 45
Nancy 45
William 45
Cable, Alfred C. 144
Martha E. 144
Cage, Benjamin M. 5,13
Claiborne 3
Jesse 97,99
John 13,88
Mary P. 3,5,13,25
Wilson 3
Cahal, Mary 67
Cain, George S. 95
Caldwell, C. B. 14
Calhoun, A. M. 35,36
Abigal 5
Agness 35
Alexander J. 116
Emily 62
Ewing F. 116
Fannie 62
Hezekiah 62
James 5,11
James M. 62
John 5,11
Lydia E. 116
Mary 113
Mary O. 116
Nancy E. 116
P. B. 116
Ralph 35
Samuel 116,121
Sarah W. 118
Thomas 62,116
Thomas P. 116
William 62
William C. 116
William W. 61,118
Calin, Hugh 15
Isham 15
Callis, Nancy M. 114
Campbell, Anis 169

Campbell cont.
David 71,148
Fannie A. 71
George H. 62,80
Hugh 95
Jane 148
John B. 71
Joseph A. 71
Lemuel R. 71
Margaret L. 148
Robert 8,12,26,29
W. B. 71,129
William 23,95
William B. 71
Canady, Alfred A. 134
Cannon, Abram 105
James 105,121
Canon, James 111
Cantrell, Elizabeth 184
George W. 73
Martha E. 73
R. 78
Capart, Laura 77
Caple, Elizabeth 29
Lucinda E. 149
Nancy 29
Rufus 29,30
Sally E. 149
Sarah 29
William 29
Caplenor, Martha 135
Capliner, Henry 56
James 56
Julia 56
Lavina 56
Samuel 56
William 56
Caplinger, Solomon 8
Caplinor, Rebecca 138
Caraway, Elihu 36
Elizabeth 27
Lovit 107
Merrett 27
Carlin, Elizabeth 17
Evaline 17
Hugh 17
Isham 17
Jane E. 5
John 17
Louisa 17
Martha 17
Spencer 5
William 93
Carlos, Archelaus 110
Carne, Edward 90
Carney, A. C. 71
D. J. 71
Carr, D. 109
Dabney 124,140
Jackey 71
James 71
Jemima 124
John 71,140
John O. 140
Martha J. 124
Mary B. 140
Matthew 3
Saphronia C. 71
Thomas H. 140
Tolbert 140
Walter 3
Carroll, George W. 140
Susan 140
William 84
Carruth, Walter 22
Carson, Henry 95
James 118,121
John D. 133
Louisa 54
Carter, Adline 178
Amanda L. 178
Annie J. 138
B. A. 183

196

197

198

Conyers cont.
  Mary J. 108
  Sarah 108
  Thomas 108
  William 75
  William F. 108
Cook, A. E. 73
  C. H. 72
  Charles H. 171
  Cleopatra 170
  James B. 79
  John 146
  John P. 79
  L. M. 128
  L. N. 126
  Margaret 79
  N. G. 73
  Rachel C. 168
  Sarah 79
Coonrod, Elvira 36
  Mrs. 36
  Newton 36
Cooper, Abram 97
  Christopher 97
  George 95
  Henry 85
Corder, Azariah 10,13,75
  Benjamin 64
  James 64
  John 64
  Margaret 64
  Mary E. 64
  Nancy E. 64
  Parthenia 64
  Sarah 64
Corke, Henry 87
Corley, Austen 93
  E. B. 9
  Elisha 108
  Robert 108
  William 108
Cornelius, James 87
  Nancy E. 184
Cossett, F. R. 59
  Franceway R. 139
  Matilda 139
Cothern, Amanda 166
  Isaiah M. 166
  Rachel E. 166
Cotther, Charlotte C. 121
Couch, Elvis P. 131
  Martha 131
  Mary 131
  W. G. 131
Cowan, Ann 44
  Docea 44
  George W. 71
  James 44
  Martha J. 44
  Mary M. 3,10
  Nancy 44
  Sarah 44
  William M. 10
Cowen, George W. 3
  Joseph W. 3
  Mary M. 4
  Samuel M. 3
  William 4
Cowgill, George W. 72
  James 72
  James P. 72
  John P. 72
  Maud 72
  Peyton C. 142
  William A. 72
Cowper, Elizabeth 151
Cox, A. 113
  Anderson 120
  Berry 35
  Berry W. 73
  Elizabeth 39,76
  Henry R. 39
  John 39

Cox cont.
  John B. 60
  Jordan 39
  Robert 70
  Sally C. 120
  Thomas 93
  William 39
Craddock, N. 94
Cragwall, William J. 110,
  115
Crapper, James 111
  William 111
Craton, Rachel 8
Crawford, C. 174
  Edmond 14,18
  Edward 35
  William 87
Creswell, Henry 104
  Rosannah 104
Crisman, Sarah 76
Criswell, Adline 101
  Halen 98
  Henry 148
  John A. 46
  John A. Jr. 46
  Mary J. 127
  Robert 148
Crittenden, John J. 53
Cropper, Benjamin 29
  Elizabeth 29
  James 26
  James C. 29
  James E. 28
Cross, E. 93
  James 84,96
  Margaret 149
  Uriah 96
  William 96
  William R. 96
Crosser, James 93
Crudup, John 69,73,119,
  121,138,142
  Josiah 57,77
  Louisa 57
  Margaret 57,169
  Pamelia C. 57
  Robert 57,77
Crunk, John 148
Crutcher, Edmund 88,96
  Mary C. 138
Crutchfield, Elizabeth J.
  19
  Esther 6
  George 6,12
  H. C. 19
  John 6,12
  Lucy 6,12
  Nancy 12,122
  Nancy A. 6
  Richard J. 127
  S. B. 6
Cummings, Charles 91
  Charles W. 91
  George 105
  Hugh 91
Cummins, A. 78
  Araminta 78
  James K. 78
  James W. 78
  Joseph 78
  Martha A. 78
Cunningham, Alexander 87
  D. 74
  J. P. 184
  James 24
  Jane 165
  Prudence 87
  Sally W. 87
  Samuel 9,16
  Sarah 87
Curd, Andrew P. 34
  Elizabeth 168
  John 167

Curd cont.
  John H. 34
  John N. 136,170
  Josephine 34
  Nancy 168
  Price 34,114
  Richard D. 34
  Susan 119,168
  Thomas 2,6
  William 23,30
  William E. 136
Currey, Abner B. 148,157
  Elijah 148,157,159
  Elizabeth 148,157,160
  Ezekiel S. 160,162,164
  Isaac N. 33,34,161
  Isaiah 148,157
  James H. 160
  Jane 148,157
  Jane S. 160
  John 84,148,157,180
  John B. 160
  Lavina B. 160
  Margaret 157,163
  Margaret C. 148,159
  Moses M. 33,143,161,163
  Nancy 160
  Rebecca 162
  Robert B. 160
  Sarah 148,157,180
  Sarah H. 148,157
  Susannah B. 148,157
Curry, Benjamin D. 175
  I. N. 174,175
  Isaac N. 174
  Jane 174
Dabney, John 148
Dale, George W. 49
  James K. 49
  William R. 49
Dance, Drury 125
  John E. 125
  John R. 125
  Mary E. 125
Danteridge, Lewis 83
  Milberry 83
Daughtry, Henry 72
David, J. B. 78
  K. 78
  Martha J. 78
  Mary S. 78
  Victoria F. 78
Davidson, Francis P. 105
  James 83
  Martha P. 105
  W. P. 105
  William P. 9
  Wilson 105
Davis, A. L. 122
  Acenith 55
  Alfred R. 141
  America A. 39
  Anderson L. 17,25,122
  Anderson T. 13
  Andy 71
  Aseneth 39
  Benjamin 101,148
  Benjamin H. 112
  Benjamin R. 44
  Catherine 137
  Cintha 164
  David 39
  Doshea 23
  E. A. 78
  Elijah 102
  Elizabeth 39,92,103
  Elizabeth J. 137
  Elizabeth M. 150
  F. M. 119
  Fanny 44
  Frances 55
  Frances B. 39
  Harriet 55,138

Davis cont.
Harriet F. 39
Ira P. 164
Isham F. 41,92,121
J. F. 119,138
J. Harvey 79
J. M. 23
J. S. 107
James 101
James E. 81
James H. 38,63,87,92,
122
Jane 164
Jane D. 149
Jesse S. 112
John 92,119
John N. 47
John R. 114
John W. 38,122
Kittie 71
Littie 44
Locky 78
Lucinda F. 148
Lucretia E. 148
Lucy 38
Lucy G. 13,17,25
M. Z. 190
Maggie 81
Marian 23,30
Marriott 103
Martha 39
Martha C. 137
Mary L. 122
Matilda T. 148
Morgan 71
Nancy A. 39
Nancy C. 13,17,25
Nancy E. 115,131
Nathaniel 47,92,106,
174
Octavia A. 148
Phoney I. 148
R. A. 119
Robert 71
Robert A. 23,47
Robert C. 97
Sally 78,128,164
Samuel 81
Sarah 81,103,174
Sion W. 148
Solomon 40
Thomas 61,67,87
W. C. 79,119
Walter 81
William 13,15,17,25,38,
39,107,119
William B. 137
William C. 39,122
William H. 63
Dean, Fannie J. 188
Dearing, Abner W. 37
Amelia 37
Elias H. 37
Robert J. 37
William L. 17,18
Willis B. 37
Debow, A. 7
A. A. 26
Ann 7
Ann E. 21,26
Bird 46
Elizabeth 7,14
Evaline N. 107,117
James 7,14,21,26
James B. 117
John 7,14,21,26
Margaret 7
Solomon 14,21,26
Sols 7
Delay, F. 184
H. H. 79
Infant 184
Jonas L. 79

Delay cont.
Mary C. 79
Nancy D. 79
Susan W. 79
Dellis, Benjamin 26
Joshua 29
Phebe 29
Robert 26,29,94
Thomas 124
Deloach, Jerusha 84,87
Joseph 87
Lucretia 87
Polly 87
Samuel 87
Solomon 84
Denny, Agnes 148
Nancy 148
Denton, Albert Y. 50
Ann E. 48
Edward 48,50,51,103
Eleanor W. 48
Emily R. 50
John E. 48
Mary E. 48
Temperance 48
Thomas 101,103
W. E. 130
William 48
William E. 50
William W. 48
Devault, Henry 163
Martha J. 166
Dew, Arthur 148
Elizabeth 148
John M. 18
Matthew 18,22
Nancy J. 18
Thomas B. 18
William C. 18
Dews, Elizabeth 105
Sarah B. 105
William W. 105
Dial, Dennis 88
Rubin 88
Sinna 88
Dias, John 55
Ruth J. 55
Dice, Jacob 86
Dickens, Elijah 14
Joseph W. 14
Mary M. 150
Samuel 103
Dickerson, Mrs. 33
John E. 34
Dies, David 52
James S. 52
Jesse 122
Lovet 52
Lovick 71,122,124
Matilda 122
Dill, Asa 83
John 83
Thomas 83
William 83
Dillard, A. R. 9
Allen 145
Elizabeth 108
Selety A. 145
Dixon, Samuel 97
Doak, John F. 128,129
William 125
Dobson, A. E. 166
Benjamin 15,71,143,155,
174
Caroline 165
Elisha 166
Elizabeth 155,165,174,
175
Esther J. 28,166
Hiram 28
Jane 155
John 94,174
Margaret 155

Dobson cont.
Martha 174
Matilda 174
Minerva J. 143
Nancy J. 71
Patsy 164
Randy 166
S. 175
Sarah A. 28,59,166
Sarah J. 153
Tho. B. 165
V. C. 174
Virginia T. 71
William 28
William R. 77,155,174
Dodd, David 27
Samuel 22
Dodds, Samuel 7
Dodson, Agness 57
George W. 69
I. J. 111
Isaac J. 57
Julia A. 57
Lavina 111
Nancy J. 69
Sarah 57
Sarah E. 71
Timothy 57
Virginia L. 69
Donaho, Bettie 77
Ed 77
Henry B. 77
Mary B. 77
Donaldson, Elizabeth 118,
133
James 126
John 118
Mary A. 133
Patrick 133
Peloney 133
Robert 133
Susan 133,168
Donalson, Elizabeth 119
Humphrey Sr. 102
James 64,65
John 68,77
Melessark 68
Patrick 70
Polena 70
Robert Jr. 70
Stokeley 77
Stokes 68
Donnell, Aceneth 40
Adlai 49,67
Adlai C. 117
Adnah 10,41,149
Agness 42
Alfred E. 50
Allen 34
America 67
Andrew K. 40
Betsy 117
Cleopatra 145
David M. 40
George 40
George E. 70
George F. 42
James 49,50,148
James A. 34,41
James E. 50
James M. 40,143
Jane 92
Jane F. 123
Jesse 85
John 40,105,117,148
John A. 50
John D. 117
John H. 41
John W. 42
Josiah 41,149
Leo 16
Levi 5,9
Lyle 149

200

201

Hardwick, William H. cont.
129
Hardy, Catherine 113
Edmund 103
James 48
Mrs. 48
Pleasant 87
Sterling B. 48,140
William 47
Harelson, Margaret A. 119
Harkreader, Catherine 173
George G. 53
John 53
John F. 53
Maggie 176
Harlaine, Fount 171
Harlan, Robert 80
Samuel 80
Harlin, Robert 141
Thomas 61,119
Harpole, George 109
Johanna 168
John 83,150
John Sr. 83
Harrelson, Ephraim 6
William 6
Harrington, Thomas 87,98
Harris, Abner 88
Alfred 4
Amelia 55,65,107,133
America E. 37
Andrew 91
Arastus C. 109
Arthur P. 68
B. W. 126,129
Baker W. 60
Charles L. 37
Coleman 4
E. A. 54
Edith L. 37
Edward 37,88,90,91,107
Eli 88,90
Eli A. 104
Eli M. 126
Eli R. 108
Elie 92
Elizabeth 68
Elizabeth E. 1
Elizabeth F. 68
Erastus C. 54,107
Fergus S. 85,88,104,129
Finis A. 126
Frances W. 37
Hannah 79
Harriet F. 55,107
J. 125
J. C. 48
J. P. 126
James 90
James H. 107
James L. 37
James S. 59,129
John 104
John B. 4
John F. 68
John G. 126
John P. 129
Joseph B. 107
Joseph H. 37
Lelia V. 54
Lilia V. 109
Lucy J. 68
Martha A. 48
Martha M. 32
Mary E. 79
Mary L. 107
Mary P. 126
Mary S. 54
Michael 1,4,5
Michael M. 1
Monroe 4
Nancy 1,4,129
Nancy A. 68

Harris cont.
Nancy J. 138
Nancy L. 1
Patsy S. 104
Polly 107,109
Richard F. 48
Richard W. 55,67,107
Robert 91
Robert E. 126
Robert J. 79
Sally 104
Samuel 83,84,88,92
Samuel H. 68,79
Samuel L. 68
Samuel P. 91
Spencer C. 1
Susan E. 55,65,107,133
Susan F. 48
Tacitus E. 37
Temple O. 32
Thomas W. 79
Virginia 107
W. 65
W. B. 108
Wesley 11
Westley T. 5
William 4,88,129
William W. 126
Harrison, A. O. 183
A. O. Jr. 179
Answorth 41,50,138
Betsy 17
Clack S. 50
Dicy F. 11
E. K. 46
E. R. 5,11
Elizabeth 1,16,18,26,28,
165
Henry A. 50
Ida J. 182
Infant 174
James C. 104
James G. 136
James P. 50,81
John 150
John P. 136
Joshua 96
Kitty 2,17,18
Landon 1,91
Lansdon 16
Margaret S. 50
Martha 136
Peter 17
Petro 2
Petro Q. 18
R. G. 174
Sally F. 136
Sterling 16,26,91
Temperance 16
Thweatt 17,18,86
Vicy F. 5
W. P. 182
W. W. 81
William 92
Harsh, George 46
Hartman, John J. 183
Mary A. 183
Hartsfield, Solomon 11,32,
96,98
Harvey, C. L. 189
Isaac 108,141
Mattie H. 189
Nancy 141
T. W. 189
Haskins, William N. 92
Hass, Albert G. 59
James W. 57
John 57,58
John E. 57,59
Joshua 59
Louisa 59
Luise A. 59
Mary A. 57,59

Hass cont.
Mary J. 59
Nancy F. 59
Phillip 57,59
Sarah J. 57,59
Thomas H. 59
William D. 59
William H. 59
Hatcher, Elizabeth 44
John 44
Lucy A. 138
Nancy 124
Polly P. 138
Robert P. 44
Sarah 44
Thomas W. 44
William 33,44
Hatton, Robert 136
Sophia 136
Hawkins, Albert G. 60
James A. 117
Jane 117
Laura 60
Hawks, John 110
Robert W. 110
Sarah 110
Haynes, Harriet 45
Manerva 45
Moody P. 45
Samuel 45
Hays, Fanny 140
Frederickson 142
Henry D. 72
James H. 142
James T. 72
Jane 6
John W. 142
Leander 142
Malinda 142
Mary 142
Mary M. 72
Mary P. 112
Nathaniel 142
Sampson 72
Samuel 72,142
Samuel A. 6
Sarah 136
Tennessee 142
William P. 136
Hazard, C. W. 128
Elizabeth 128
J. R. 30
Hearn, Alfred G. 33
Brunetta 53
C. R. 32
Catherine 137
Drucilla B. 32
Ebenezer 33,85
Elizabeth 54,109
Elizabeth S. 151
George 47
Granderson L. 33
Grandfather 122
Hardy 137
Hardy M. 145
Henry L. 137
James 137
James W. 25,137
John M. 37
Joseph M. 7
Lurana A. 32
Margaret C. 32
Martha A. 33
Mary C. 137
Mary G. 32
Mathew 32
Milbrey 24,25
Milbrey P. 137
Milby 85
Orren D. 33
Purnell 137
Rachel C. 24,32
Robert E. 33

Major cont.
 Samuel 141
 Samuel D. 127
 Samuel W. 22
Majors, Captain 95
Malone, David 110
 Fed 99
Manley, David 104
 Joseph 104
 Levi 104
 William 104
Manning, Bettie 69
Manor, Lewis 126
 Mrs. 126
Mansfield, Granville 133
Manson, J. T. 108
 Joseph T. 129,130
Markham, Jane 162
 John 123
 John R. 39,58
 Nancy 123
 Pleasant M. 39
 Plesent M. 162
Marks, Bailey 136,141
 Elizabeth 60,124,137,
 141
 George 38,52,60
 J. B. 77,81
 James 1,62
 James A. 52
 John 29,38,115,124
 Joseph 109
 Lewis 52
 Louiza J. 115
 Martha J. 52,124
 Thomas 38,60,115
Marler, Anthony 78
 Gideon P. 78
 Harrison B. 188
 J. W. 189
 Jasper 78
 John L. 187
 John R. 78
 Joseph 78
 Mary 189
 Minnie 190
 Mollie T. 186
 Rachel 188
 Robert W. 188
 Samie 187
 Z. F. 190
Marrs, Alexander 92,124
 Anna 4,15
 Catharine 12
 Hugh 101
 Hugh H. 15
 Katharine 4
 Martin 15,92,101
 Mary 15
 Nancy 4
 Robert A. 124
 Samuel 64
 Samuel E. 124
 William 4
 William D. 124
Marshall, Ann 131
 David 89,97,102
 John 97
 John W. 55
 William 97
Martin, Adaline 70
 Albert G. 49
 Amanda J. 54
 Amos 117
 C. L. 142
 Dabney 86
 David 88
 Dayton 172
 Dorcas 168
 Dosha 105
 E. B. 54,123
 Eliza D. 53
 Elizabeth 168

Martin cont.
 Elizabeth E. 54
 George 171
 J. D. 54
 J. F. 170
 James 54
 James L. 54
 James T. 114
 John 86,88,172
 John C. 54
 John H. 54
 Joseph 83
 Lindsey C. 70
 Maria 70
 Martha A. 111
 Martha E. 54
 Martha R. 168
 Martin 105
 Mary E. 70,153
 Mary J. 70
 Mathew 88
 Nancy 105
 Robert W. 54
 S. A. 142
 Sarah 49,126
 Sarah E. 49
 Susan 70
 Susan A. 105
 Thomas 171
 Wesley 70
 William 70
 William D. 49
 William L. 128
Massey, A. A. 60
 Abraham A. 122
 Albert W. 60
 Alice 65
 Benjamin L. 122
 Eli 143
 Eli M. 122
 Eli P. 143
 Elizabeth J. 122
 Ely 60
 Etheldred P. 60
 George W. 122
 Henry Y. 65
 John T. 143
 Joseph 65
 Mahaley 65
 Margaret 65
 Margaret A. 122
 Martha M. 122
 Mary 62,143
 Mary E. 122
 Matthew 60
 Nancy M. 60,66,122
 William L. 65
Massie, Martha M. 150
Mathews, Lucy E. 51
Matthews, J. L. 178
 Nancy J. 178
 William 93
 William E. 93,94
 Willie D. 178
Mattock, Amzy 48
 Elizabeth S. 48
 Henry B. 48
 Margaret H. 48
 William H. 48
Maxwell, Jesse 83
Mays, James 46
Meador, John 95
Measles, Jacob 74
 James 74,137
 Nancy 74
 Susan 74,137
 Tennessee 74
 Virginia 74
Medlin, Amand S. 47
 Charlotte L. 47
 Frances 43
 John 43
 Martha A. 47

Medlin cont.
 Mary E. 47
 R. S. 47
 Robert H. 47
 Susan 47
Michie, James 94
Mickel, N. J. 144
Miers, G. W. 165
Mildham, Jacob 84
Miles, Thomas 2,7
Miller, Caroline 170
 Esther 150
 Harriet J. 170
 Hary J. 170
 Henry 89,175
 J. P. 171
 James 171
 Rachel 175
 Rachel D. 149
Milligan, Sam 140
Mills, Robert L. 18,32,33,
 40
 Robert S. 28,30
Milton, James 94
 Thomas 91,94
Mires, Charity 181
 Cordelia A. 166
 Dinah 181
 Eveline 166
 Lorena T. 181
 Morgan 181
 T. F. 181
 William 166,181
Mitchell, Edward 150
 Everett 90,91,99
 John 54
 Mrs. 117
 Taswell 90,91,102
 Thomas 100,102
Monnet, Mathias 67
Montgomery, Alexander 95
 James 95
 Jennett 95
 Mary E. 95
 Michael 95
Moody, E. W. 76
 Sarah W. 76
Mooningham, H. B. 122,129
 Mrs. 45
Moor, Larkin 171
Moore, A. F. 189
 Abner 25,28,94
 Amanda J. 27
 Andrew K. 48
 Benjamin 94
 Benjamin F. 27
 Catharine 75
 Catherine F. 149
 Cynthia 75
 Deca 116
 Elizabeth 36
 Elizabeth B. 116
 Frances 116
 Israel 10,14,22,116
 Isreal 19
 James D. 48
 Jane 116
 Jasper 116
 John 48,122
 Joseph 75,118
 L. B. 13,14
 Lucinda 75
 Lucinda H. 141
 M. E. 189
 Maria 116
 Marion 116
 Mary A. 48,128
 Nancy 122
 Samuel 75,116
 Sarah 116
 Solomon 27,28
 Susannah 118
 Susanna F. 116

Organ cont.
J. F. 110
James F. 118
John 8,38,46,55,58,62,
64,69,70,75,78,81,109
John C. 113
Simpson 87,94
O'Rian, John R. 75
Orion, Martin 140
Orr, William H. 68
Orrand, John 44
Orston, Edny 114
Osborn, Alfred 180,181
Elizabeth E. 164
Hester A. 164
Martha 181
Osment, Amanda 169
Harrison 171
J. S. 175
John 170
Josephus 175
Martha 175
Owen, Anthony 6,14,120
Archibald A. 126
B. R. 33,47
Benjamin R. 32,47
Caledonia 53
David 28
Elizabeth 47
Fanny 47
James C. 53
Jane 28
John D. 33
Josaphine 53
Joseph 94
L. W. 28
Mary J. 107
Moses 28
Phebe 94
Richard 28
Samuel 28
Stephen W. 53
Theodora 53
Ozment, Elizabeth E. 149
J. W. 177
Jasper 177
Jonathan 5
Maud 173
P. G. 77
Sally 5
Padgett, Henrietta 51,56
Page, America 47
Ann 47,138
John S. 47
Lavice 47
Lavisa 138
Martha A. 138
Merica 138
William 47,127
Palmer, Frances 125
Francis 72,96,151
Frank 74
Henry 151
James 86
John 29,123,125
Margaret 123,125
Phillip 151
Sarah 123
Susan 151
W. R. 80
William 74,123,150,151
William K. 125
Parham, Lewis N. 139
Thomas 90,96
Cherry 134
Elizabeth 121
George 134
Hanley 134
Mary C. 134
Susannah 122
Parks, John M. 102
Parrish, Eliza F. 127
Elizabeth S. 127

Parrish cont.
Francis 131
Howell G. 127
J. C. 119
John D. 132
Joseph J. 127
Mary J. 127
Nancy 127
Nancy C. 132
Sally A. 132
Samuel E. 127
Tursa E. 132
Will 87
William K. 127
William L. 132
William R. 132
Parrott, Arving 83
Daniel 83
Partain, Andrew W. 42
Dovy 42
James 42
Martha 42
Partlow, Ann D. 149
Ann F. 153
Benjamin E. 153
Chloe 53,55
James W. 153
Johnathan N. 153
Jonathan N. 63
Joshua 130,153
Mary E. 63,152
Nancy E. 153
Rebecca F. 54,55,153
Robert D. 54,55,153
Sarah J. 54,55,153
Thomas 54,55,63,89,153
Thomas A. 63,153
William A. 153
Parum, Demaris 164
James 164
Pasley, John H. 94
Patey, W. L. 79
Patterson, A. J. 74
Aley 121
Amos J. 49
Burrell 19,114
Elizabeth 126
Elizabeth P. 14
Green 114
H. G. 73
J. S. 55
James 73,78
John T. 78
Joseph L. 178
Kinchen 114
Lewis 7,14
Lucinda 73,78
Marinda 19
Martha 19
Martha A. 134
Mary 73,78
Mary J. 14
Nancy 14
Nathaniel G. 78
Philfin 49
Robert 88
Samuel 88
Samuel P. 111
Tilman 114
Uriah 14
William 19,83,88
William C. 14
Z. S. 78
Patton, A. A. 186
Agnes 185
Andrew 188,189
Ann A. 187
Annie 185
Arthur M. 145
C. M. 185,189
Charles 70
Cornelia A. 187
Dee R. 184

Patton cont.
Dessie 186
Donnell 186
Dora M. 184
Ed 187
Edward 187
Effa 187
Elender C. 187
Elizabeth 187,189
Etter B. 187
Fanny E. 187
Fate 184
Gallie 189
J. B. 185
J. G. 188
J. H. 185
J. Wilson 185
James G. 187
James H. 145
James L. 118
James N. 185,188
James T. 75,143,186,187
Jimmie W. 187
John 187,189
John A. 143
John F. 188
John L. 76
Johnie 190
Jonathan 187
Joseph 112,130,187
Joseph S. 187
Julia A. 184
L. J. 187
L. T. 187
Lassie 190
Laura A. 187
Lucy F. 186
M. 189
M. E. 188
M. J. 187
Malinda 187
Mandie A. 184
Margaret 130
Margaret A. 188
Margret 187
Martha 188
Martha J. 189
Martha T. 188
Mary 118,145,186
Mary E. 187
Mary J. 189
Minnie M. 185
Nancy 70,187
Nancy E. 187
Nancy L. 185
Nancy M. 187
Napoleon B. 12,13,14
Phillip S. 186
R. H. 186
Rachel J. 143
Ruth 187
S. D. 187
S. E. 185
Sallie J. 186
Samuel 187
Samuel H. 189
T. E. 185
T. M. 70
T. W. 188
Tom D. 189
Turney 186
W. 189
William 14
Paulden, Lucus 109
Payne, Alfred B. 39
D. F. 71,77
Daniel H. 139
E. J. 185
Henrietta 77,139
Henry 190
Hubbard 77
Infant 189
J. C. 185

216

218

Sweatt cont.
W. C. 113
William 12,21
Sweeney, W. G. 171
Swift, Martha D. 122
Swindell, L. A. 111
T. A. 127
Tailor, Mary J. 142
Talley, Dan G. 186
Eudora E. 186
Freddie 186
Jane E. 185
Laurence E. 185
M. J. 186
Robert E. 184
Vina M. 185
W. C. 186
W. T. 186
William H. 184
Tally, Betsy 92,95
Caroline A. 68,122
Coleman 5,11,53,92
E. 6
E. C. 124
Edwin 12
Edwin C. 6,16
Emily 6
Ephraim 12,16
Frances 92
Hannah 92,95
Henry 16
Henry J. 68
Jane 6
John A. 62
John C. 68
John G. 186
Larance E. 112
Martin 93
S. B. 81
Sam E. 12
Spencer 95
Spencer B. 69
Spencer W. 96,114
William 95
William W. 92
Tanner, Elizabeth J. 46
Tapp, John L. 99
Tarpley, Elzie H. 185
Ernest L. 190
John 190
Lucretia 126
Sarah 141
Shelvie E. 185
Sterling 126
William T. 190
Tarver, B. J. 107
Benjamin 39,151
Benjamin F. 32,34
Benjamin J. 60,136
Edmund D. 151
John B. 79,136
Louisa M. 150
Lucinda 136
Nancy M. 150
Silas 3,4,32,34,36,51,
60,136,151
Silas N. 32,34
Sophrona 68
Sophronia 58
Susannah P. 118
Tabitha 151
William 8,58,68
Tate, James 125
James J. 11,18,31
John W. 47,112,121
Rachel J. 11,18
Rebecca W. 152
Richard J. 11
Zachariah 121
Zidekiah 18
Tatom, Asa 99
Bernard 99
Tatum, Ann E. 44

Tatum cont.
Dabney 120
Martha E. 141
Patsy E. 149
Taylor, Anny D. 98
Armstead J. 40
Elizabeth 40
Elizabeth S. 42
Francis A. 18
Hester A. 40
James A. 61,73,120
James B. 18,25,40
James C. 42
James D. 73
James H. 133
James P. 61
Jeremiah 18
John 37,39,56,75
John D. 37,59,62
John P. 25
Josaphine 53
Joshua 18
Joshua B. 18
Joshua V. 24
Josiah 42,53
Louisa 24
M. W. 143
Martha 24,40
Martha L. 61,120
Mary 37,56,68
Mary F. 129
Mary J. 174
Milton 139
Mortimore W. 42
Moses L. 61, 120
Paris 139
Patterson 53
Robert 56,68
Solomon 39
Sophia S. 120
Susan 135
Tennessee C. 39
Thomas 9
Thomas B. 9,100
W. W. 77
William B. 61,120
Teag, William 151
Telford, Andrew J. 159
Ann 155,159
Elizabeth 155,157,159,
164
Elizabeth A. 159,164
Elizabeth S. 159
Esther H. 157
G. W. 123
H. 7
Hugh 123,151,155,157,
159,163,181
Hugh A. 155,159
Hugh B. 163
Isabel C. 157
James H. 124
James W. 180
Jane 123,155,157
John 95,98,99,100,124,
155,159
Joseph 124
Julia A. 163
Louiza 159
Margaret 164
Margaret A. 123
Margaret O. 157
Mary 155,159
Mary A. 140,176
Mary W. 159
Maryan F. 157
Nancy 157
Rachael 157
Rachel 164
Rebecca E. 163
Richard B. 163
Robert 1,155
Robert A. 123,157

Telford cont.
Samuel 124,155
Samuel B. 163
Samuel K. 159
Sarah 155
Sarah E. 166
Sarah G. 149
T. C. 123,176,177
Thomas 7,12,39,58,123,
155,157,176
Thomas C. 1,58
Thomas E. 155,159
Thomas F. 157
Tirzah 155
Washington 12,155
William 159
William G. 159
William T. 163,166
William W. 159
Terrell, Anthony 42
John 105
Richard 42
Thomas 42
William 42
Terrence, Alexander 91
Terry, J. C. 108
Nancy J. 64
Tharp, Drury 69
John T. 68
Thomas, Amy E. 17
Catharine 17
Hugh 17
J. B. 108
James 17
John W. 138
Lucinda 17
Mary E. 17
W. B. 17
Thomason, Jacob 62,110
William 101
Thompkins, James 127
Thompson, Amelia A. 120
Andrew 112,120,188,189
Andrew J. 59,112
Andrew Jr.112
Andrew W. 9,112
Ann 189
Ann F. 153
Anne K. 150
Diantha 76
Dudley H. 120
E. M. 188
Eli W. 76
Elizabeth 150
Elizabeth J. 188
Elizabeth M. 61
Elizabeth S. 50,134
Emanuel S. 61
Esther 185
G. G. 189
G. W. 55,61
George 112
Haynie 118
Henry C. 112
Henry F. 61
Henry R. 1,42
Isaac L. 76
J. 190
J. G. 188
Jack 79
James 58,59,112
James G. 64
James O. 184
James P. 4
James R. 1
John 1,4,9,59
John B. 134
John G. 184
John N. 184
John P. 112
Lavina 75
Louisa D. 64
Lucy A. 109

219

Vaughan, Abram 151
  H. B. 120
  M. S. 140
  Birdie I. 177
  Edward W. 87
  Elisha 93
  Elizabeth 134
  Ola M. 177
  Thomas 24,93,129
Vaught, E. T. 188
  Elizabeth J. 188
  G. H. 82
  J. M. 188
  John M. 188
  Josephine G. 188
  Samuel 82
  T. B. 82
Vaughter, D. K. 142
Vernum, Alfred 165
Vick, A. W. 60,114
  Alex W. 72
  Martin 178
  Samuel 8
Vivrett, Drewry 50
  Elizabeth 84,134
  Henry 53,55
  Henry J. 55
  J. B. 121,133
  Jacky A. 50
  John B. 75
  Lancelot 83
  Lucrecy 53
  Margaret L. 134
  Mary F. 134
  Micajah 55,83,84
  Nancy 40
  P. H. 53
  Polly 122
  Rebecca 134
  Thomas 113
  W. D. 69
  William D. 40
  William H. 55
Wade, Charles 2,18
Walden, Elizabeth 189
  Joe M. 190
  Margaret 190
Waldran, Jesse 100
  Sally 100
Walker, Amanda 166
  Ann 15
  Caroline 42,45
  Celea L. 46
  Celia F. 29,33
  Clinton 30,36
  Eleanor 3
  Eleanor D. 4
  Elisha 29,33
  Elizabeth J. 29,33
  Frances 122
  Frances C. 140
  Frances W. 72
  Francis G. 146
  George W. 52
  Henry 3,4,46
  High C. 15
  J. W. 105
  James D. 46
  James H. 30,36,72,140
  John 90
  John J. 32
  Josaphine C. 45
  Julius 103
  Kesiah 3
  Kiziah 16,23
  Louiza J. 112
  Lureny 15
  Martha 15,46
  Martha A. 27
  Mary 29
  Mary C. 33
  Mary F. 169
  Mildred A. 124

Walker cont.
  Milner 30,36,45
  Mourning 15
  Nancy 4
  Nancy W. 72,146
  Nathan 42
  Noah 15
  Parthena 15
  Phereby F. 34
  Polly 3,27
  Radford 27
  Saleno 27
  Samuel 11,27
  Susan 42
  Susan D. 47
  Thomas 11
  Thomas P. 3,30,170
  W. B. 135
  Washington B. 46
  William 3,15,16,30,42,
    83,103
  William C. 46
  William E. 3,4
  William H. 30,36
  William L. 36
  William S. 30
  Wilson Y. 32
Wall, Bird 2,10
  Christian 10
  Frederick 2
  Manerva 2
  Sarah 10
  William 2,10
Wallace, J. William 105
  Laura A. 134
  Polly 122
Waller, Elizabeth 105
  Richard 105
Walsh, David A. 33
  Mary 33
  Norman 25
Walton, Josiah 104
  R. J. 79
Wammack, Ann R. 69
  Elijah 42,88
  Erixon E. 63
  Frances P. 69
  J. S. 63
  Richard 69
  Sarah P. 69
  Wrepps 69
Ward, Bryan 86
  Edward 96
  George R. 51
  George W. 73
  Henry 100
  James 51
  John 86
  Jonathan 102
  Jourdan 97
  M. G. 33,40
  Mary A. 51
  Mary E. 73
  Meredith F. 33
  Meredith G. 33
  Phillip 87
  Ransom 12
  Sally 164
  Sarah 33
Ware, Cintha 10
  Devy 10
  Dudley 7,10
  Granberry 10
  James 10
  Jerusha 10
  John R. 10
  Lovell 10
  Polly 10
  Thomas 10
Warren, Adelea D. 16
  B. W. 61
  Ball E. 84
  Benjamin 129

Warren cont.
  Benjamin W. 57
  Booth M. 84
  Charles 5,11
  Eliza J. 11
  Elizabeth 11
  Elvira 11
  Green 16
  James 84
  Jesse 87,94
  John A. 129,142
  Lina 5,11
  Martha 16
  Mary 115
  Polly 81
  Rebecca A. 84
  Richard L. 84
  Robert B. 84
  William G. 129,142
Wasan, Abner 92
Washburn, Ada 76
  Catherine 76
  Sarah 118
  Vesparia 76
  W. W. 76
  William 76
Waters, Etha 67
  George 91
  George W. 111
  John 27
  John F. 67,111
  John H. 27
  Jonnie F. 67
  Kiziah 27
  Polly 110
  Robert 27
  Shela 15
  Shelah 9,33,91
  Thomas 57,64
  Tom 110
  W. L. 78
  W. T. 2,6
  William L. 27
  Wilson C. 15
  Wilson F. 110
  Wilson L. 22,47
Watkins, Elizabeth 117
  Richard 96
Watson, Joseph 102
Weatherly, Darthula 142
  Deretha 142
  Gideon 142
  Harriet 142
  Parallee 142
Weatherspoon, Alexander 8
  Calvin 13
  Emeline 13
  Wilson 13
Webb, Allen 8,26
  Elizabeth 8,24,26
  George 13
  George C. 48
  John 17,25
  John S. 48
  Martha 48
  Mary 48
  Mickie 48
  Nancy 42,45
  Susan 48
  Susan D. 47
  Thomas 24
  Thomas J. 24
  William 8,95
  Wilson 97
  Woodson 92
Webber, Eliza H. 168
  Margaret 117
Welch, Delilah 164
  Mitchell 164
Welles, Edward 134
  Sarah 134
West, Albert J. 130,131
  Charles M. 191